NUMB]

Yale French Studies

The Place of Maurice Blanchot

THOMAS PEPPER 1 Editor's Preface: The Law—The Not Good Enough Father

I. *Law, Death, Community*

JAMES SWENSON 11 Revolutionary Sentences

HENT DE VRIES 30 "Lapsus Absolu": Notes on Maurice Blanchot's *The Instant of My Death*

JEAN-POL MADOU 60 The Law, the Heart: Blanchot and the Question of Community

II. *In Time, Among Contemporaries*

DOMINIQUE RABATÉ 69 The Critical Turn: Blanchot Reads des Forêts

MICHAEL SYROTINSKI 81 Noncoincidences: Blanchot Reading Paulhan

DENIS HOLLIER 99 Timeliness and Timelessness

SIMON CRITCHLEY 114 Who Speaks in the Work of Samuel Beckett?

III. *Voices, Persons*

ANN BANFIELD 133 The Name of the Subject: The "il"?

LYNNE HUFFER 175 Blanchot's Mother

DAVID R. ELLISON 196 Narrative and Music in Kafka and Blanchot: The "Singing" of Josefine

IV. *Attentions*

THOMAS SCHESTAG 221 Mantis, Relics

HANS-JOST FREY 252 The Last Man and the Reader

Yale French Studies

Thomas Pepper, *Special editor for this issue*
Alyson Waters, *Managing editor*

Editorial office: 82-90 Wall Street, Room 308.
Mailing address: P.O. Box 208251, New Haven, Connecticut 06520-8251
Sales and subscription office:
Yale University Press, P.O. Box 209040
New Haven, Connecticut 06520-9040
Published twice annually by Yale University Press

Designed by James J. Johnson and set in Trump Medieval Roman by The Composing Room of Michigan, Inc. Printed in the United States of America by the Vail Ballou Press, Binghamton, N.Y.

ISSN 044-0078
ISBN for this issue 0-300-07375-5

THOMAS PEPPER

Editor's Preface
The Law—The Not Good Enough Father

It could have been *The Name Maurice Blanchot.* Or *The Topos: Maurice Blanchot,* the topos of topos, the space of space, the place of place or space, etc. One could go on and write an inordinate number of sentences *that* way. One has become weary of these things. And it doesn't really make much difference, does it?

Or does it?

In order to answer, we would have to seriously engage a bygone era—as Heidegger would say, an era that stands ever before (it amounts to the same parabolic mode). This volume was planned at a very specific historical moment. The moment happened after the two deaths of Paul de Man, after High Theory began to die its living death, the death rattle of an indestructible feminine figure in one of Blanchot's books—that is to say after it started to be called High Theory, with the monumental ruination of those petrifying Majuscules. Now the very mention of names such as Blanchot, Heidegger, de Man—I need not go on—provokes a kind of fond nostalgia or a hateful sense of relief at a pastness of the past that should, according to the laws of the American populist anti-intellectual marketplace of ideas, never happen again. Plunges *à corps perdu* into the abyss of reflection on language are not the rage; one might in fact say that a sort of fundamental ontological inquiry that thrived briefly in departments of literary study in the United States has given way to an apparently never-ending series of ever more manic attempts to corner the market with offerings of regional ontologies, usually known under the names of various kinds of identity politics.

In the literary academy, this in fact has dire consequences: virtually no one wants to be associated with lyric poetry anymore, with the

YFS 93, *The Place of Maurice Blanchot,* ed. Thomas Pepper, © 1998 by Yale University.

genre that always produced the furthest-going reflections on literary language. In short, few are interested in difficulty. Twenty minutes at the MLA has become our answer to Hollywood's twenty words or less. Capital, by the byways of clouds of administrators (one is reminded of Bataille on the village wedding of philosophy, of Kafka and of Benjamin on him), has produced a situation of multimedia numbness in which everything has to be done quickly: dissertations, books, articles, in short, production. In the university—which has never, in any case, been particularly hospitable to anything passionate or original—this is the time of the reign of the hordes of vice-presidents, provosts, deans, and development officers. If Blanchot's books had not been written in French and by an aging figure of authority, it is scarcely imaginable that anyone in the United States would publish them now. An unknown figure producing collections of essays such as *La part du feu, L'espace littéraire, Le livre à venir, L'entretien infini* would be stillborn or on the lines of unemployed negativity. Who, in any case—what publisher? what journal?—would have kept such a figure alive so that the essays could be written, published, collected into books?

Blanchot himself has something to say about this situation, and it dates, in a prescient manner, from 1969. Here are some words from the "Note" at the beginning of *The Infinite Conversation*[1]:

> When I speak of "the end of the book," or better "the absence of the book," I do not mean to allude to developments in the audio-visual means of communication with which so many experts are concerned. If one ceased publishing books in favor of communication by voice, image, or machine, this would in no way change the reality of what is called the "book"; on the contrary, language, like speech, would thereby affirm all the more its predominance and its certitude of a possible truth. In other words, the Book always indicates an order that submits to *unity,* a system of notions in which are affirmed the primacy of speech over writing, of thought over language, and the promise of a communication that would one day be immediate and transparent. [*IC,* xii]

Such thoughts are borne out by the degree to which, in order to be recognizable to an academic idiocy (disciplinary—in all senses) *unit* one must write on the most standardized topics, now more than ever, so as to be capable of being recognized and recognizable. Clearly this is

1. Maurice Blanchot, *L'entretien infini* (Paris: Gallimard, 1969), translated by Susan Hanson as *The Infinite Conversation* (Minneapolis: University of Minnesota Press, 1993), henceforth *IC,* followed by page number.

not what Blanchot had in mind with his statement about the unity of the book—this empirical factoid of our present-day obsession with the unity of a project, to be legible on the title page (controlled by that extension of the viceregal apparatus: the editor). And indeed it is more than worthwhile to think what the unity of the book has become in our time: a parody of the unity of the Book. The internet has not changed this at all.

But Blanchot goes on:

> Now it may be that writing requires the abandonment of all these principles, that is to say, the end and also the coming to completion of everything that guarantees our culture—not so that we might in idyllic fashion turn back, but rather so we might go beyond, that is, to the limit, in order to attempt to break the circle, the circle of circles: the *totality* of the concepts that founds history, that develops in history, and whose development history is. Writing . . . supposes a radical change of epoch: interruption, death itself—or, to speak hyperbolically, "the end of history." Writing in this way passes through the advent of communism, recognized as the ultimate affirmation—communism being still always beyond communism. Writing thus becomes a terrible responsibility. . . . [*IC*, xii]

Capitalism is not, in its terrifying triumph of the end of the millennium, the end of history. Only for the reigning cynicism of today could it be thought to be so. Communism, "hyperbolically," would be this end, a "communism . . . still always beyond communism." The utopic project of communism, spurned and abandoned, is the correlate of writing, which "thus becomes a terrible responsibility." Both are names here for the hyperbolic limit of our culture. We might say that our cynical moment is the moment of a kind of forgetting of this hyperbology. Thus it is not a coincidence that both communism and writing—in the strong senses Blanchot gives to both of these words here—figure as the strongly repressed elements of our political and (what passes for) intellectual discourses today. The attempted total destruction of civil society in the creation of a war of all against all called a free market mirrors the other scene, the intellectual market, where the -isms and identities fight it out. The university has been reduced to an extremely vulgar mirror. And it no longer seems possible even to dream of anything more.

But: such futures (think commodities) cannot be the future, even by virtue of their sheer instantaneity, their lack of—dare I say it?—the vision thing. What is it to have a vision—of society, of writing? Certainly it means one must have *some* relation to totality, some notion of the way in which systems—institutions, language—function. This notion of totality must be reconstructed upon the critiques of totality and of totalization which we have endured following upon the advent of fascism as a certain dark limit. But such reconstruction does not occur by pretending to ditch totality and its history. For the concept of writing, and the necessity of a reconstruction of a communism beyond communism cannot take place without a conscious working through of what happened to totality itself, to the total social fact, to the thinking of writing.

* * * * *

And this indestructible place—of community, of writing—is very much the sovereign space of Maurice Blanchot. Every time he puts, has put pen to paper—maybe he types, maybe he dictates now; maybe he doesn't write at all, which is to say, he doesn't exist (the proof of god by his effects), every time he has written, he opens this indestructibly fragile space, simply, absolutely, immediately, without warning. He opens the space, and we enter, like Abraham setting out for Mount Moriah or like Kierkegaard's actor Beckmann on the stage of the Königstädter Theater in Berlin, who not only walks on stage, but who *comes walking,* and brings the entire world in tow.[2]

So here we are, in this demiurgic, terrifying space. Terrifying and of course reassuring, because the one thing one can know about it is: it is there. Never here. Always there. It is also the space of *Yale French Studies* itself, to which Blanchot has contributed over and again. It is here.

Still.

This writing begins at the beginning, at the leveling, neutralizing destruction that allows a beginning to happen. It happens all the time: Witness Thomas sitting and looking at the sea, and then among the waves: "and, at the same time, there reigned a silence and a calm which gave the impression that everything was already destroyed."[3]—Or else, another beginning: Now we are in those ravishing-in-their-ravaging pages after the opening "Note" of *The Infinite Conversation,*

2. See Søren Kierkegaard, *Fear and Trembling* and *Repetition,* trans. Howard and Edna Hong (Princeton: Princeton University Press, 1983), 163.

3. Blanchot, *Thomas l'obscur* (nouvelle version, Paris: Gallimard, 1950), translated by Robert Lamberton as *Thomas the Obscure* (New York: David Lewis, 1973), 7.

those pages in italics, those paragraphs prefaced with their ± ±, those redoubled mathematical tombstones.

What is simulated in this pseudomathematical attack? It is blindingly lucid, just like mathematics (but not). If a single ± says, what follows can go either way, can either be, say, what is the case or is not the case, asserted or denied, depending, then the reduplication, like an aorist, something out of a very old verb, the oldest of the old ('something happened once': but this is a fable without a moral),—±± says, like an absolute construction, what follows can only be neutral-ized, that is to say, what follows *this mark* is suspended in the space of, that is to say, under the name or sign of something like this giddy paraphrase: it cannot be asserted or denied that what follows these marks can be asserted or denied, the case or not the case; it cannot be established that what follows is or is not the case,—or even *that* it follows, and so on. Etc.

But what, if anything, does follow? What comes on stage, as soon as the *creatio ex nihilo* is proffered, as soon as this space, this place, is opened up under this sign or name? What follows here is exhaustion, fatigue—and this at and as and from the beginning. Fatigue and exhaustion follow. What is it to follow? It should not be to be a disciple or a follower, but one who goes and comes with—by the way, who came with?—it should be one who reads, but not one who kneels. And certainly not one who begs.

Fatigue follows. From the very beginning:

> ±± *"If you were not there, I believe I could not bear the weariness."—"And yet I also contribute to it."—"That is true, you weary me very much, but precisely very much, within human limits. Nevertheless, the danger is not averted: when you are there, I still hold on, I have the desire to spare you, I do not give up appearances entirely. This will not last long. I ask you, then, to go. Out of respect for weariness."—"I will go then."—"No, don't leave yet."*
>
> *Why does he give the name weariness to what is his very life? There is a certain imposture there, a certain discretion. In the same way, he can no longer distinguish between thought and weariness, experiencing in weariness the same void, perhaps the same infinite. And when thought and speech disappear one into the other, identical, not identical, it is as though weariness passed into another weariness, the same, nevertheless, to which, ironically, he gives the name rest.*
>
> *Thinking weary.*
>
> *The weariness grows insensibly; it is insensible; no proof, no sign*

> *altogether sure; at every instant it seems to have reached its highest point—but, of course, this is a lure, a promise that is not kept. As though weariness kept him alive. For how long still? It is endless.*
>
> *Weariness having become his sole way of living, with the difference being that the more he is weary, the less he lives, and yet living only though weariness.*
>
> *If he rests, then weariness has already, in advance, taken possession of this rest.*
>
> *It seems that at every instant he appears before his weariness: You're not as weary as all that, true weariness awaits you; now, yes, you are beginning to be weary, you are beginning to forget your weariness; is it possible for one to be as weary as this without offence? And never does he hear the liberating word: All right, you are a weary man, nothing but weary.* [*IC*, xix–xx]

This fragment, surrounded by its others, sits on the sill of Blanchot's most extensive book of essays. What is one to do with these paragraphs, which look forward to the books of fragments, aphorisms (which are they?—the two are not the same), *Le pas au-delà* and *L'écriture du désastre,*[4] with their black lozenges? It is as though each "fragment" opens up and specifies a possible world. We know this from the antecedents: Pascal, Kafka, Wittgenstein, who do it in their own way. But an attempt at the construction of the specificity, of the singularity of the *Blanchot effect* has to account for the way in which these sentences, written in the language of the everyday and which yet seem to suspend any sense of the ordinary, induce interpretative hysteria, a kind of auratic and unending transference neurosis. Like negative theology, the work is done in the accomplishment of the ascesis, the image of the hermit writer (no photographs, please) who produces these paradivine utterances, rewrites his fictions, pares them down.

* * * * *

To inflect what has been said above differently: we could say that the Blanchot reception has to move and change. It must move from being simply hysterical, in the face of a confrontation with such a father-text, of supporting its desire, to an analysis of that hysteria. We have to work through the discipleship, to work away at—without the possibility of ever effacing it—the relation to the Law of the Father.

4. Blanchot, *Le pas au-delà* (Paris: Gallimard, 1973) and *L'écriture du désastre* (Paris: Gallimard, 1980).

But the holy name of the Father—as any name—is always defaulting. The Father, from Abraham to the dreamer of Freud's Dream of the Burning Child, the one who sustains the children in being unable to sustain them, allowing them to die before their time, or to be stillborn, is never good enough.[5] And that is, this is, our salvation. Because it gives us space of our own. It gives us a space of quiet breathing—unsteady, always capable of apnea, of a cutting syncope or caesura. But *it is a space,* a space our own breath only increases.

It will have been necessary to become the parent of the parent and forgive him for not having been good enough in his blinding, castrating greatness. I said forgive, but not forget, never.

That is to say: Thanks.

* * * * *

This project could not have been realized without the essential interventions of many people. From before the very beginning, Liliane Greene blessed it with her characteristic graciousness. Jacques Derrida, Shoshana Felman, Denis Hollier, and Kevin Newmark were all there as witnesses. The Søren Kierkegaard Research Centre at the University of Copenhagen and Danmarks Grundforskningsfond provided work space and access to the world. And all the authors, who paid with brilliance and, most of all, patience.

5. It is impossible for me to mention the Dream of the Burning Child (see Sigmund Freud, *The Interpretation of Dreams* [London: Hogarth Press and The Institute for Psychoanalysis, 1953], chapter 7) without thinking of Mary Quaintance (1963–1995).

I. Law, Death, Community

JAMES SWENSON

Revolutionary Sentences

For Mary, who negated the world with her language

"Literature and the Right to Death"[1] occupies a distinctive place in the development of Blanchot's critical career. Both its length (more than twice that of any other essay in *La part du feu*) and its placement at the end of the collection, printed in italics, mark out this status. Of the essays that precede *L'espace littéraire*,[2] it is the one that most seems to escape the book-review format in which these writings were originally published. While the specificity of Blanchot's critical practice may well reside in the rapidity with which an account of a particular work passes to general considerations on the nature of literature, in this case we begin on this level.

"Literature and the Right to Death" represents the explicit introduction into Blanchot's critical vocabulary of a thematics (already present in his fiction) that will come to dominate later critical work such as *L'espace littéraire, Le pas au-delà* and *L'écriture du désastre*,[3] namely the equivalence of death as the impossibility of dying and of literature as the impossibility of writing. The conjunction of the title can equally well be understood as a copula (*et/est*), but the "right" referred to is one that, while it must be claimed, can never be fully exercised. Death is related to literature in an essential way, rather than merely as a possible but contingent theme, by a structure that combines obligation and impossibility.

1. Maurice Blanchot, "La littérature et le droit à la mort," in *La part du feu* (Paris: Gallimard, 1949); "Literature and the Right to Death," in *The Work of Fire*, trans. Lydia Davis (Stanford: Stanford University Press, 1995). Future citations will use the Davis translation, giving page numbers from the French edition followed by those from the Davis translation.

2. Blanchot, *L'espace littéraire* (Paris: Gallimard, 1955).

3. Blanchot, *Le pas au-delà* (Paris: Gallimard, 1973); *L'écriture du désastre* (Paris: Gallimard, 1980).

YFS 93, *The Place of Maurice Blanchot*, ed. Thomas Pepper, © 1998 by Yale University.

The reflection on Revolutionary Terror in the middle of the essay represents the culmination of a set of appearances of this theme in Blanchot's writing that are of key importance in understanding his career. A number of critics have recently emphasized the importance of the theme of Terror in the transition that takes place in Blanchot's career during the Occupation, a theme that links the far-right agitation of the prewar years and the turn to literature in a short book (later included in *Faux pas*) dedicated to Paulhan's *Les fleurs de Tarbes*, entitled *Comment la littérature est-elle possible?*[4] In the prewar period, this theme appears most clearly in one of Blanchot's most virulent essays of the 1930s, published in the right-wing journal *Combat* under the title "Le terrorisme, méthode de salut public." Here Blanchot called for "illegal and, if necessary, fanatical action" against the Blum government, judging that all means of legal opposition (if they ever had any genuinely oppositional value) had been thoroughly co-opted.[5] This sort of violent action, Blanchot argued, was rendered necessary by the fact that a "degenerate people" [*un peuple aussi aveuli que le nôtre*] cannot be reformed by peaceful means but requires "bloody convulsions" [*des secousses sanglantes*] to shake it out of its lethargy. The entrenchment of the corrupt regime makes revolution both impossible and necessary. In an earlier essay entitled "Le marxisme contre la révolution," Blanchot had characterized this conjunction of impossibility and necessity as the hallmark of any true revolution, which "is rigorously deducible from the movement of all the facts which it must contradict."[6] The Terror represents a violent *passage à*

4. See Jeffrey Mehlman, "Blanchot at *Combat:* Of Literature and Terror," in *Legacies of Anti-Semitism in France* (Minneapolis: University of Minnesota Press, 1983), 6–22; Michael Syrotinski, "1941: How is Literature Possible?" in *A New History of French Literature,* ed. Denis Hollier, et al. (Cambridge: Harvard University Press, 1989), 953–8; Allan Stoekl, "Paulhan and Blanchot: On Rhetoric, Terror, and the Gaze of Orpheus," in *Agonies of the Intellectual: Commitment, Subjectivity, and the Performative in the Twentieth-Century French Tradition* (Lincoln: University of Nebraska Press, 1992), 145–73; Steven Ungar, *Scandal and Aftereffect: Blanchot and France since 1930* (Minneapolis: University of Minnesota Press, 1995); Jean Paulhan, *Les fleurs de Tarbes, ou la terreur dans les lettres* (Paris: Gallimard, 1941); Blanchot, "Comment la littérature est-elle possible?" in *Faux pas* (Paris: Gallimard, 1943).

5. Blanchot, "Le terrorisme, méthode de salut public," *Combat* 1/7 (July 1936), reprinted in *Gramma* 5 (1976): 61–63. It is difficult not to conclude that these measures would include the assassination of elected officials.

6. Blanchot, "Le marxisme contre la révolution," *La revue française* 4 (April 1933), also reprinted in *Gramma* 5 (1976): 58.

l'acte that provides not a resolution but a way out of the contradiction generated by the simultaneity of necessity and impossibility.

The second moment in this series of appearances of the theme of Terror is Blanchot's encounter with Paulhan. *Les fleurs de Tarbes* divides literature into two attitudes, designated by the terms "Rhetoric" and "Terror," and roughly corresponding, in terms of literary history, to classicism and romanticism (thus almost all major French poets since Hugo, with the possible exception of Valéry, qualify as terrorists). The book presents a defense of "Rhetoric" and its use of "commonplaces," clichés and set forms against the attacks of the "terrorists" and their demands for a purity of expression. For Paulhan this priority given to thought over language is ultimately self-defeating and paralyzing for literature, since it leads in the end to an even more obsessive concern with words than with thought. This defense, however, is ultimately based not on the falseness of the Terror, but on the fact that Rhetoric already contains its moment of truth, that Rhetoric is in fact a "perfected Terror" (*Fleurs,* 140–56). Blanchot's "Comment la littérature est-elle possible?" takes its point of departure from the dual and fundamentally contradictory nature of the terrorist accusation against literature: Terror demands both an absolute originality of expression and an absolute transparency of language to thought. For some of Paulhan's terrorists, Blanchot points out, "language's mission is to correctly express thought, to become its faithful interpreter, to be submitted to it as to a legitimate sovereign. But for others, expression is only the prosaic destiny of everyday language; language's true role is not to express but to communicate, not to translate but to be" ("Comment la littérature," 95). The unity of these two attitudes can be characterized as the properly terrorist activity of accusation. No aspect of literature is spared in this *épuration.*[7] The two forms of terror "put language as such, and literature as such, on trial." But this trial is in fact what is most essential in literature; Terror, the accusation of literature, "is literature, or at least its soul" ("Comment la littérature," 96–97). Contrary to Paulhan's apparent argument, it is Terror that contains Rhetoric within it. Or, as "Literature and the Right to Death" puts it, "literature begins at the moment when literature becomes a question" (300).

7. On Paulhan's writings on the series of the postwar trials of intellectuals known as the *épuration,* see Syrotinski, "Some Wheat and Some Chaff: Jean Paulhan and the Post-War Literary Purge in France," *Studies in Twentieth-Century Literature* 16 (1992): 247–63.

But this question is not Sartre's "What is Literature?," a question that Blanchot says "has received only meaningless answers" (294/302). Blanchot's question is a *how* rather than a *what*, an interrogation of possibility or existence rather than of being or essence. The answer he gives to the question of how literature is possible is that it is not. But literature nevertheless does exist, not merely despite but precisely *as* its own impossibility. "Literature continues to be, despite the internal absurdity that haunts it, divides it, and renders it properly speaking inconceivable ("Comment la littérature," 99). It is this relation to its own impossibility that constitutes literature as a specifically terrorist activity for Blanchot.

This characterization in fact contains a fundamental insight into the nature of the Revolutionary Terror. When Saint-Just writes, "republican government has virtue as its principle; if not, terror,"[8] Terror is precisely a response to an impossible exigency. Rousseau's republicanism, to which the revolutionaries were strictly faithful in this respect at least, rests upon a logical circle: only a virtuous people can make just laws, but only just laws can make a virtuous people.[9] The circularity is that of means and ends, in which, as Hegel says, "each moment presupposes the other."[10] The Terror can thus be described as a *passage à l'acte* in which the immediacy of violence provides an exit (or entrance) to the closure of the circle, to the impossibility of a beginning. The Republic, like literature, is both necessary and impossible: it presupposes, as a condition, what can only exist as its result. In "Literature and the Right to Death," Blanchot cites Hegel (making him speak of the writer just as we are making him speak of the terrorist): " 'For that very reason,' Hegel remarks, 'he has to start immediately, and, whatever the circumstances, without further scruples about beginning, means, or End, proceed to action' " (296/304).

The first problem that a reading of "Literature and the Right to Death" must confront is that of the essay's unity. The essay was originally

8. Louis-Antoine de Saint Just, "Fragments d'institutions républicaines," in *Œuvres complètes*, ed. Michèle Duval (Paris: Gérard Lebovici, 1984), 978; my translation.

9. On this "virtuous circle," see particularly the section on the Legislator in Jean-Jacques Rousseau, *Du contrat social*, in *Œuvres complètes*, vol. 3, ed. Bernard Gagnebin and Marcel Raymond (Paris: Gallimard, Bibliothèque de la Pléiade, 1964), 381–84, and Carol Blum's commentary in *Rousseau and the Republic of Virtue* (Ithaca: Cornell University Press, 1986), 108–32.

10. G. W. F. Hegel, *Phenomenology of Spirit*, trans. A. V. Miller (Oxford: The Clarendon Press, 1977), 240.

published in the journal *Critique* in two parts. The first section appeared in November 1947 (no. 18), under the title "Le règne animal de l'esprit" (the spiritual animal kingdom, the heading of a chapter from Hegel's *Phenomenology of Spirit*); the second half appeared under the definitive title two months later, in January 1948 (no. 20). There are no changes in the text other than the soldering together of the two halves. This joining occurs, in the final text, in the middle of a paragraph:

> Literature contemplates itself in revolution, it finds its justification in revolution, and if it has been called the Reign of Terror, this is because its ideal is indeed that moment in history, that moment when "life endures death and maintains itself in it" in order to gain from death the possibility of speaking and the truth of speech. This is the "question" that seeks to pose itself in literature, the "question" that is its essence. [Here ended "Le règne animal . . ."] Literature is bound to language. Language is reassuring and disquieting at the same time. When we speak. . . . [311–2/321–2]

Once one has been alerted to the circumstances of the first publication, it is impossible not to read the apodictic statement "Literature is bound to language," the first sentence of the article appearing in *Critique* 20, as a genuine point of departure, and therefore as a real division in the essay's structure. The first part concerns the "situation of the writer"—whether in 1947, 1807, or 1793—and is developed through a commentary on two moments of the *Phenomenology of Spirit*. In the second part, the character of the writer has disappeared to the benefit of a reflection on language. The most apparent link and source of unity between the two halves of the essay is provided by the use of Hegel's *Phenomenology*, largely read through the commentary provided by Kojève in his *Introduction à la lecture de Hegel*.[11] A some-

11. The period immediately following World War II constituted the high watermark of Hegelianism in France. The debate centered around two publications: Jean Hyppolite's *Genèse et structure de la 'Phénoménologie de l'esprit'* (Paris: Aubier, 1946), and Kojève's *Introduction à la lecture de Hegel* (Paris: Gallimard, 1969 [1947]). These two publications gave rise to an extensive debate in the pages of the ambitious journals that dominated the intellectual life of the time, most notably in *Les temps modernes* and *Critique*. There are two important studies of this debate available in English, both containing extensive bibliographies: Judith P. Butler, *Subjects of Desire: Hegelian Reflections in Twentieth-Century France* (New York: Columbia University Press, 1987), and Michael S. Roth, *Knowing and History: Appropriations of Hegel in Twentieth-Century France* (Ithaca: Cornell University Press, 1988). Particular attention should be given to Kojève's "Hegel, Marx, et le christianisme," *Critique* 3–4 (August–September 1946): 339–66; his letter to Tran duc Thao of 7 October 1948, cited in Dominique Auffret's biography, *Alexandre Kojève. La philosophie, l'état, la fin de l'histoire* (Paris:

what less apparent, but equally important link is provided by the essay's main polemical target. Without ever mentioning Sartre by name, "Literature and the Right to Death" is an insistent confrontation with *Qu'est-ce que la littérature?*, doubtless the most influential essay in literary theory of the period, which had just appeared in serial form in *Les temps modernes.* Blanchot clearly if indirectly indicates his polemical stance in the initial considerations, cited above, on the nature of literature as a question. His critique of Sartre concerns first of all the concept of commitment [*engagement*] and the idea of literature as action, and then proceeds to a reversal (or, more precisely, a making-reversible) of the privilege given by Sartre to prose over poetry. The verbal marker of this polemic is the use of "cat" as an example of referential language. Sartre had cited Boileau's claim to referential directness—"*j'appelle un chat un chat et Rolet un fripon* [I call a cat a cat and Rolet a rascal]—as the health against which the modern sickness of words could be measured:

> The function of a writer is to call a cat a cat. If words are sick, it is up to us to cure them. Instead of that, many writers live off this sickness. In many cases modern literature is a cancer of words. It is perfectly all right to write "horse of butter" but in a sense it amounts to doing the same thing as those who speak of a fascist United States or a Stalinist national socialism.[12]

Blanchot's most direct and most polemical reference to this passage is in the first half of the essay, where he castigates talk of the sickness of

Grasset, 1990), 249; Jean Hyppolite, "Situation de l'homme dans la phénoménologie hégélienne," *Les temps modernes* 19 (April 1947): 1276–89; Henri Niel, "L'interprétation de Hegel," *Critique* 18 (November 1947): 426–37; Louis Althusser, "L'homme, cette nuit," *Cahiers du sud* 286 (1947), reprinted in *Écrits philosophiques et politiques*, vol. 1, ed. François Matheron (Paris: Stock/IMEC, 1944), 239–42; translated as "Man, That Night," in Althusser, *Early Writings: The Spectre of Hegel*, trans. G. M. Goshgarian (London: Verso, 1997), 170–72; Tran duc Thao, "La *Phénoménologie de l'espirt* et son contenu réel," *Les temps modernes* 36 (September 1948): 492–519; Georges Canguilhem, "Hegel en France," *Revue d'histoire et de philosophie religieuses* 28–29 (1948–1949), reprinted in the *Magazine littéraire* (1991): 26–29. "Literature and the Right to Death" occupies an eccentric place in this debate. It is overlooked in bibliographies of Hegel studies of the period, and avoids the two major problems of the controversy: Hegel's relation to Marx, on the one hand, and to Christianity, on the other.

12. Jean-Paul Sartre, *Qu'est-ce que la littérature?* (Paris: Gallimard, collection Folio/essais, 1985), 281; *What Is Literature? And Other Essays* (Cambridge: Harvard University Press, 1988), 228, translation modified to maintain the reference. The cat is taken from Boileau's first *Satire;* the "horse of butter" comes from Georges Bataille's *L'expérience intérieure* (1943), in *Œuvres complètes*, vol. 5 (Paris: Gallimard, 1973), 157, and is cited by Sartre on more than one occasion.

words as a misunderstanding of the nature of language, of what their "health" depends on, and restores the denunciatory (that is, terrorist) subtext of the Boileau reference.[13] It is in the second half of this essay, however, that the example of the cat comes to motivate a reflection on the relation between literature and the referential function of language.

Blanchot's reflections in this second part of the essay are organized around a distinction between two directions or "slopes" of language (he uses both the words *versants* and *pentes;* the importance of these terms, in implicit opposition to "sides" [*côtés*] is that they avoid a static conception). In a first moment the distinction would seem to obtain between everyday language and literary language, but this first opposition soon disappears behind a distinction between poetry and prose. Blanchot traces these distinctions with respect to the question of denomination, understood as the fundamental characteristic of language in its relation to the world. Denomination is first and foremost an act, namely an act of murder. The word—the name—kills the thing it names.

The appropriation of reality that gives language its power depends on this suppression of the real existence of the world. Blanchot here cites Hegel's *First Philosophy of Spirit:* "The first act, by which Adam established his lordship over the animals, is this, that he gave them a name, i.e., he nullified them as beings on their own account, and made them into ideal [entities]."[14] In an "immense hecatomb," the cat is suppressed in favor of the idea of a cat. In the vocabulary Blanchot will generally use in this part of the essay, this cat's "existence" is suppressed, leaving us with its "being."[15] Language's ability to perform

13. "Naturally a writer can always make it his ideal to call a cat a cat. But what he cannot do is then believe he is on the way to health and sincerity. On the contrary, he is causing more mystification than ever, because the cat is not a cat, and anyone who claims it has nothing in mind but this hypocritical violence: Rolet is a rascal" (302/311). This passage from "Situation de l'écrivain en 1947" originally appeared in the July 1947 issue of *Les temps modernes.*

14. Cited from H. S. Harris's translation, Hegel, *System of Ethical Life and First Philosophy of Spirit* (Albany: State University of New York Press, 1979), 221–22.

15. Anne-Lise Schulte Nordholt suggests that we should understand being [*être*] as *essence:* "The term 'existence' designates . . . being in its poorest possible state, in its greatest indigence, what remains of a being when everything, even its essence, has disappeared. This is why, for Blanchot, who is here calling essence 'being,' existence is 'existence without being,' which is to say, in terms of classical metaphysics, existence without essence" (*Maurice Blanchot, L'écriture comme expérience du dehors* [Geneva: Droz, 1995], 54). The explicit identification made by Blanchot is between *être* and *sens.*

this ideal and idealizing murder is ontologically grounded in the mortality of the object. This grounding ultimately requires a shift of examples to the human realm, in which this mortality takes on its full significance.[16] Mallarmé's often-cited description, in "Crise de vers," of the enunciation of the word *fleur* as calling forth *"l'absente de tous bouquets* [the one absent from every bouquet]"[17] is rewritten by Blanchot as "je dis: cette femme [I say: this woman]."

> Of course, my language does not kill anyone. And yet, when I say, "this woman," real death has been announced and is already present in my language. . . . If this woman were not really capable of dying, if she were not threatened by death at every moment of her life, bound and joined to death by an essential bond, I would not be able to carry out that ideal negation, that deferred assassination which is what my language is. [313/323]

What is more, insofar as I implicitly name myself as the subject of my speech every time I speak, each speech act is a suicide as well as a murder. "When I speak, I deny the existence of what I am saying, but I also deny the existence of the person who is saying it" (313–4/324). It is because "we"—"I" and "this woman"—are "the life that endures death and maintains itself in it" that we can be named. It is thus no exaggeration to say, as Blanchot does, that the name, and by the same token the murder, is the truth of the thing. Language names the truth of finitude. It is thus, in the most complete sense of the Hegelian *Aufhebung,* not only a suppression but a *fulfillment* of what is suppressed.

Now, it is important to emphasize at this point that this murderous action of the name is characteristic of both slopes of language. Everyday language is every bit as abstract, idealizing, and murderous as literary language, prose as poetry. The distinction of everyday language is

16. See the parallel passage in Kojève, *Introduction à la lecture de Hegel,* ed. Raymond Queneau (Paris: Gallimard, 1969), 372–73; *Introduction to the Reading of Hegel,* ed. Alan Bloom, trans. James H. Nichols, Jr. (Ithaca: Cornell University Press, 1980), 141, where mortality is identified with finitude: "However, Hegel says, if dogs were not *mortal*—that is, not essentially *finite* or limited with respect to duration—one could not *detach* its concept from it—that is, cause the Meaning (Essence) that is embodied in the *real* dog to pass into the *non*living word."

17. Stéphane Mallarmé, "Crise de vers," in *Œuvres complètes,* ed. Henri Mondor and G. Jean-Aubry (Paris: Gallimard, Bibliothèque de la Pléiade, 1945), 368. "Crisis in Poetry," trans. Mary Ann Caws, in Mallarmé, *Selected Poetry and Prose,* ed. Caws (New York: New Directions, 1982), 76.

that it recoils from the consequences of this murder. Everyday language believes "that once the nonexistence of the cat has passed into the word, the cat itself comes to life again fully and certainly in the form of its idea (its being) and its meaning: on the level of being (idea), the word restores to the cat all the certainty it had on the level of existence" (314/325). This attitude, Blanchot notes ironically, is healthy: the cat may be dead, but understanding marches on. Literary language, to the contrary, does not accept this limitation. It is not only murderous, it is morbid. What it resuscitates is the stinking corpse of Lazarus, "the one who already smells bad, who is Evil" (316/327), Baudelaire's stifling, malodorously perfumed flowers and his *charogne.* Everyday language is in fact more abstract and less realist than literature in that it ignores this corpse. This leftover or remainder of the act of nomination is implicitly identified by Blanchot with another remainder, that of the reality or materiality of the word itself.

The division that interests Blanchot here, then, is not between literature and everyday speech, but between poetry and prose. These two *versants* can be described as two attitudes or strategies that can be adopted with respect to the double remainder. Like everyday language, prose is entirely concerned with meaning, and it perceives the reality of the word as an embarrassing opacity that blocks the ideality of meaning. But unlike everyday language, prose is marked by the "disquiet" that literature is, and therefore cannot content itself with the reconversion of determinate negation into positive meaning, but continues and seeks to grasp the very movement of negation that gives rise to meaning.

> One side of literature is turned toward the movement of negation by which things are separated from themselves and destroyed in order to be known, subjugated, communicated. Literature is not content to accept only the fragmentary, successive results of this movement of negation: it wants to grasp the movement in itself and it wants to comprehend the results in their totality. [318–9/330]

Prose is a permanent negation. It seeks, on the one hand, to negate the entirety of existence—whence its predilection for the novel, wherein the totality of the world is negated and replaced by a fiction—and on the other, it seeks to negate its own products, whence its terrorist (in Paulhan's sense) "distrust of words." Prose seeks to represent, or more precisely to *be,* the endless negating movement of consciousness itself, to go beyond the truth of things to the source of truth.

> On the one hand, its only interest in a thing is in the meaning of the thing, its absence, and it would like to attain this absence absolutely in itself and for itself, to grasp in its entirety the infinite movement of comprehension. What is more, it observes that the word "cat" is not only the nonexistence of the cat but a nonexistence made *word*, that is, a completely determined and objective reality. It sees that there is a difficulty and even a lie in this. [315/325]

Prose goes beyond the negation of the thing by the word to negate the word in turn. It is prose, in this movement of negation, that invents the figure, the negation of the name by the metaphor. Blanchot's supreme examples of *prosateurs* are thus Lautréamont and Sade, writers in whom the absolute clarity of each sentence, of each group of sentences only leads us further into the night of obscurity. The infinite, restless character of this movement implies in turn that prose becomes what had at first seemed to be its opposite, poetry.

Poetry today is habitually defined, in the wake of Jakobson, in terms of the autonomization of the signifier. This characterization is certainly true for Blanchot as well. But in this essay, the emphasis on the material nature of language is in fact a consequence of poetry's true nature, "a concern for the reality of things." The preoccupation with the reality of language therefore appears, not as a closed self-referentiality, but rather as a means to attain this reality of things. The materiality of language is that "thing" that can never be completely negated as meaning, since it is the necessary vehicle of such a negation:

> The language of literature is a search for this moment that precedes literature. Literature usually calls it existence; it wants the cat as it exists, the pebble *taking the side of things* [*le galet dans son* parti pris de chose],[18] not man but the pebble, and in this pebble what man rejects by saying it, what is the foundation of speech and what speech excludes in speaking. . . . What hope do I have of attaining the thing I push away? My hope lies in the materiality of language, in the fact that words are things, too, are a kind of nature. . . . Everything physical takes precedence: rhythm, weight, mass, shape, and then the paper on which one writes, the trail of the ink, the book. [316–7/327]

It is in the signifying material, "a bit of bark, a sliver of rock, a fragment of clay [that] the reality of the earth continues to exist" (317/328). From

18. The reference, which will be taken up more explicitly by Blanchot a page later, is to Francis Ponge, "Le galet," in *Le parti pris des choses* (Paris: Gallimard, collection Poésie, 1967), 92–101.

this point of view, which is that of brute existence, the word is no longer what destroys the thing but what preserves it. It does this at the price of turning its back on meaning, seeking to be rather than to mean. Now, this does not lead to a perfectly symmetrical becoming-prose of poetry. But this flight from meaning does in fact lead back to meaning. "When literature refuses to name anything, when it turns a name into something obscure and meaningless . . . signification in general appear[s] in its place, . . . what asserts itself now is the very possibility of signifying" (318/329). But this possibility is in fact an impossibility for Blanchot: the impossibility of ceasing to be, the impossibility of ceasing to mean, and what Blanchot will call, for the rest of the essay, the impossibility of dying.

The opposition between poetry and prose is extremely volatile and unstable. In fact the two terms relate to one another in the way Paulhan's Terror and Rhetoric do: each of them bears within itself the division that opposes them. They are indeed different, but they are not separate. It is not even possible to segregate literary works empirically into two clearly defined categories. Blanchot multiplies examples that do not fit. "An art which purports to follow one slope is already on the other" (321/332). The "ambiguity" that makes them indistinguishable and capable of reversing positions at any moment will, in the end, be identified with literature as such, and, in a final repetition of the essay's key phrase, will be named "the life that endures death and maintains itself in it."

The first half of the essay is built around a commentary on Hegel's "Spiritual Animal Kingdom." Blanchot's analysis here is based upon Kojève's interpretation, which identifies the "individual" Hegel speaks of in this chapter with "the intellectual."[19] Blanchot takes this allegorization one step further and makes the intellectual "the writer." Kojève's commentary on this passage has the great virtue of giving a strong interpretation of the animality that characterizes this individuality. The ontological separation between man and animal (or between man and nature more generally) is one of the major starting

19. This sort of interpretive move can also be found, although much less insistently, in Hyppolite's *Genesis and Structure of Hegel's 'Phenomenology of Spirit'*," trans. Samuel Cherniak and John Heckman (Evanston: Northwestern University Press, 1974), 305: "The artist expresses his original world view in his work, a world view that is specifically and exclusively his; the intellectual puts his labor and the result of his research into the work—he is entirely in the work."

points of Kojève's interpretation of the *Phenomenology.* Kojève's reading is based on a radical anthropologization of *Geist:* spirit, he repeatedly contends, is human spirit. Such an interpretation requires that Hegel's monist ontology—and with it both his philosophy of nature and the ruse of reason—be discarded in favor of a historical dualism (the human emerges out of nature but once it exists is completely irreducible to natural life).[20]

The difference between man and animal can be expressed most clearly in terms of desire. Animal desire is immediate—it finds its satisfaction in the consumption of a natural object—whereas human desire is fundamentally mediated. Even desire of natural objects is only truly human to the extent that it is *mediated* by another desire, a point Lacan resumed in his formula, *le désir de l'homme est le désir de l'autre* ["man's desire is the desire of the other"]. Animal desire, like human desire, always negates its object, but it does so *immediately.* "Even the animals," writes Hegel, "are not shut out from this wisdom [concerning the nothingness of sensuous being] but, on the contrary, show themselves to be the most profoundly initiated into it; for they do not just stand idly in front of sensuous things as if these possessed intrinsic being, but, despairing of their reality, and completely assured of their nothingness, they fall to without ceremony and eat them up" (*Phenomenology,* 65). The phrase "without ceremony" [*ohne weiteres*] marks this immediacy. Kojève's animals do not labor, that is, defer enjoyment; they do not exchange, that is, establish the value of the object in the eyes of an other; most of all, even if they occasionally fight for the possession of an object, they never struggle for prestige.

Kojève treats the intellectual as an animal because he lacks self-transcendence. What the intellectual seeks to express is merely his "talent" or his "nature," that which is given and which he has not himself created. Thus the intellectual's activity "alters nothing and opposes nothing" (*Phenomenology,* 237). Because he operates in a purely literary mode, the individuality that expresses his talent does not achieve any self-transcendence through a genuine and therefore creative negation. The nature that is expressed remains a given, animal

20. As Charles Taylor has noted, a revolutionary Hegelianism must necessarily anthropologize *Geist,* to do away with the cunning of reason. See *Hegel* (Cambridge: Cambridge University Press, 1975), 424–25: "What is conservative, or at least non-revolutionary, in Hegel has its source in the thesis that the rationality of the real is not that of man, but of Geist. This view of cosmic spirit as the subject of history rules out the possibility of a revolutionary praxis founded on reason. Revolutions are only understood and justified by reason ex post facto."

nature; it is not dialectically transformed in the process of expression. "The intellectual negates nothing; he therefore creates nothing, only manifests his 'nature': he is a 'spiritual' animal [*das geistige Teirreich*]" (Kojève, 93). Even more fundamentally, the intellectual is an animal because his literary mode leaves him always short of the struggle for recognition that is the constitutive moment of human, or more precisely, for Kojève, *anthropogenic* desire. As Michael Roth puts it, the intellectual "only speaks . . . [he] neither triumphs as a master nor works as a slave" (Roth, 106). He pretends to be disinterested and only concerned with the impersonal purity of what Hegel calls "the matter in hand" [*die Sache selbst*]. He fails to insist on recognition, the hallmark of human desire in Kojève's interpretation of Hegel. Rather than forcing the others to recognize his value, the intellectual withdraws into the posture of disinterestedness. This implies that there is no such thing as an *intellectuel engagé,* because the intellectual *risks* nothing. Both commitment and disinterestedness are moments of a dialectic of deception and imposture. This point can also be expressed by saying that there is nothing *social* in the action of the intellectual. Hegel ends "The Spiritual Animal Kingdom" by emphasizing that what is essential is the "action of each and everyone." For Kojève, however, because the intellectual sidesteps the mediation of struggle and labor, both of which necessarily involve a social dimension, the universalization that he is engaged in is inevitably false. "The action of the intellectual is purely *thought:* for him the *Tun Aller und yeder* [*sic*], collective *action,* means that his *thought* must become universal, universally valid" (Kojève, 94). This universalization is false not because of its content, but because it is too immediate; it neglects to pass through the action of the collectivity, to become effective (*wirklich*) in the social life of a people, to engage in the struggle of history.

This analysis allows us to see what is most paradoxical in Blanchot's use of Kojève. Blanchot rejects any opposition between literature and action, any account of literature as a pure passivity. Against Kojève's account of the animality of the intellectual, Blanchot deploys Kojève's own definition of labor as an activity of transformation and negation.

> But what is a writer doing when he writes? Everything a man does when he works, but to an outstanding degree. The writer, too, produces something—a work in the highest sense of the word. He produces this work by transforming natural and human realities. . . . In order to write, he

> must destroy language in its present form and create it in another form. . . . [305/314]

This analysis of writing as labor—simultaneously transformation and negation—implies that there is no such thing as a "mere intellectual," or if there is, it would be one who does not write. The writer is not an animal in Kojève's sense. Blanchot's writer fundamentally chooses human death over animal life. On the basis of this reversal, the rest of Kojève's critique of the intellectual is accepted, or more precisely, assumed—that is, it ceases to be a critique and becomes a positive characterization of the literary project. Like the animal, the writer operates in a domain of immediacy. He negates, but he negates too easily (no matter how difficult it may be to write). His mode of negation sidesteps empirical conditions and possibilities of realization and proceeds immediately to "absolute freedom."

> Insofar as he *immediately* gives himself the freedom he does not have, he is neglecting the actual conditions for his emancipation, he is neglecting to do the real thing that must be done so that the abstract ideal of freedom can be realized. His negation is *global.* This is why this negation negates nothing, in the end, why the work in which it is realized is not a truly negative, destructive act of transformation, but rather the realization of the inability to negate anything. [306/315]

The labor involved in Blanchot's literary freedom fails to create because it is insufficiently destructive. The relations it entertains with the world of productivity and politics—of determinate means and ends—can only be based on a mutual misunderstanding. This misunderstanding is indicated by the second half of the title of Hegel's chapter, "deceit, or the 'matter in hand' itself [*der Betrug oder die Sache selbst*]." Blanchot quite accurately summarizes the sense of this term as "no longer the ephemeral work but something beyond that work: the truth of the work" (300/308). Hegel's characterization of *die Sache selbst* appears as the unity of individual action and the objectivity that the work gains from existing for other individualities; thus it stands above the various moments that make the work something contingent and ephemeral (circumstances, means, reality), and therefore can be taken to represent the higher purpose, the truth of which the work may only be an imperfect realization. And in principle, this higher purpose is what author and readers can agree on as genuinely important, as the source of their interest in the work. Other individuals take an interest in the work and "disinterestedly" offer their opinions and their aid. But this interest in the "matter in hand" displayed by all the individualities is in fact merely a cover for their true interest in their own action. While Hegel expressly qualifies this attitude as honesty or integrity [*Ehrlichkeit*], it is clear that it is fundamentally an alibi. The retreat into a consideration of one's own action as the true matter at hand, however, is equally deceptive, for the work continues to exist for others. "It is, then," Hegel concludes, "equally a deception of oneself and of others if it is pretended that what one is concerned with is the 'matter in hand' alone" (*Phenomenology*, 251).

Blanchot gives a number of possible versions of the "matter in hand" as higher purpose: art, the ideal, the world, values, authenticity, etc. Even failure, silence, or nothingness can be figured as the essence of literature and therefore as the truth behind the work. But the dialectic of deception that takes place around this notion is best illustrated by the example of engagement in a political "Cause" (which is, moreover, an excellent translation of *Sache*):

> For example: [an author] writes novels, and these novels imply certain political statements, so that he seems to side with a certain Cause. Other people, people who directly support the Cause, are then inclined to recognize him as one of themselves, to see his work as proof that the Cause is really his cause, but as soon as they make this claim, as soon as they try to become involved in this activity and take it over, they realize that the writer is not on their side, that he is only on his own side, that what interests him about the Cause is the operation he himself has carried out—and they are puzzled. It is easy to understand why men who have committed themselves to a party, who have made a decision, distrust writers who share their views; because these writers have also committed themselves to literature, and in the final analysis literature, by its very activity, denies the substance of what it represents. [301/309–10]

The writer cannot commit himself to a cause because the activity through which this commitment would be expressed, namely literature, nullifies any particular purpose it would represent.

On the basis of this passage, we can describe the central question of the first half of the essay as a critique of Sartrean *engagement* in terms of the negativity constitutive of literature. "The right to death" therefore appears as a different relation to politics. This makes the section on the Revolution, in the middle of the essay, its culmination. For Blanchot, the relation between literature and politics—that is to say, the question to which *engagement* is one possible response—cannot be understood in immediately political terms. A relation can only be established between these two terms by beginning with an understanding of the character of the literary project as such. We have seen that this project, for Blanchot, implies an *immediate* and *total* negation of the world as it is given to us. Therefore a commitment to a *particular* political project, a Cause, is impossible for a writer as *writer:* it is an act of imposture or bad faith, which is in fact perceived as such by both writers and *militants.* This is true whatever the writer's political sympathies may happen to be. There is, however, a political *analogue* to this immediate and total negation of the world, namely, the Revolutionary Terror. The writer's relation to the Terror, however, cannot be described in terms of commitment; rather, it appears as an *identification.*[21] The writer *recognizes himself* in the Terror. This is no more a question of the individual writer's particular political sympathies than is the imposture of commitment. Instead, this recognition is founded on the nature of the literary project as such and the relation to politics that literature allows or indeed demands. This is in fact the fundamental point of the example of Sade: despite his noble family background and his attachment to the ways of the *Ancien Régime,* despite his relatively humanitarian behavior in 1792–1794, the fundamental meaning of his writing as writing is to be found in an infinite movement of negation. Blanchot's contemporaneous essay, "La raison de Sade," (1947) describes this movement of negation that accepts no limit: if at a certain moment nature appears as a positive name for the very movement of negation, and thus becomes the totality that contains this movement and reconverts it into positivity, it must be negated in its turn.[22]

This infinite movement of negation is also the essence of the Revolution, which is the meaning of Hegel's phrase, "*absolute* freedom." There is no social reality that cannot be freely transformed. "At this moment," writes Blanchot, "freedom aspires to be realized in the *immediate* form of *everything* is possible, everything can be done." It is

21. In a later essay entitled "L'insurrection, la folie d'écrire," Blanchot abandons this term in favor of "coincidence." See Blanchot, *L'entretien infini* (Paris: Gallimard, 1969), 330; translated by Susan Hanson as "Insurrection, the Madness of Writing," in *The Infinite Conversation* (Minneapolis: University of Minnesota Press, 1993), 222. This essay was originally published under the title "L'inconvenance majeure," as the preface to D. A. F. de Sade, *Français, encore un effort si vous voulez être républicains* (Paris: Jean-Jacques Pauvert, 1965).

22. Blanchot, "La raison de Sade," in *Lautréamont et Sade* (Paris: Éditions de Minuit, 1963), 40–42.

precisely this combination of immediacy and totality that makes the Revolution a literary event. Reality no longer resists. It "sinks effortlessly, without work, into nothingness." Everyone can propose his or her own constitution, attempt to immediately universalize his or her own consciousness as reality. The classic question of the relation between literature and the Revolution concerns the "influence" of Enlightenment thinking. Blanchot's description of the Terror bypasses this unresolvable question, and points to what is most fundamental in Hegel's analysis: the extent to which the Revolution, as event, has the form of literature. The Revolution is a fabulation: a new world, with new men and new laws. "The speech of fable becomes action. . . . Revolutionary action explodes with the same force and the same facility as the writer who has only to set down a few words side by side in order to change the world" (309/318–19). It is therefore not so much that the writer identifies with the Revolution—he does, but this is in fact secondary. *The Revolution* realizes *literature. But because it realizes* literature, *it is in fact completely derealizing.* It is in the Revolution as revolution, or more precisely, as permanent insurrection, and not as the realization of particular if universalistic values, that this literary ambition comes to pass. The Revolution is not a state, but an infinite movement of negation.[23]

Blanchot's most direct and most important borrowing from Kojève is the title phrase, "the right to death." Kojève had written, in one of his most deliberately provocative formulations:

> We have seen that death voluntarily confronted in a negating struggle is precisely the most authentic realization and manifestation of absolute individual freedom. It is thus indeed in and by the Terror that this freedom spreads throughout society, and it cannot be attained in a "tolerant" state which does not take its citizens sufficiently seriously to assure them of their political right to death. [Kojève, 558]

The right to death is therefore something that must be claimed, and that must be claimed precisely because it represents the highest fulfill-

23. See "L'insurrection, la folie d'écrire," 330; "Insurrection, the Madness of Writing," 222: Sade "says that living in a republic will not suffice to make a republican, nor will a republic be made by having a constitution, nor, finally, will laws make this constitutive act that is the creative power endure and maintain us in a state of permanent constitution. We must make an effort, and still always another—this is the invisible irony. . . . But what sort of effort will it be? . . . Sade calls this permanent state of the republic insurrection. In other words, a republic knows no state, only movement."

ment of human (literary?) freedom. The terrorist is one who has already claimed his right to death, claimed it for himself before claiming it also for others, and is therefore speaking as one already dead. The frequent invocations made by Robespierre and Saint-Just (as well as by a score of less notorious orators of the period) of their impending deaths are thus not "mere" (that is to say, dispensable) rhetorical flourishes. They in fact define the *lieu d'énonciation* of their discourse, and the possession of this rhetorical position is one of the major sources of their political power. The terrorist speaks from beyond the grave, as one who is already dead.

> Robespierre's virtue, Saint-Just's relentlessness, are simply their existences already suppressed, the anticipated presence of their deaths, the decision to allow freedom to assert itself completely in them and through its universality to negate the particular reality of their lives. Granted, perhaps they caused the Reign of Terror to take place. But the Terror they personify does not come from the death they inflict on others but from the death they inflict on themselves. . . . The Terrorists are those who desire absolute freedom and are fully conscious that this constitutes a desire for their own death. [310/319–20][24]

The Terror suppresses individuals, killing them off as if their particular lives had no meaning. It is, indeed, *because* rather than *in spite of* this fact, that the Terror is the fulfillment of humanity for Kojève (Humanism *as* Terror), just as, for Blanchot, it is the fulfillment of literature. But an essential difference must be remarked here. Whereas for Kojève the historical function of the Terror is to prepare for the universal (Napoleonic-Hegelian-Stalinist) state, in which humanity will be fully satisfied and thus history at an end, for Blanchot what remains after this moment is *poetry.* If prose is the most truly murderous form of literature, poetry's concern for what remains after this hecatomb is inhuman, but perhaps thereby more humane. "Ponge's descriptions," writes Blanchot, "begin at that hypothetical moment after the world has been achieved, history completed, nature almost made human, when speech advances to meet the thing and the thing learns to speak."

24. For a historiographical interpretation of the Terror that reaches remarkably similar conclusions, see Claude Lefort, "The Revolutionary Terror," in *Democracy and Political Theory,* trans. David Macey (Minneapolis: University of Minnesota Press, 1988), particularly 86–87: "The Terror is revolutionary in that it forbids anyone to occupy the place of power; and in that sense, it has a democratic character. . . . Robespierre was constantly obliged to cover up the paths that had brought him to power, but this was not because of some character trait; as we said above, it was because everyone who sought power was under an obligation to disappear as an individual."

They express "not existence as it was before the day but existence as it is after the day, the world of the end of the world" (323/335). Literature, Blanchot says in conclusion, is "the life which supports death and maintains itself in it" (330/343). But while this death may be what is most human in the world, indeed "a power that humanizes nature" (325/337), the life that survives it is not our life. Literature is what survives humanity.

HENT DE VRIES

"Lapsus Absolu": Notes on Maurice Blanchot's *The Instant of My Death*

> Dying means: you are dead already, in an immemorial past, of a death which was not yours, which you have thus neither known nor lived, but under the threat of which you believe you are called upon to live; you await it henceforth in the future, constructing a future to make it possible at last—possible as something that will take place and will belong to the realm of experience.
>
> —Maurice Blanchot, *The Writing of the Disaster*

It has always been risky to speak of the conceptual underpinnings of a corpus of texts—Blanchot's "oeuvre"—in which critical commentaries have not only accompanied and commented upon the fictional writings (the novels and *récits*) from early on, but in which these seemingly separate kinds of writing have increasingly interpenetrated each other to the point of becoming virtually indistinguishable from each other. Indeed, the greatest challenge of Blanchot's writing, for any philosophical interpretation, as much as for any other reading, might be posed by the more recent fragmentary meditations and *récits* in which the common distinctions between the genres of fictional narration, literary criticism, the philosophical aphorism, as well as of autobiography seem to have been all but erased. One of the most puzzling examples of this recent writing is Blanchot's *L'instant de ma mort* (*The Instant of My Death*), published in 1994, and which is the main focus of this essay.[1] It is in this recent text that one finds the elements of literature, philosophy, historical engagement, testimony, and, it seems, autobiography; the interplay, or rather entanglement, of these elements calls for a reading that is at once philosophically astute and sensitive to the text's apparent fictionality. This fictional status first appears in the curious role of the voice of the narrator and, as always, in

1. Maurice Blanchot, *L'instant de ma mort* (Montpellier: Fata Morgana, 1994). Translations from this work are my own.

YFS 93, *The Place of Maurice Blanchot,* ed. Thomas Pepper, © 1998 by Yale University.

the relationship between the "je" and the "il," in which one takes the role of the other, and indeed substitutes for the other. *L'instant de ma mort* provides us with a meditation on the meaning of death, of its impossibility and of its necessity, its irreplaceability and its apparent universality. It does so in a short narration which, for all its singularity or idiosyncracy—suggested already by its very title—entails an oblique interrogation of the philosophies of death, from Plato (whose *dictum* "For of death, no one has knowledge" Blanchot had already quoted in the opening sentence of *Le dernier à parler*, the text devoted to Paul Celan) through Hegel and Heidegger, and others as well.

One of the contemporary authors on whom Maurice Blanchot has had a decisive and lasting influence and in whom he has arguably found in turn his most patient and formidable interpreter is Jacques Derrida. The work of Derrida provides us with an important key to the reading of the suggestive text of *L'instant de ma mort*, which, for all its brevity, conjures up not only an immense tradition of thought and an engagement with the forces of history, but also the depths of an inwardness that seems "indestructible" or at least marked by a sublime indifference, and that neither historiography nor autobiography can capture.

Derrida is one of the contemporary French thinkers who, together with Michel Foucault, Emmanuel Levinas, and Jean-Luc Nancy, has payed homage and devoted extensive attention to the inexhaustable richness of Blanchot's oeuvre and, more particularly, to intricacies and indeterminacies of its literary, fictional or narrative, and critical challenge of the concept and the practice of genre. In addition, it could be argued that, like no other reader, Derrida has, from the outset of his career, insisted on the philosophical pertinence of Blanchot's writing to any responsible discussion of the relationship between literature and critical thought (not to be confused with the Heideggerian *Denken* and *Dichten*[2]), and to any discussion of literature and critical thought in relation to the elusive notion that will interest us here. This notion forms the extreme limit—the end or, rather, the very beginning—of all narration, of discourse, and, if this could be said, of experience in general. In Blanchot's writings, as has often been noted, this peculiar notion is given different names, and the same name may evoke radically different associations, descriptions, analyses, and conjure up

2. See Timothy Clark, *Derrida, Heidegger, Blanchot: Sources of Derrida's Notion and Practice of Literature* (Cambridge: Cambridge University Press, 1992).

other names. But all of them, in some way or another, revolve around the nondialectical negativity of *death* or, more precisely, around the singular mode of our relation—*dying* (*le mourir*)—to this death, which never gives or presents itself to us, here and now, in any experience, or as such. It is in addressing this absolute singularity, whose very idiom even absolves itself from language—without, therefore, becoming unsayable or idiosyncratic—that Blanchot, throughout his long career as a writer, has touched upon the central myths and theologemes of the Western, Judeo-Christian tradition as well as upon some of its most irreducible philosophemes. It is first of all in speaking of death—and in the wake of the death that, he argues, characterizes and enables all writing, especially the writing called literary whose privileged *instance* is the *récit*—that Blanchot enters into a philosophical dialogue with Hegel and Heidegger, Levinas and Derrida. Their work, I would argue, forms the philosophical backdrop against which to place the Blanchotian leitmotif that I will attempt to discuss here by drawing on merely one decisive insight of the recently published *L'instant de ma mort*.

Derrida has devoted several major analyses to Blanchot's novels and *récits*. The most explicit and elaborate of these readings have been collected in *Parages*.[3] This volume is in the first place dedicated to the intractable forms taken by such fictional writings as *Thomas l'obscur*, *L'arrêt de mort*, and *La folie du jour*. But other references to the more essayistic and theoretically or philosophically oriented texts of Blanchot abound, from Derrida's earliest up to his most recent writings. The list of allusions to the name and the work of Blanchot ranges from *L'écriture et la différence* to *Spectres de Marx*, *Politiques de l'amitié* and *Aporias*. All of these writings, it could be argued, pursue the response to Blanchot collected in *Parages*. These extend Derrida's reading well beyond the *récits* and address the whole spectrum of Blanchot's other texts, from *L'entretien infini* (notably the essay "La pensée et l'exigence de discontinuité"), *La part du feu* (in particular the chapter "La littérature et le droit à la mort"), and *L'amitié* (especially the parts entitled "Les trois paroles de Marx" and "La facilité de mourir"), to name only the most significant examples. The latest of these readings is "DEMEURE: fiction et témoignage," published most recently in *Passions de la littérature*.[4]

3. Jacques Derrida, *Parages* (Paris: Galilee, 1986).

4. Derrida, "DEMEURE: fiction et temoignage," in *Passions de la littérature. Avec Jacques Derrida*, ed. Michel Lisse (Paris: Galilée, 1996), 13–73.

Taken together, these analyses necessitate an interrogation of an intellectual filiation that no one could pretend to be able to reconstitute fully, here or elsewhere. Paradoxically, the first task of any such inquiry should consist in examining the difficulty, indeed the very impossibility, of determining a rigorous concept of influence, of intellectual inheritance, of translation, and even of interpretation. Such an examination might well establish that the complex, yet far from random processes that govern the relationships between authors and texts do not permit us to establish a simple, let alone unilinear, mode through which ideas are transmitted. For if there is any dialogue between them, it is characterized by transference and belatedness, among other things. This is the very structure of the leitmotif that interests me here: death, the impossible being toward the impossibility that is death.

It should come as no surprise, then, that Derrida's *Parages* begins with a preliminary consideration of precisely this interpretive and analytical problem as it is encountered by any genuine reading of Blanchot's work. This difficulty pertains to his fiction—novels and *récits*—as well as to the critical and philosophically oriented work that has accompanied these literary writings from the very outset of Blanchot's career. They entail the suggestive effect of a writing praxis that resists the categories commonly attributed to the world of letters. Nonetheless, Derrida argues, they testify to a formalizable logics of singularity, of the singular, a logics that is at once exact and elusive, paradoxical and aporetic. And, it is precisely in their tendency toward a relentless formalism and impersonalism, Derrida goes on to suggest, that Blanchot's writings acquire their surprising and often unsettling intensity.

This is nowhere clearer than in their fictional evocation and in their critical analysis of the notion, the figureless figure, and the impossible experience of so-called death. The most recent and most telling example of this preoccupation with death and everything for which it stands can be found in *L'instant de ma mort*. This text contains a host of indirect or oblique "references" to the modern philosophical traditions, references of the kind mentioned above. But it is also marked by what Derrida, in his most recent discussions of death or the being-towards-death, has come to term the "culture" and the "politics of death." In this, I would claim, it departs from the long tradition of meditations on death, of the *memento mori*. Neither a reconcilation *with* nor an appropriation *of* death is attempted in Derrida here.

Given the limited space available in this context, I take my point of departure from a compressed citation that Derrida takes from Blanchot's *L'écriture du désastre* and that can be found in one of the final notes to *Aporias:*[5]

> Dying means: you are dead already, in an immemorial past, of a death which was not yours. . . . This uncertain death, always anterior—this vestige of a past that has never been present—is never individual. . . . Impossible necessary death . . . one lives and speaks only by killing the *infans* in oneself (in others also).[6]

Derrida's elliptical commentary in this particular context is revealing and will guide this discussion of *L'instant de ma mort:*

> Here as elsewhere one can recognize the reference to Heidegger, notably to the thinking of death as the "possibility of impossibility" [the well-known formulation from *Sein und Zeit* that Blanchot addresses in the same context, in a discussion of the specific case of the death called suicide]. . . . The apparent neutrality of this reference (neither an approbation nor a critique) deserves a patient and original treatment that we cannot undertake here. [*Aporias,* 87 n. 18]

Yet with reference to the earlier reading of *L'arrêt de mort* in "Survivre," the main text of *Aporias* echoes this by recalling the leitmotif that interests us here and that, as Derrida reminds us, we find most

5. Derrida, "Apories. Mourir—s'attendre aux 'limites de la vérité,'" in *Le passage des frontières. Autour du travail de Jacques Derrida,* ed. Marie-Louise Mallet (Paris: Galilée, 1994), 309–38. *Aporias. Dying—awaiting (one another at) the "limits of truth,"* trans. Thomas Dutoit (Stanford: Stanford University Press, 1993).

6. Cf. Blanchot, *The Writing of the Disaster,* trans. Ann Smock (Lincoln: University of Nebraska Press, 1986), 65; 66; 67; The figure of the *infans* is borrowed from Serge Leclaire. Blanchot explains: "One lives and speaks only by killing the *infans* in oneself (in others also); but what is the *infans?* Obviously that in us which has not yet begun to speak and never will speak; but, more importantly, the marvelous (terrifying) child which we have been in the dreams and the desires of those who were present at out birth (our parents, society in general)" (67). I will not analyze this motif here, but only note that it allows one to engage with at least three related discussions: first, the one that Blanchot has in this very context with psychoanalysis; second, and more obliquely, with Heidegger, more precisely with the latter's privileging of being-toward-death over and against a being-toward-birth that seems to be marked by an almost similar structure, by an analogous possibility of impossibility; and, third, even more indirectly, with the very figure of the sacrifice of the child that haunts Derrida's interpretation of the sacrifice of Isaac, of Kierkegaard's *Fear and Trembling,* and, more generally, of the giving oneself (and others) death, in *Donner la mort.* In addition to "Pas" and *Apories,* I consider this text to be of crucial importance for any attempt—however provisional, as it is undertaken here—to unravel the enigmatic texture of *L'instant de ma mort.*

clearly expressed in *L'attente l'oubli, Le pas au-delà* and, again, in *L'écriture du désastre:*

> When Blanchot constantly repeats—and it is a long complaint and not a triumph of life—the impossible dying, the impossibility, alas, of dying, he says *at once the same thing and something completely different from Heidegger.* It is just a question of knowing in which sense (in the sense of direction and trajectory) one reads the expression of the possibility of impossibility. [*Aporias,* 77; my emphasis]

Death, the impossible experience and endless agony of death, forms the subject of many of Blanchot's novels and critical essays. *Thomas l'obscur, L'arrêt de mort,* and *Le dernier homme,* no less than the studies on Mallarmé and Rilke collected in *L'espace littéraire,* abound in analyses of the modification of time and space in light of the relation toward a death that seems unable to arrive—or to be experienced—*as such.*[7] Speaking of the *arrêt* of death, Blanchot evokes this paradoxical, indeed aporetic, structure by suggesting that one's being sentenced to death does not exclude but, on the contrary, presupposes the suspension of its actual arrival. More precisely still, death does not stop to arrive. Yet a death that at every instant goes on to arrive never arrives as such. Put otherwise, its arrival as such retains an element or structure of ineffaceable delay or postponement. Its distance is a measure of its imminence, it retreats the more one comes near to it.

What to think, then, against the backdrop of this well-known schema, of the title and the content of Blanchot's *récit* entitled *L'instant de ma mort?* Does this title seem to contradict all the central features that had dominated the earlier writings? Does it not bid farewell to the endless analysis of an indefinite, it not necessarily infinite, suspension of death, an analysis that would seem to undermine the very evocation, in the title and the text that interest us here, of an apparent punctuality of the notion rather than the concept of the "in-

7. Many excellent analyses have been devoted to the relationship between literature, philosophy, writing, and death. See, for example, Anne-Lise Schulte Nordholt, *Maurice Blanchot. L'écriture comme expérience du dehors* (Geneva: Droz, 1995), chapters 2 and 10; John Gregg, *Maurice Blanchot and the Transgression of Literature* (Princeton: Princeton University Press, 1994), chapter 3; Evelyne Londyn, *Maurice Blanchot. Romancier* (Paris: Éditions A.-G. Nizet, 1976), chapter 1; Françoise Collin, "Arrêts de morts," *Magazine littéraire* 197, special issue on "La littérature et la mort" (July/August 1983): 34–38; and Collin, *Maurice Blanchot et la question de l'écriture* (Paris: Gallimard, 1971), notably 120 ff. and 190 ff., to name only a few examples. None of these authors, however, was able to address *L'instant de ma mort.*

stant" and *a fortiori* of the concept or, again, the notion of "death" and "dying" in the sense Blanchot has given to these apparently all too familiar words? Can there be an "instant" of death, especially of *my* death, of which I can be the witness or to which I myself can testify, in the present, here and now, or after the fact? Can this "instant" be anything else but always—and always already, from birth and earlier on—in coming, at least *for me:* an "instant forever pending," that is to say, *"en instance"*?[8] Moreover, does the phrase *ma mort* not undercut the very impersonality of the experience of death, which nonetheless continues to subtract itself from any relation between a preestablished or fixed subject that could be said to "be" and its supposed destination, termination, and nonbeing? In other words: how does the text of *L'instant de ma mort* situate itself with respect to the Heideggerian description of death in terms of anticipation or *Vorlaufen,* to be distinguished from the expectation of a determinable event, an anticipation, moreover, characterized by an indelible mineness or *Jemeinigkeit,*[9] rather than by *le neutre?*

The structure of the relation to death or, as Heidegger puts it in *Being and Time,* to our being-towards-death, is one of waiting, awaiting, expectation, and anticipation alone. Or so it seems. For some essential conceptual differentiations have to be made here. They all revolve around the understanding of the most paradoxical or even aporetic features of the "waiting" that all thinking and all experience tend to suppress and forget. It is precisely to these features that Blanchot already points in his contribution to the *Festschrift* for Heidegger's seventieth birthday, published in 1959, in a short text entitled "L'attente" and later included in his *L'attente l'oubli.* And *L'instant de ma mort,* whose *récit* we are about to read, follows a similar path—similar also to the ones taken by *L'arrêt de mort* and *L'écriture du désastre*—in that it sets out our common interpretation of time, of human temporality, both in its vulgar (objective, historical) sense and, I would add, in its supposedly originary, ontological sense (as defined by Heidegger in the Second Division of *Being and Time*). Some indications may suffice to make this clear.

If the voice of the narrator recalls that the young man who undergoes the near-execution is "still young," then the subsequent interrupted experience and the haunting character of this event or nonevent

8. See also Derrida, "DEMEURE," 34.
9. See also Derrida, "DEMEURE," 38.

is a process of sudden aging or *vieillissement,* to use the phrase to which Levinas has given new philosophical significance. This apparent detail is not without relevance for the general argument here. Whereas *Being and Time* invokes the saying that as soon as man is born he is old enough to die—"Sobald ein Mensch zum Leben kommt, sogleich ist er alt genug zu sterben"[10]—Blanchot's *récit,* by contrast, strikes an almost Levinasian tone by implying that man is—like the unlucky sons of the farmers—either *too young* (that is to say, *not old enough*) or, conversely, *already too old* to die. One never dies on time. While one dies at some time or another, one never dies in a timely way or, indeed, *in* time. More generally speaking, the text of *L'instant de ma mort* can be read as an exploration of the untemporality, or atemporality, or countertemporality, of the instant, that is to say, of the instant of death or, as we shall soon see, of the very *instance* and instantiation of this instant. For while it is clear that the text seems to be centered around a few incisive historical dates (1807 and 1944), and in fact displays an almost comic excess of chronological detail—e.g., in its portrayal of the family of the young man: "the aunt (94 years old), his much younger mother"—the scene that is evoked or remembered is also one of detemporalization. Thus, the still young man is said to age or grow old overnight. By contrast, the Germans who make up the firing squad at the very moment when the forces of the *maquis* intervene are depicted as frozen, immoblized, when the *arrêt de mort*—the undeclared death sentence—comes to a halt (*arrêt*). What is arrested is time alone.[11] In addition, there is a general insecurity on the part of the voice of the narrator (or ascribed to the main protagonist of the narration) with respect to the time that has elapsed between the different actions and situations that punctuate the story. As a consequence, the *récit* seems to provide us with what are finally conflicting indices concerning the time taken up by the course of the events that are related. Let me give yet another revealing example. It is in the woods that the voice of the narrator says:

> *Suddenly* [*tout à coup*], and *after how much time* [*après combien de temps*] he found a sense of the real. Everywhere, there was fire, a *sequence* [*une suite*] of *continuous* [*continu*] fire, all the farms were burning. *A little later* [*Un peu plus tard*] he learned that three young

10. Martin Heidegger, *Sein und Zeit* (Tübingen: Max Niemeyer Verlag, 1979), 245.

11. See Blanchot, *L'instant de ma mort:* "Les allemands restaient en ordre, prêts à demeurer ainsi dans une immobilité qui arrêtait le temps" (12).

> men, sons of farmers, who had been strangers to the struggle, and whose wrong was only their youth, had been slain.
>
> Even the swollen horses, on the road, in the fields, testified to the fact that a war *had raged for some time* [*avait duré*]. In fact, *how much time had elapsed* [*combien de temps s'était-il écoulé*]? [*L'instant de ma mort*, 13; my emphasis]

Even while the face-to-face with death inspires a sudden, unanticipated sentiment of "lightness" and "extasis," this mood is less an appropriation of the young man's being-there than a freedom from being. More significantly, it is presented as the momentary—or, rather, less than momentary and *im*mediate because *in*temporal and *non*-dialectizable—flight from the very weight that life, the war, and the responsibility for others (in the first place for the family in the castle and for friends in the resistance) impose. Thus, the "instant" of evasion is not only followed by the "instant" of the return to the world of affairs, the two instants are, in a sense, one and the same. As in the Platonic parable of the cave that is related in the *Republic*—the philosophical counterpart, if one can say so, of the myth of Orpheus and Euridyce, analyzed in *L'espace littéraire*—the care for the soul, of that soul, that is, in its very preoccupation with death, is in essence an uplifting yet blinding movement of ascent—and a return to light and life—followed by the equally blinding movement of the soul in its descent back into the dark. The young man steps forward out of the castle, faces his death, only to disappear in the woods. What thus comes to interrupt the everydayness of his experience does not spare him from rediscovering this everydayness in an even more disconcerting manner than ever before. Yet, the return of what the words of the narrator describe as *le sens du réel* is not so much the real in an empirical, ontic, or historical sense, let alone the real of which much is made by Lacanian psychoanalysis. It is a heightened and irrefutable sense of responsibility, of a responsibility even or especially for those who are not one's direct concern, one's relatives or neighbors, but whose sociopolitical status is unmistakable. The three young men from the country who die instead are those whose only "wrong" (*tort*) had been their age and, it would seem, their class. The "torture of injustice" that the one who lives on suffers, from this moment on, is grounded in the mere fact of his living on alone, which, it should be added, is also the condition of his testimony and of testimony in general ("DEMEURE," 33–34). *De facto* and *de iure* his life takes the place of theirs. That also is the mistake made by justice, "the error of injustice" (*L'instant de ma mort,* 7), of which the narrator is immediately reminded (even though this error is mentioned only after the dying [*mourir*] of the still young man which has been prevented by death itself [*la mort même*], that is to say, by the "sentiment of lightness" but also—perhaps [*peut-être*]—by death of the others). No ecstasis of death and, at the same time, more of this ecstasis—*Plus d'extase*—both characterize the existence and the conscience of the one who had been given death, were it not for the intervention of others, and who gives death to others, in turn. Young men take the place, in this narration, of the feminine figures whose agonies and corpses populate Blanchot's novels and *récits*. Here, in *L'instant de ma mort,* the women are spared and move silently back into the house, "a long and slow cortège, silent, as if everything had already been accomplished" (*L'instant de ma mort,* 10).

In all this the opposition between the castle, a designated place of exception and social distinction, or between what is called the castle (*le Château, disait-on*), and what surrounds it is crucial. It reinscribes the seemingly abstract, existential, and ontological problem of death and finitude into what Derrida will come to call the culture and the politics of death.[12] Without ever raising the issue directly, the *récit* makes one wonder whether the young farmers have sensed the same lightness when confronted with their death or whether even this very sentiment that is supposed to signal a step beyond being and not-being, beyond life and death, is not itself already tainted or prejudged by social privilege. *Il faut bien mourir,* Derrida writes in *Aporias,* a formulation

12. Two further observations should be made here. First, it is no accident that it is precisely in Blanchlot's reading of Franz Kafka that the relationship between writing and death is analyzed. And the direct or oblique reference to the latter's second major novel, *The Castle,* is never absent here. In the second place, it is tempting and, I would add, imperative also to treat Derrida's well-known reading of Kafka's "Vor dem Gesetz" ["Before the Law"], in "Préjugés—devant la loi," as a reading *avant la lettre*—more precisely, after *Parages* but well before *Aporias* and "DEMEURE"—of *L'instant de ma mort.* Conversely, Blanchot's *récit* can be considered as an *instantiation* or *re-instantiation* of the formal schematics, if one may say so, that Derrida's reading puts in place. "Préjugés," at least as much as *L'instant de ma mort,* is a thorough, some would say fatal, rearticulation of the existential analytic of the being-toward-death in light of a relentless exposure of its inherent aporias. Interestingly, the evocation of an endless deferral of waiting, as in the case of the man from the country in Kafka's parable, and of instant *en instance,* forever pending, comes down to the same: in both places it indicates the relation-without-relation to death. Perversely, they each say the same thing as Heidegger and *something completely different.*

that brings into play all the ambiguity of the necessity of dying (one has to die anyway, one way or the other) and the need or desire of dying well expressed by so many discourses *de bene moriendi. Il faut bien mourir,* but, we might add, not everybody dies as well. The death, then, whose instant is related in this *L'instant de ma mort,* is perhaps not just any other death, it is hardly the death of everyone. It is a guilty death, albeit not as a general rule or universal quality, but in the singularity of *my* death. Blanchot touches here upon the logic of substitution that is developed in the later writings of Levinas, which center around the enigmatic phrase that speaks of *ma substitution,* in the middle chapter of *Autrement qu'être ou au-delà de l'essence.*[13]

In saying this, however, we have reached the point where a Levinasian *récit*—or, for that matter, a Levinasian reading of Blanchot's *récit*—must presumably also come to a halt since there is nothing more to say.[14] Such a reading could not but affirm the most cynical note on which Blanchot's text seems to conclude—"That was it, war: life for some, death for others, the cruelty of assassination" (*L'instant de ma mort,* 16). What is more, it could not but locate whatever remains other in the other (*autrui*) and the Other (the trace of "God" left in the face of this other) alone. For the narrator of *L'instant de ma mort,* by contrast, something else remains as well. It is here that, in spite of its essential untranslatability, the "infinite" seems to open itself in the first place (or for the first time). What remains is an interiorization and introjected "death" in relation to which—or, paradoxically, in comparison to whose immeasurability—the first death, no less than the ones to come, loses much, perhaps all, of its ontological privilege:

> Neither happiness, nor unhappiness. Neither the absence of fear and perhaps already the step (not) beyond [*le pas au-delà*]. I know, I imagine that this unanalyzable sentiment changed what remained to him of existence. As if the death outside him could not but clash with [or find itself limited by] the death inside him. "You live. No, you are dead."[15]

13. Emmanuel Levinas, *Autrement qu'être ou au-delà de l'essence* (The Hague: M. Nijhoff, 1974).

14. See Collin, "La peur. Emmanuel Levinas et Maurice Blanchot," in *Cahiers de l'Herne: Levinas* (Paris: L'Herne, 1991), 313–27; Schulte Nordholt, *Maurice Blanchot: L'écriture comme expérience du dehors,* 334 ff.; Paul Davies, "A Fine Risk. Reading Blanchot Reading Levinas," in *Re-Reading Levinas,* ed. Robert Bernasconi and Simon Critchley (Bloomington and Indianapolis: Indiana University Press, 1991), 201–26.

15. *L'instant de ma mort,* 16–17. Needless to say, one is reminded here of the striking motto taken from Poe that opens Derrida's *La voix et le phénomène. Introduc-*

Contrasting the death inside and the one outside, overcoming or counterbalancing the latter with the help of the former, and this to the point of erasing—giving death to—their very distinction, all this comes down to the repetition of a classical topos. It is the topos of the *memento mori* that informs a whole tradition from at least Plato through Christianity up to Heidegger. This, it would seem, is the only thing that remains and the sole thing that counts:

> What remains is solely the sentiment of lightness which is death itself or, to put it more precisely, the instant of my death which is from now on always pending [*en instance*]. [*L'instant de ma mort*, 20]

It should be noted that the voice of the narrator does not project this mode of relating to death—or *as dead*—onto an ontological and originary modality of being-there or existence. Not only is the mode in question one that never comes into its own and, as a consequence, remains forever in suspension, imminent or, more precisely, *en instance*. The new mode of relating to death is also opened up by an event that, for all its historical specificity, apparently never took place as such or whose actual violence was first of all or in fact inflicted upon others. Moreover, everything here is a matter of memory, of the power of recollection. It is no accident that the sole capitalized words—"*I REMEMBER*" [*JE ME SOUVIENS*] (*L'instant de ma mort*, 7)—mark the very beginning of the *récit*, which struggles throughout with the distinction between the "essential" and the "empirical" (*L'instant de ma mort*, 15)—a distinction that, as the text ironically states, was still possible for a Hegel—only to resign by stating that, in the end, subtleties of this kind matter little: "Qu'importe." What remains is what remains alone—trauma, if one wishes, but the concept as well as its psychoanalytic reverberations are conspicuously absent here, as if they were still too comforting, too serious, too schematic also, for the understanding (without understanding) of what is at issue in the "sentiment of lightness," that is to say, of that which alone remains, as it were, as our (mine, his) sole *habitat* (*seul demeure*). And yet, it is in spite of (or thanks to) its very elusiveness that what remains "is" *from now on* also something "indestructible":

> Man is indestructible and . . . can none the less be destroyed. This happens in affliction [*malheur*]. In affliction we approach the limit

tion au problème du signe dans la phénoménologie de Husserl (Paris: Presses Universitaires de France, 1967); see also 108.

> where, deprived of the power to say "I," deprived also of the world, we would be nothing other than this Other [*Autre*] that we are not.[16]

We can now understand—again, without fully understanding, for an aporia, especially this aporia, the *sans issue* of death, marks precisely the limit (in Levinas's words, the *sans réponse*) of all understanding—why Derrida's assertion that Blanchot "says at once the same thing and something very different from Heidegger," gives an exact description of the difficulty of situating Blanchot *vis-à-vis* Heidegger, in particular where the question of death is concerned. Derrida writes, we recall:

> When Blanchot constantly repeats . . . the impossible dying, the impossibility, alas, of dying, he says *at once the same thing and something completely different from Heidegger.* [*Aporias,* 77, my emphasis]

As a matter of fact, the passage goes further by adding a minor qualification that makes all the difference in the world. Or so it seems. Derrida continues:

> It is just a question of knowing in which sense (in the sense of direction and trajectory) one reads the expression of the possibility of impossibility. [*Aporias,* 77]

If one reads the expression in the sole way Heidegger would have approved of, namely as the formal indication of *Dasein*'s innermost and utmost possibility, as the possibility that alone allows *Dasein* to appropriate itself—all by itself and first of all for this very self that it potentially is—then Blanchot says indeed "something completely different from Heidegger." The death of which our text speaks is, in spite of its title, irreducible to the structure of mineness and appropriation articulated in *Being and Time.* This is an almost ironic response to Derrida's intriguing assertion, noted above, that *il faut bien mourir,* one must die all right, and which suggests that, while everybody must die, not everyone dies as well as everyone else.

If, on the contrary, the relation to death is the relation to a possibility that is experienced *as* impossibility, that is to say, not experienced at all (or properly speaking); if death marks the limit of both the actual and of the possible or of possibilization as long as it is thought as an actual or actualization to be (or to come); and if death is thus *itself* or *as such* never faced, directly or indirectly, frontally or obliquely, liter-

16. Blanchot, *L'entretien infini* (Paris: Gallimard, 1969), 192; *The Infinite Conversation,* trans. Susan Hanson (Minneapolis: University of Minnesota Press, 1993), 130.

ally or figuratively, by myself or in others; if this is what one can make Heidegger say by reading him against the grain, perversely, aporetically—then Blanchot does indeed say "the same thing" as Heidegger. On this reading, the proper death is at the same time the least proper, the least appropriable, and the one that is already invaded—and, indeed, haunted—by the actual or possible death of others (including the other that the "I" is to itself).

The instant of death, thus encountered, however, is also and at once an *instant death,* the death of death, death to death, death without death, a being always already one step beyond death, a "being," if one can still say so, that is otherwise than the being-towards-death and other than the being toward the death that is *mine.* Perhaps this is precisely what the final words of *L'instant de ma mort* seek to convey or evoke: the *instant as instance,* the instance *qua* instance, names the structure and the aporia of what does not let itself be appropriated, of what does not properly belong to anyone, of what is proper to no one, and therefore, in a sense, the property of no one, of nobody, *personne.* Death, then, the relation to death, to a death that has not yet taken place or that has taken place in others or in myself as the other alone, could be said to "be" the very "event" of singularization. But this singularization, which is a singularization of the self in the very determination of its mineness, is one that, in turn, singles nothing out. Nothing, or, rather, almost nothing is singled out. Neither *Dasein* in its resoluteness, as Heidegger would have it, nor the self made responsible to the point of alienation and being hostage of and for the other, as Levinas suggests, exhausts the meaning or, rather, the meaninglessness of this nothing or almost nothing that the *récit* singles out as the realm in which everything else may appear or not, disappear or not.

This indecision, it seems, plays itself out between the very title of the narration, *L'instant de ma mort,* which would seem to affirm the structure of mineness—*ma mort,* confirming both the structure of *Jemeinigkeit,* according to Heidegger, and that of *ma substitution,* according to Levinas—and the text "itself." For in this last, the familiar transition from the "I" to the "he" is respected whenever the subject of the imminent death is at issue. The voice of the narrator substitutes the voice of the soon-to-be-dead and hesitates to speak in his place:

> I know—do I know [*le sais-je*]—that the one whom the Germans faced already, waiting for nothing but the final order, thus experienced an extraordinary sentiment of lightness, a kind of beatitude (nothing

> happy, by the way)—sovereign drunkenness? The encounter with death and of death [*La rencontre de la mort et de la mort*]? [*L'instant de ma mort,* 10]

The indecision or twilight of Being and beings, of selves and others—an indecision that is signaled even by the ambiguity of the different possible intonations of the *le sais-je* (suggesting "*do* I know?" or "do I *know?*" and the affirmative "do *I* know!" or "who else would know besides or better than myself!" respectively)—is inaugurated by that most enigmatic of Blanchotian phrases, namely that of the *pas au-delà.* This "step (not) beyond" evokes not only the not yet dead, the living, the no longer simply living, the living on, the haunt, etc. It describes the very mode (not modality) of the instant *qua* instance in which an "I" is and is not death, ontologically, existentially, and semantically speaking.

> In his place, I will not attempt to analyze this sentiment of lightness. He was perhaps suddenly invincible. Dead—immortal. Perhaps ecstasy. Much rather the sentiment of compassion for suffering humanity, the happiness of being neither immortal nor eternal. From now on, he was linked to death, by a surreptitious friendship. [*L'instant de ma mort,* 11]

Death and dying are, from here on, the "silent companion" of all speech and of all agency: the instance of an "originary affirmation" as much as of a passion, more passive than any passivity. It is precisely because of this ontological and linguistic indeterminacy that only one last option remains—or, in fact, is necessary: that of testimony or attestation. This might well be what it means to respond to an impossibility ("répondre à l'impossible" is the expression adopted in *L'entretien infini*). It has been noted that this responsibility *vis-à-vis* the impossible is also an impossible, paradoxical, and aporetic, responsibility, one that is possible to the extent that it is impossible and vice versa. In this it resembles the very structure of death, of being toward the anteriority, the immemorial pastness, rather than some imminent yet indistinct futurity called death. In the terminology of *The Writing of the Disaster:*

> Impossible necessary death: why do these words—and the experience to which they refer (the inexperience)—escape comprehension? . . . Thought cannot welcome that which it bears within itself and which sustains it, except by forgetting. [67]

To use a Kantian formulation: what is comprehensible is this incomprehensibility alone, not what it stands for, the incomprehensible "itself." This singular "fact," not of reason but of an existence without or beyond existence in the very ontological determination that is typified and revolutionized by the Heideggerian existential analytic of *Being and Time:* it is this bare fact and nothing else that will remain what Blanchot calls "indestructible." Yet this "indestructible" is neither a new existential mode nor an always already there. It only comes into being—without, however, ever attaining this being as such—on the basis of an event that it outlives. Its *survie,* its being more and other than life (that is to say, more and other than mere life) is founded by an act of testimony, by an attestation, whose ontological status is uncertain, warranted by this testimony alone.

The word "indestructible" doesn't appear in the text. However, this word may well serve our purpose to clarify what is at stake in *L'instant de ma mort* and enable us to establish a certain continuity between this quasi-autobiographical fiction and some of the so-called critical writings that have preceded it, that silently comment on it, that have made it possible, and that, in turn, are made possible or at least more intelligible by it. I am referring here to the remarkable first section from the chapter of *L'entretien infini* entitled "L'indestructible," whose two parts are titled "être juif" ["Being Jewish"] and "l'espèce humaine" ["Humankind"], and published for the first time in 1962 in the *Nouvelle revue française.* Like "L'attente," this text opens with yet another fragmentary phenomenology of waiting and of the intricate relationship between attentiveness and *malheur* ("affliction," as it is translated, but surely also unhappy consciousness in the very Hegelian sense of this expression that is put to work by the *Phenomenology of Spirit*).

* * * * *

Let me return to the letter of the text of *L'instant de ma mort.* It should be noted that the death of which this *récit* speaks is neither a so-called natural death nor, for that matter, a suicide (so often discussed in Blanchot's other writings) but, on the contrary, a death that announces itself and, more precisely, threatens in the name of a specific culture and politics of death. The pending death, whose instant will forever transfigure the existence of the main protagonist of the narration, is not just any death. It is an execution, a failed, delayed and, finally, a delegated execution. And while the reference to the (unpronounced and, perhaps, unpronounceable) verdict, to the death sentence, has always been a connotation of Blanchot's repeated use of the phrase *arrêt de mort,*[17] its explicit articulation here in terms of war crimes is remarkable in itself. That the instant of death of which the *récit* speaks takes place (without taking place) in the context of the Nazis' war against France and the Allies, that this war, in its turn, conjures up the Napoleonic wars that would leave their mark on Hegel's philosophy of history—all this is central to the understanding of this text. And yet, while these references should be taken for what they are, as indices of an irreducible historico-political and, perhaps, biographical specificity or singularity, they do also have a broader relevance. It is almost as if the state of exception that typified the war here becomes the very measure and the central ontological feature of everydayness, of our always already being condemned to death itself. This generalization, or even universalization—the transformation of the *arrêt de mort* into an existential structure—could thus be said to qualify and transform the Heideggerian analytic of death (of my being-towards-death) by inscribing an almost Levinasian moment in it. Yet, I note that Blanchot says, *mutatis mutandis,* "at once the same thing and something completely different" from Levinas, just as he says "at once the same thing and something completely different" from Heidegger, from Freud, and, perhaps, from Derrida. Indeed, with respect to each of these authors, Blanchot's own "position"—if we can speak of a position—no longer deserves the name of either "approbation" or "critique." For, as in the case of his translation of certain motifs taken from the traditions of Judaism, a certain cautiousness should govern any reading at this point. And let us not forget: what is addressed throughout *L'instant de ma mort* is precisely the difficulty for the narrator to "translate" (*traduire*) the "sentiment of lightness," ascribed to the main protagonist when faced with his imminent execution (or *fusillade*) (*L'instant de ma mort,* 16).

Now, does not this generalization, aside from respecting the historical specificity that it commemorates, also result in an irresponsible trivialization, that is to say, in the betrayal of the very singularity to which it seems to attest? No simple answer—other than "Yes and no"—is to the point here. Without a minimum of translation (and thus betrayal), historical singularity would be condemned to death and no longer speak to us, haunt us. Yet were a translation without remainder

17. See Derrida, *Parages,* 161–64.

(and thus a total betrayal) possible at all, then this singularity would be even more surely put to death.[18] It is in this very tension that Blanchot's writing, together with that of so many of his contemporaries (Levinas and Derrida included), finds its element, its disturbing force, and, indeed, its sublimity. The "instant" of death conjures up this "at once" or "and . . . and" of translatability and untranslatability, of substitutability and nonsubstitutability, all of which reveal not only the structure of repetition and of iterability in general, but receive an exceptional intensity where death (the death of the other or of the self as the other) is concerned. The intensity of this sentiment has as its effect a desubjectivization and depersonalization that signal a desocialization and, paradoxically, also mark the very constitution of a "community of the dying."[19] Each of these interdependent movements helps to explain what is meant by the statement, cited earlier, that death is "not individual."

By the same token, death is hardly the ultimate possibility of my being-there, the possibility of *Dasein*'s impossibility, which for Heidegger obtains all the qualities of pure and purely purifying possibility—of an absolute possibility, that is—which allows *Dasein* to come into its own and to appropriate its essence, that is to say, its existence. Rather, death, in Blanchot's sense, "is" an "absolute lapsus,"[20] an exemption and exile from the "cosmic order" as well as from the realm of the possible. What is more, this singular structure of singularity, signaled by the very title of the text in question, reveals the inherent ambiguities that destabilize the relationship between history and literature, autobiography, whether fictional or not, and responsibility. The text, it would seem, taken as a fiction or otherwise, absolves as much as it accuses.[21]

18. See Derrida, *Parages,* 146–149.

19. See Schulte Nordholt, *Maurice Blanchot. L'écriture comme expérience du dehors,* chapter 10.

20. Blanchot, *Le pas au-delà* (Paris: Gallimard, 1973), 85; *The Step Not Beyond,* trans. and with an introduction by Lycette Nelson (Albany: State University of New York Press, 1992), 60: "absolute slip." I prefer to retain the French (and Latin) *lapsus* since it allows one to insert Blanchot's text in the series of commentaries on originary guilt, from the Biblical myth, through Nietzsche's genealogy, up to Heidegger's formally indicative use of this phrase in *Being and Time,* to say nothing here of Freud and Levinas. Blanchot's account of the fall (and the *Verfallen*) is different from each one of them. Or, more precisely, he says "at once the same thing and something completely different" from them.

21. It should be noted that this is also a central concern of the postface, entitled "Après coup" ["After the Fact"] that Blanchot added to (and superimposed on) the two

* * * * *

That the death of which *L'instant de ma mort* speaks is interrupted by chance,[22] that it does not take place as such, by no means lessens its subsequent, momentary, and belated effect. As with trauma, we are indeed dealing here with an experience that is an experience without experience, that does not take place in the present, in some past present, or at which we are present, but that is always coming and therefore not coming at all or as such, and remains *toujours en instance.* And in the latter, the sentiments of elation and lightness are necessarily juxtaposed with an instantaneous return to the real and to an unbearable weight of guilt.

If the instant of which and from which *L'instant de ma mort* speaks is one that "is" always in coming, always to be instantiated and always its very own stand-in, then we are dealing with paradoxical and aporetic "logics" of the instant (of the "at the same time," "at once," and "each time again," "always yet to come" or *à venir*) in which a tantalizing tautology and a restless radical heterology coincide or become virtually indistinguishable. The very singularity of "my death," of an event that never comes into its own, that does not enter into an experience here and now—and that is therefore not "mine" in any rigorous sense—but continues to gaze at me at every instant, this singular singularity is one that never gives itself as such or once and for all but only as infinitely repeatable. Death is a shadow of itself. And this holds true as long as I continue to live, as long as I am bound to die, that is to say, *always* (or at least as long as the enunciation "I" in the first person singular or as long as its gestural equivalents continue to make any sense at all). The instant of my death, more precisely, the instant *qua* instance, in its very difference from itself, expresses the *alpha* and

"fictions" from the thirties entitled "L'idylle" and "Le dernier mot" respectively—"innocent stories that resound with murderous echoes [*présages*] of the future"—and republished under the title *Après coup, précédé par Le ressassement éternel* (Paris: Éditions de Minuit, 1983), see 92; *Vicious Circles: Two Fictions & "After the Fact,"* trans. Paul Auster (Barrytown: Station Hill Press, 1985), see 64. On these and related issues, see Steven Ungar, *Scandal and Aftereffect: Blanchot and France since 1930* (Minneapolis: University of Minnesota Press, 1995).

22. See also Blanchot, *The Madness of the Day,* trans. Lydia Davis (Barrytown: Station Hill Press, 1981), 6: "Shortly afterwards, the madness of the world broke out. I was made to stand against the wall like many others. Why? For no reason. The guns did not go off. I said to myself, God what are you doing? At that point I stopped being insane. The world hesitated, then regained its equilibrium." As Derrida notes in "DEMEURE," the two *récits* narrate, perhaps, "au fond" the same thing (35).

omega of experience.[23] *It says nothing and all.* It describes the nothing of death as all there is or, conversely, rethinks everything that is in the light of this nothing.

Rather than being a *hic et nunc* that is determinable in time and space, the instant of which Blanchot speaks resembles the "*no-time-lapse*"[24] that Derrida, in *The Gift of Death,* attributes to the instant of the Abrahamic resignation to sacrifice or to give death to the *infans* that is his son. The instant of Abraham's decision, Derrida recalls with reference to Kierkegaard, is "madness":

> The paradox cannot be grasped in time and through mediation, that is to say in language and through reason. Like the gift and "the gift of death" it remains irreducible to presence and to presentation, it demands a temporality of the instant without ever constituting a present. If it can be said, it belongs to an atemporal temporality, to a duration that cannot be grasped: something one can neither stabilize, establish, *grasp, apprehend,* or *comprehend.* . . . [I]n the act of *giving death,* sacrifice suspends the work of negation and work itself, perhaps even the work of mourning. [*The Gift of Death,* 65]

L'instant de ma mort addresses death in its relation, not only to the multifaceted and paradoxical temporality of the instant whose instantaneous character is that of a haunting *instance,* but first of all in so far as all of these are intrinsically linked with the question of justice or, rather, injustice. Even where "my" death is concerned, death is in the first place the death of the other, of others (in this case of the peasants who are forced to take the place of the young man from the castle according to a logic that seems obvious to the German officer and the Russian soldiers alike and that determines the dialectical logic of history—as thought by Hegel, as enacted by Napoleon—itself).

Could this last aspect or concern be taken as an oblique indication of the often debated Levinasian turn to the format of dialogue or polylogue with the Other and the fragmentation of writing that can be discerned in Blanchot's oeuvre from the publication of *L'entretien in-*

23. See Derrida, *Parages,* 176–77. Somewhat earlier in this text, Derrida discerns a "temptation" of Blanchot's writing in its tendency to develop a "logics" that permits one to say all and to do so out of the most singular and "aleatory" details ("tentation du côté de Blanchot: à partir de *L'arrêt de mort,* point de départ à la fois aléatoire *et* nécessaire, reconnaître une 'logique' qui permette de *tout* dire, dans *L'arrêt de mort* et ailleurs, jusqu'à l'élément le plus petit, le grain de sable, la lettre, le blanc, etc." [166–67].

24. Derrida, *The Gift of Death,* trans. David Wills (Chicago: University of Chicago Press, 1995), 95–96.

fini, in 1969, on? Does it signal the supposed turn to Judaism or even the "philosémitisme"[25] that seems to mark the writings of the 1960s and that would seem to have culminated in *L'écriture du désastre* (published in 1980)? How is one to understand these aphorisms, which abound in reflections on exile, on the desert, on the messianic, and on the Shoah? And to what extent do they reflect on the narration of *L'instant de ma mort?*

Even if the invocation of injustice does seem to organize the *récit* of *L'instant de ma mort* from beginning to end, it should also be noted that this text's evocation of the meaning-without-meaning of death continues to differ radically from the one encountered in Levinas's texts, from *De l'existence à l'existant* and *Le temps et l'autre* through the main works *Totalité et infini* and *Autrement qu'être ou au-delà de l'essence,* up to one of the last lecture courses recently published by Jacques Rolland under the title *La mort et le temps.*[26] Even though the earliest of these writings already presents us with a seemingly parallel interpretation of the notion of the "instant" in terms of an ontological rupture, Levinas's oeuvre nevertheless explores a different type of questioning of death, of being-towards-death, of my-being-towards-my-death, and substitutes this very relation to the unsubstitutable with an obsessive testimony of my "being" toward the other's mortality *to the point of* substitution.[27] On numerous occasions Levinas has clarified this distant nearness that characterizes his relation to Blanchot's writing no less than their common relation to Heidegger. In Blanchot's work, Levinas notes:

> Literature is neither the approaching of ideal Beauty nor one of the events of our life, nor the testimony of the epoch, nor the translation of its economic conflicts, but the ultimate relationship with being in a virtually impossible [*quasiment impossible*] anticipation of what is no longer being.[28]

25. Julia Kristeva, in the program "Sur les traces de Maurice Blanchot," broadcast by France Culture in 1995.

26. Emmanuel Levinas, *La mort et le temps,* ed. Jacques Rolland (Paris: Éditions de l'Herne, 1991).

27. Levinas, it seems, does not—or cannot—claim that substitution takes place, here and now or in some past present. The intrigue of responsibility is more complex than that and, in its very absoluteness, expressible by a hypothetical clause alone: if there will have been responsibility, it will have had the structure of substitution. But no one could say, speaking for others, let alone speaking for himself, that responsibility *is* to be *seen* in this particular instance. To say this is precisely what would be irresponsible.

28. Levinas, *En découvrant l'existence avec Husserl et Heidegger* (Paris: Vrin, 1974), 144 n. 1; my translation.

In the same vein, Blanchot's preoccupation with the instant is hardly the return to the Greek *nun* that, as Derrida demonstrates in "Ousia et grammè," is already infinitely more complex than the simple *now* to which Heidegger would seem to reduce it at times.[29] The final words of *L'instant de ma mort* thus seem to invoke an instant that is neither a *hic et nunc* nor a *thisness* or *haecceitas*, but a singularity that singularizes beyond the *individuum*, beyond the "one" or the "I;" in other words, an instance that remains always on the verge of its own instantiation, that is "*toujours en instance*," that *is*, strictly speaking, *not*, and therefore remains "indestructible." We would be dealing here with a "subject-position" that can best be described in terms of "an instance (without stance, a "without" without negativity)," to cite a formulation used by Derrida in an interview with Jean-Luc Nancy, entitled "Il faut bien manger."[30] The instance thus marks the resistance against time and temporality in its vulgar *and* authentic, improper *and* proper or kairological sense—a thinking that characterizes so many of Blanchot's other writings as well.

Not a "triumph of life," then, but rather an incisive articulation of the perturbation of the most unquestioned of all "border lines," namely, that between life and death. This conclusion could already have been drawn on the basis of Derrida's "Survivre—Journal de bord," the horizontally divided text that comments on two of Blanchot's *récits* that are most relevant to any discussion of *L'instant de ma mort*, to wit: *La folie du jour* and, of course, *L'arrêt de mort*. The point of reference, if one may say so, in Derrida's reading is Shelley's *The Triumph of Life*, but much more is at stake than a loosely or merely associative commentary on this poem in the light of Blanchot's texts. Derrida analyzes all the complexities involved in the phrase *arrêt de mort*, whose meaning is not exhausted by the ambiguity between the "halt" and "the stopping" of death, on the one hand, and the "death sentence," on the other, but whose semantic effects urge upon us a careful reading of all the different modalities or, rather, traits of the "living on," the *survie* or *survivre*. Thus, Derrida writes,

29. The *nun*, Derrida argues in "Ousia et grammè" (in *Marges de la philosophie* [Paris: Minuit, 1972]), is commonly translated as "*instant*." Yet, in Greek it takes the function of our word *now* (*maintenant*). See *Parages*, 197.

30. See Derrida, *Points de suspension. Entretiens* (Paris: Galilée, 1992), 269–301; 290; *Points . . . Interviews, 1974–1994* (Stanford; Stanford University Press, 1995), 255–87; 275–76.

> Living on can mean a reprieve or an afterlife, "life after life" or life after death, more life or more than life, and better; the state of suspension in which it's over—*and* over again, and you'll never have done with that suspension itself.[31]

According to this reading, Blanchot thus comes close to what Roland Barthes, as Derrida reminds us in the concluding pages of "Les morts de Roland Barthes," had indicated when he spoke of the "impossible enunciation" of the sentence that states one's own death. Derrida cites an essay from 1973, titled "Analyse textuelle d'un conte d'Edgar Poe," in which Barthes says of Valdemar's famous phrase:

> It is in fact a banality to enunciate the phrase "I am dead!" . . . The reversal of the metaphor in a literal meaning, *precisely for this very metaphor,* is impossible: the enunciation "I am dead," according to its literal meaning, is foreclosed. . . . We are dealing therefore, if one wishes, with a scandal of language. . . . We are dealing here with a performative, but one, to be sure, that neither Austin nor Benveniste had foreseen in their analyses. . . . [T]he unheard phrase "I am dead" is hardly an unbelievable statement but much more radically the *impossible enunciation.*[32]

We would be dealing here, then, with an "absolute performative" or "perverformative," to cite Derrida's *La carte postale,* whose contextual requirements are never fulfilled. Dying is an impossibility for my being-there and the phrases "I am dead" or "I am dying at this very moment" make no sense at all. This is not to say that I live forever or that even beyond this present life I am supposedly immortal. The reason is simply that the name death indicates the very moment where an I can no longer take the word or speak for itself.[33] This explains why Blanchot's texts, in speaking of death, are marked by the transition from the first- to the third-person singular, substituting the "il" for the "je." It is as if—contrary to what Heidegger thinks—the event of death can only be grasped by analyzing the death of the other or, more precisely, by appropriating my own death as the death of an other, that is to say, by not appropriating it at all.

31. Derrida, "LIVING ON: Border Lines," in Harold Bloom et al., *Deconstruction and Criticism* (New York: The Seabury Press, 1979), 75–176, 77.

32. Cited after Derrida, *Psyché. Inventions de l'autre* (Paris: Galilée, 1987), 302. See also Derrida, "DEMEURE," 34.

33. See Schulte Nordholt, *Maurice Blanchot,* 273.

In one of his most striking, lapidary statements, in the metaphysical mediations that conclude his *Negative Dialektik* (*Negative Dialectics*), Theodor W. Adorno formulates an insight that may well sum up the central argument that guides this reading of Blanchot's *L'instant de ma mort.* In the section entitled "Dying today" (*Sterben heute*), we read:

> It is impossible to think of death as the last thing pure and simple. Attempts to express death in language are futile, all the way into logic, for who should be the subject of which we predicate that it is dead, here and now.[34]

For Adorno, this lack of semantic reference, which is a respectful "irreverence" in its own right, is inseparable from a larger process that only a dialectical philosophy of history that is fully aware of the Hegelian temptation could hope to articulate. And it is this thinking of *Vergängnis* and of the instant of the *Jetztzeit* rather than of "world history" (*Weltgeschichte*) or, for that matter, "historiality" (*Geschichtlichkeit*) that differs considerably from the *récit* concerning the *instant* of death that we have been discussing here. The latter is not so much indifferent with respect to the philosophical underpinnings of the very concept of the historical—the reference to Hegel teaches us otherwise—but presents this instant of death as radically *ab*solute, in the etymological sense of this word. The instant is not a moment in or of history, even though it has no being elsewhere. It leaves its trace on history, as it were, or permits history and historiality to be thought or experienced in ways that escape common understanding, the collection, addition, and archivization of data, Hegelian dialectics as well as Heidegger's ontology or thought of Being.

In *Sur Maurice Blanchot,* Levinas singles out the position taken vis-à-vis Hegel and Heidegger as the watershed that separates a fundamentally incommensurable way of understanding the word, the experience, and the event of Being, of the nothing or the not, of death and dying, as well as of the anxiety and lightness these notions continue to inspire.

> The poetic language that has removed the world lets the incessant murmur of that distancing reappear, like a night manifesting itself in the night. It is not the impersonality of eternity, but the incessant, the

34. Theodor W. Adorno, *Negative Dialectics,* trans. E. B. Ashton (New York: Continuum, 1973), 371.

> interminable, recommencing below whatever negation of it may be undertaken. . . .
>
> To Blanchot, death is not the pathos of ultimate human possibility, the possibility of the impossibility, but the ceaseless repetition of what cannot be grasped, before which the "I" loses its ipseity. The impossibility of possibility. The literary work brings us closer to death, because death is that endless rustle of being that the work causes to murmur. . . . Death is not the end, it is the *never-ending ending.* As in certain of Edgar Allan Poe's tales, in which the threat gets closer and closer and the helpless gaze measures that ever still distant approach [*toujours encore distante*].
>
> Blanchot thus determines writing as a quasi-mad structure, in the general economy of being by which being is no longer an economy, as it no longer possesses when approached through writing any abode—no longer has any interiority. It is literary space, that is to say, absolute exteriority—exteriority of the absolute exile.[35]

At times Levinas suggests that this death is more distant, farther out than any God ever was or will be. But it is also suggested that the otherness of death is otherwise than Being. Even if it seems to share with this Being an absolute neutrality[36] (a dark light instead of the fluorescent luminosity of the clearing), it resembles at least the formal structure of that other otherwise-than-being-and-not-being that Levinas calls the Infinite or *Illéité* and that he introduces as the counterpart of the mere murmur of the so-called *il y a.*[37]

L'instant de ma mort allows us to consider other encounters and confrontations as well. The most important of these is a certain resemblance to and departure from the traditions of mysticism and negative theology. To speak of an instant without instant, to address a death that is mine without therefore being appropriable in any rigorous sense of these words—all this is reminiscent of the discourses on death and God that characterize the tradition of apophatic, mystic speech. It may suffice here to recall that the logics of the *sans,* the *without*—mostly in the form of "X sans X," "X without X"—resembles the very structure and abstractions of the *via negativa.* As is well known, the formulae in

35. Levinas, *On Maurice Blanchot,* trans. Michael B. Smith (London: The Athlone Press, 1996), 132–33.

36. See Levinas, *Sur Maurice Blanchot* (Montpellier: Fata Morgana, 1975), 49.

37. See my essay, "Adieu, à dieu, a-Dieu," in *Ethics as First Philosophy: The Significance of Emmanuel Levinas for Philosophy, Literature and Religion,* ed. Adriaan T. Peperzak (New York and London: Routledge, 1995), 211–20.

question are used by Blanchot to circumvent the formal-logical and dialectical determinations and deployments of the concept of the negative. The Blanchotian rearticulation of this "negative without negative" should be distinguished from Heidegger's rethinking of the "not," the "not yet," as well as of the *Nicht,* against the backdrop of a more fundamental reconsideration of the "nothingness" that the latter terms the *Nichts.* But Blanchot too recalls a certain experience of "night" and "dark light." And while these central motifs pay tribute to the *expérience intérieure* of Georges Bataille, with whose writings Blanchot was intimately familiar, they conjure up other references as well.

Thus, it could be claimed that *L'instant de ma mort* occupies—envelops or opens up—the literary and, perhaps, no longer simply literary space that is inhabitated by the writings containing Blanchot's most explicit reflections on the Jewish tradition. Again, one is first of all reminded of "L'indestructible," the section in *L'entretien infini*—to which I alluded earlier—that considers the question "what remains?" in a way that anticipates the "instance" or the perennial *re-instantiation* of the "instant" of which *L'instant de ma mort* speaks. Yet the way in which this motif is thus articulated against the backdrop of tradition also reveals some remarkable differences between this rearticulation and other attempts at establishing the logics of the instant or, rather, of instantiation. At times it would seem that, whereas for Blanchot (as well as for Heidegger) an ultimate possibility is given in and beyond the impossible experience of death, Levinas—and in his wake Derrida—goes one step further in rethinking the relation without relation between self and other. They do so by deconstructing even the nonepistemic certainty of whatever it is that remains. What remains, if anything, even less than a possibility, a potentiality or force of being or of being-there, less than a sentiment, less than a lightness, appears (as) "the indestructible."

Finally, a certain continuity, or at least contiguity, could be established between this reading of *L'instant de ma mort* in the light of "L'indestructible," on the one hand, and Blanchot's meditation on the giving of the Torah, in "Grâce (soit rendue) à Jacques Derrida." In this contribution to the special issue of the *Revue philosophique* devoted to Derrida's oeuvre,[38] Blanchot responds not so much to the former's

38. Blanchot, "Grâce (soit rendue) à Jacques Derrida," *Revue philosophique* 2

incessant reflection on his own work, but to that which, in Derrida no less than in his own writing, with ever more persistence escapes and resists the parameters and, perhaps, the very element of Heideggerian thought. It is not an interpretation of Derrida that is attempted here—"how pretentious," Blanchot writes—but an invocation of a singular structure of singularity whose ethico-political or, rather, religious overtones demand a redescription of the "not yet" that governs Heidegger's fundamental ontology or existential analysis of death. Not unlike the substitution of the toward-death with the *à dieu* encountered in Levinas and in Derrida, this rearticulation consists in a reinscription of the figure of death—indeed of its very instant—into the traditional scene whose singular and historically overdetermined nature is hardly fortuitous: the writing of the Tablets and the relationship between Moses and Aaron. At the surface this relationship would seem simply to illustrate the well-known theses that Derrida has advanced since the publication of *De la grammatologie* and *La dissémination,* notably in "La pharmacie de Platon." However, much more is at stake here.

What is interesting about this reading is that it establishes a formal analogy between the doubling of death and the doubling of the Torah, between the impossible phrase of the absolute performative of finitude—"I am dead"—and the absolute performative "I am who I am," which the Biblical text reserves for God, for JHWH, alone. This is another way of saying that the structure of the instance of death, an instance that cannot be experienced or enunciated as such, extends itself well beyond the realm of human beings and finite history and into the auto-affirmation of God Himself. And this, in its turn, is another way of saying that human finitude was premised all along on the singular nature of what (or Who) has been deemed infinite, unpronounceable, secret, sacred, and, to that extent, precisely, indestructible. Speaking of the "indeterminacy of death," in *Aporias,* Derrida suggests as much:

> Fundamentally, one knows perhaps neither the meaning nor the referent of this word. It is well known that if there is one word that remains absolutely unassignable or unassigning with respect to its concept and to its thingness, it is the word "death." Less than any noun, save "God"—and for good reasons, since their association here is probably

(1990): 167–73; "Thanks (Be Given) to Jacques Derrida," trans. Leslie Hill, in *The Blanchot Reader,* ed. Michael Holland (Cambridge: Blackwell, 1995), 317–23.

> not fortuitous—is it possible to attribute to the noun "death," and above all to the expression "my death," a concept or a reality that would constitute the object of an indisputably determining experience. [*Aporias,* 22]

For Blanchot, as for Levinas and Derrida, the towards-God, the *à dieu,* comes down to a towards-death, an *adieu.* This not only presupposes a *kenosis* of and vis-à-vis God (a motif Blanchot introduces at a crucial moment of this text); it also shows itself in the following meditation on Moses's death:

> It is sometimes said, in analyses of Deuteronomy, that Moses was incapable of telling the story of his own death, writing it (critical scepticism). Why not? He knows (with knowledge that is never elucidated) that he dies through "God," "on God's mouth," thereby carrying out a last, final commandment in which there is all the sweetness of the end—but an end that is hidden from view. The death that is necessarily in life (since Adam) "here does not take place in life" (Derrida). And God, playing the part of the gravedigger (Levinas), in a proximity that promises no afterlife, buries him in a valley in the land of Moab, in an (atopical) place without place. "No man knows of his sepulchre unto this day," which is what allows those who believe in superstitions to doubt his death, just as the death of Jesus will later be doubted too. He is dead, but "his eye was not dim, nor his natural force abated." He has a successor, Joshua, but he also has none (no direct heir; he himself refused this kind of transmission). *And there has not yet arisen a prophet since in Israel like unto Moses.* "Not yet." The disappearance is without any promise of return. But the disappearance of the "author" gives even greater necessity to teaching, writing (the price prior to all text) and speech, to the speech, to the speech within writing, the speech that does not vivify writing which otherwise would be dead, but on the contrary impels us to go towards others, caring for the distant and the near, without it yet being given to us to know that, before all else, this is the only path towards the Infinite. ["Thanks (Be Given) . . . ," 173]

In *L'écriture du désastre,* the most desertified of his writings, Blanchot suggests as much, once more referring explicitly to the work of Levinas, according to whom the other (*Autrui*) speaks to us from a dimension of height:

> The death of the Other: a double death, for the Other is death already, and weighs upon me like an obsession with death. [*The Writing of the Disaster,* 19]

In a sense, then, the story of Moses's death—unlike the account of his nebulous Egyptian origin at which Blanchot hints without mentioning Freud's *Moses and Monotheism* directly—is read as the prefiguration of every death to come, of the structure of impossible anticipation that characterizes the to-come of each single death, of the other, and of myself as other (to myself), and thus as "the only path towards the Infinite." What Derrida, in *The Gift of Death,* says of Abraham, of the sacrifice of Abraham, of the moment of "Abrahamic renunciation," thus holds true for Moses as well. The *adieu* is the very form and content of the *à dieu,* and vice versa.

The sentiment that accompanies the face to face with death—and subsequently with the mortality of others—is, therefore, not only that of a freedom from or with respect to life, but, if anything, also that of "the infinite which opens itself" (*l'infini qui s'ouvre*) (*L'instant de ma mort,* 16). Is it both or, on the contrary, neither of these two? *L'instant de ma mort* leaves the question unanswered. What remains is merely the nonepistemic certainty that there is neither "happiness" nor "unhappiness," nor, for that matter, an "absence of fear" here, but at best a "step"—and whether this step is actually (or potentially) a "step beyond" or "no step" at all (*L'instant de ma mort,* 16–17), must remain forever uncertain. What is certain is this very uncertainty, the condition of all speech, of all writing, of any event, of every act, whether commemorative or not, fictive or not, and, indeed, of every passion. The passage from *L'écriture du désastre* used as epigraph for this essay, and in which Blanchot challenges the common understanding of death in terms of an imminent threat and futurity—as a possibility, that is, that could or should be appropriated and mastered—thus continues:

> To write is no longer to situate death in the future—the death which is always already past; to write is to accept that one has to die without making death present and without making oneself present to it. To write is to know that death has taken place even though it has not been experienced, and to recognize it in the forgetfulness that it leaves in the traces which, effacing themselves, call upon one to *exclude oneself from the cosmic order* and to abide where the disaster makes the real impossible and desire undesirable.[39]

39. Blanchot, *The Writing of the Disaster,* 66. This passage is also cited by Derrida's "DEMEURE," 37. On "desire," see the second essay of *La communauté inavouable* (Paris: Éditions du Minuit, 1983); *The Unavowable Community,* trans. Pierre Joris (Barrytown: Station Hill Press, 1988), which discusses Marguerite Duras's *La maladie de la mort* (Paris: Éditions du Minuit, 1983).

Death and God, the "death of God," its instant or, more precisely, its being forever *en instance,* falling short of itself: both of these notions could be seen as the figures for an "absolute lapsus" that forms the matrix and the disaster (the birth and the infanticide) of all other instances where singularity translates itself into a generality beyond recognition. An "absolute fall," a "no-time-lapse," from which no return—no relief, no retrieval also—will ever be possible. What remains can hardly be remembered. Or, if it *remembers* at all, it remembers by forgetting and forgets by remembering, articulating itself all over again. Indestructible, it is at the same time (i.e., at no time) inappropriable. Improper death.

Death, then, the instant of my death, *toujours en instance,* is not an event that takes place only once and that is therefore unrepeatable and unique. Nor is it some indeterminate futurity or even futurity *par excellence.* It is first of all the "echo" resounding or the shadow cast in every word, in each gesture: "the figure of absence which haunts every figure" (Collin, 34). What is more, it is the figure of every relation to death, to the death of others, and to the instant of my death as radically other, that is to say, as dead, at the very limit of experience, of discourse, and of narration, including that of *L'instant de ma mort* itself.

JEAN-POL MADOU

The Law, the Heart: Blanchot and the Question of Community

Echoing Jean-Luc Nancy's *La communauté désoeuvrée,* which was published by Christian Bourgois in 1986, but first appeared in the journal *Aléa* in the Spring of 1983, Blanchot attempts, in his *La communauté inavouable,*[1] to trace—on the flip side of every social philosophy and in the very irruption of the political—the outlines of a community whose advent is even more urgent, to the extent that its instauration reveals itself to be impossible. A strange community this, that does not allow itself to be circumscribed by any form of sociality and is not taken up in any dialectical process. A community, I want to add, that is not capable of being conserved, nonproductive, inoperable [*désoeuvrée*], and which, emptied of all transcendence, is abandoned to an immanence just as impossible. What is more, the Hegelian manner of recognition between consciousnesses is found to be radically put into question in the first pages of Blanchot's essay:

> A being does not want to be recognized, but to be contested: in order to exist it goes towards the other, which contests and at times negates it, so as to start being only in that privation that makes it conscious (here lies the origin of consciousness) of the impossibility of being itself, of subsisting as its *ipse* or, if you will, as itself as a separate individual: this way it will perhaps ex-ist, experiencing itself as an always prior exteriority, or as an existence shattered through and through, composing itself only as it decomposes itself constantly, violently and in silence. [*CI,* 16/6]

1. Maurice Blanchot, *La communauté inavouable* (Paris: Minuit, 1993); translated by Pierre Joris as *The Unavowable Community* (Barrytown, N.Y.: Station Hill Press, 1988). Henceforth *CI,* followed by page numbers for the French and English, respectively.

YFS 93, *The Place of Maurice Blanchot,* ed. Thomas Pepper, © 1998 by Yale University

These are also the categories of Sartre's *Critique of Dialectical Reason,* which are found to be unwound, because the community in question is not a matter either of the serial collectivity (the individual as number), nor of the fusional group founded upon oath and terror, nor, furthermore, of the praxis that this group would pretend to make happen free of any inertia (the practico-inert). In effect, in Hegel as in Sartre, it is never anything other than a matter of the relation of the Same with the Same, or of the reciprocity of the Same and the Other—which amounts, in any event, to the *same.*[2] For Blanchot, as for Levinas, the dissymmetry of the Same and the Other is ineluctable. Any sublimation or transfiguration amounts to a mystification. What becomes, then, of the communitarian demand, if the I can never be on equal footing with the Other [*l'Autre*], if any other [*autrui*] is always closer to God than to myself? But whereas for Levinas the irreciprocity of the Same and the Other is experienced from the very beginning as an ethical demand [*exigence*], for Blanchot this demand is experienced in a privileged manner, as the "pure movement of loving" [*CI,* 70/41], which exceeds the pure reciprocity of an *I* and a *Thou* because it is, abandoning without limits, a movement without return, a movement that exposes lovers to the abyss and to the night of the Outside:[3] "For the Greeks, according to Phaedrus, Love is nearly as ancient as Chaos" (*CI,* 68/40). But let us not simply oppose ethics (Levinas) and love (Blanchot, Duras). Their relation reveals itself to be infinitely complex in Levinas and in Blanchot. Asking if it is a matter of the same dissymmetry, Blanchot responds:

> This is not certain, and neither is it clear. Love may be a stumbling block for ethics, unless love simply puts ethics into question by imitating it. [*CI,* 68/40]

What Blanchot calls the "pure movement of loving" is not the mortal fusion of hearts dear to romantic myth, but rather the strange relation that attracts lovers into an intimacy that makes them even more for-

2. It is the *Critique of Dialectical Reason* that is at issue here. In *Being and Nothingness,* it is rather irreciprocity that is in evidence. The other [*autrui*] is present to me without intermediary, without mediation, without distance. But this distance is not reciprocal: "The total opacity of the world is necessary for me to be, myself, present for an other [*autrui*]" (Jean-Paul Sartre, *L'être et le néant* [Paris: Gallimard, 1942], 329).

3. In Levinas, eros also leads to a beyond, beyond the beloved, beyond the face, to a future never future enough. Levinasian love leads to paternity, to fecundity: "The relation with the child—that is to say with the Other, not power, but fecundity, places into relation with the absolute future or with infinite time" See Emmanuel Levinas, *Totalité et infini* (The Hague: Nijhoff, 1971; Paris: Livre de poche, 1990), 300.

eign to each other: "Not separated, not divided: inaccessible and, in the inaccessible, in an infinite relationship" (*CI*, 72/43). Passion and the Law, while in no way identical, both reveal an infinite attention to the Other [*l'Autre*], an attraction for an other [*autrui*]. This attraction seems to be even more irresistible inasmuch as an other cannot be reached [*rejoint*]. So it goes—both for love and for friendship.

The community—which, for Blanchot, is a matter at once of the ethical demand (Levinas) as well as of political utopia (Marx), of the passion of love and of communism—would only be capable of being manifested in the faultlines of the social fabric, in the tearing or rending of ordinary communication. It would not be capable of being realized without being lost immediately. The Acéphale Group, conceived by Georges Bataille, was the most gripping example. The failure of this enterprise on the eve of the Second World War does not allow us, however, to abandon the question. Today Blanchot sees as privileged these two forms of apparently opposed communitarian manifestation: the limitless and anonymous presence of the people—May '68[4]—and the world of lovers—Bataille and Duras. Everything would lead to opposing these currents if it were not for the fact that they share a trait [*trait*]: that of being a gathering held together only by its imminent disappearance, a proximity all the more close by virtue of the fact that, at the heart of the embrace, the imminence of the retreat [*retrait*] is always already announced. Thus the idea of this community can only be grasped by default by those who brought it into existence.

How does one conceive a community in which singular beings would come to communicate amongst themselves the deconstruction of their own identity, and thus to share, in the "consummation," which is also the consumption of every social tie, the unmasterable excess of their proper finitude? How does one reconcile the communist demand for equality—which, for Blanchot, remains more than ever incapable of being superseded—with that, no less imperious, of sovereignty and of ecstasy? Must not the community refuse ecstasy on pain

4. The theme of the anonymous crowd is already present in one of Blanchot's first *récits, Le dernier mot.* But whereas, in this *récit,* the crowd, with its sinister torchlight processions and yelping dogs, seems to be linked to the advent of National Socialism, in *The Unavowable Community* it is linked to leftist insurrection. One would thus have to analyze in greater detail the relation, in Blanchot, between "the people" and "the crowd." The people is not the crowd. They are contraries. The question of the people is also that of sovereignty as the state of exception that no law circumscribes, "because [sovereignty] challenges [such a law] while maintaining [the law] as its foundation" [*CI* 56/33].

of sinking into fascist communion? In other words, how do I conceive my presence to an other, other than in the mode of intersubjective specularity, of the master-slave dialectic and its cortege of mediations? The stakes are high.[5] For Blanchot, it is a matter not only of the meaning of the political but, before all else, of *love* and of *friendship.* It is a matter of the meaning of literature:

> What, then, calls me into question most radically? Not my relation to myself as finite or as the consciousness of being towards death or for death, but my presence for another in as much as this other absents himself by dying. To remain present in the proximity of an other who by dying removes himself definitively, to take upon myself another's death as the only death that concerns me, this is what puts me outside myself, this is the only separation that can open me, in its very impossibility, to the Openness of a community. [*CI,* 21/9; translation modified]

What happens, Blanchot asks, when I take the hand of one who is dying? How can one share the solitude of the event? "I die without you with you," he responds, echoing Bataille: "'A man alive, who sees a fellow-man die, can survive only *outside himself*'" (*CI,* 21/9, translation modified). Is this to say that the essence of community, and of its eminent manner in the "community of lovers,"—the paradigm of community—is found to be revealed by and in the death of an other? In fact, it is only to the degree that the community is not up to the task of death, as Bataille says, that death reveals its truth to the community. The community only reveals its truth by putting itself to the test of its impossible immanence.

This community, ordered around the death of each [*autrui*], is what Duras gives us to read, in an exemplary fashion, in the text "On the Image of the Death of the German," published as an appendix to *Hiroshima mon amour:*[6]

5. It is a matter of articulating what Heidegger did not succeed in articulating: *Mitsein* and *Sein zum Tode,* being together and being towards death.

6. Marguerite Duras, *Hiroshima mon amour* (Paris: Gallimard, 1960), 125; hereafter *HA.* [This is the first of a series of notes Duras writes to the text of *Hiroshima mon amour,* and which are now published in the same book as the screenplay. Before the title of this particular note, on the same page, appears the word "APPENDICES," followed by the subtitle "NOCTURNAL EVIDENCES (*Notes sur Nevers*).*" The asterisk refers to a note by the author at the bottom of the page, which reads: "Without chronological order. 'Do as if you were commenting the images of a finished film,' Resnais said to me." Trans.]

> Both of them, equally, are on the verge of this event: his very own death. . . .
>
> She dies so much of his own death that one might believe her to be dead. . . .
>
> It might be said that she helps him to die. She does not think about herself but only about him. And that he consoles her, almost excuses himself for having made her suffer, for having to die.
>
> When she is alone, at this place where they were just before, grief has not yet taken its place in her life. She is simply in an unvoiceable astonishment at finding herself alone. [*HA*, 125]

How can one conceive of a community founded not upon the reproduction of identities, but on the apportionment of ecstasy, ravishment, and the forgetting of the world? Without a doubt no text has better evinced the joy of forgetting in the community of lovers than the last scene in *Hiroshima mon amour:*

> SHE
>
> I'll forget you! I'm forgetting you already! Look how I'm forgetting you! Look at me!
>
> *He holds her by the arms [the fists], she keeps herself facing him, her head turned backwards. She moves away from him with great brutality.*
>
> *He helps her in his own absence. As if she were in danger.*
>
> *He looks at her while she looks at him as she would look at the city and calls him very sweetly all of a sudden.*
>
> *She calls him "into the distance," in astonishment. She has succeeded in drowning him in universal forgetting. She is astonished at this.* [*HA*, 124]

From Rousseau to Marx, the question of community has not ceased to haunt Western philosophy. There, history is thought in terms of a community to be retrieved or reconstituted. Thus the distinction between society—*Gesellschaft*—which evokes neutral and anonymous allotments of forces and of needs, and community—*Gemeinschaft*—which, as Nancy shows, evokes the "intimate communication of its members amongst themselves, but also the organic communion of this very community with its own essence" (Nancy, 30). Society is not built upon the ruins of community. Far from being what society would have lost or broken with, community is what reaches us *starting out from* society—in the form of questions, of the imperative. In an exemplary manner, Bataille—as Blanchot reminds us—has thought the destiny of modern communities in reference to three problematics that border its horizon: communist egalitarianism, fascist communion, and the community of lovers. The question that Nancy raises and that Blanchot takes up again is thus not that of understanding how singularities compose a community, but of how a community is, from the start, the exposition of singularities. But is such a community even conceivable? How might singularity accomodate itself to the constraints of a normative society? Isn't singularity incommunicable? Blanchot writes, commenting on ecstasy and the abyss in the Bataille of *L'expérience intérieure:*

> In a certain way, the instability of illumination needed, before being capable of being transmitted, to expose itself to others, not in order to reach in them a certain objective reality (which would have denatured the reality immediately), but for the purpose of reflecting itself therein by sharing itself and letting itself be contested. [*CI,* 34–5/17; translation modified]

Inconceivable, unavowable, the unworkable community could only be the despair of the political. It is exactly this impossible community that Utopia and Apocalypse—those two great discourses of the West—have not ceased to fight over without ever being able to name it, and that, like voice-overs, have shared the soundtrack of History in the manner of a badly-dubbed film. Community—not the political, in the current meaning of the word, nor the mystical, in the theological sense, neither depending on any social contract, nor being supported by any transcendent order, nor targeting, furthermore, any fusional communion, but testing its own radical immanence—opens that which is exposed on that disputed site to the infinity of alterity, at the same time that it consecrates its own ineluctable finitude. Not for Blanchot any more than for Bataille is it a matter of a marginal community, that is to say, of a community that, in its deviation from any social norm, would still remain the parodic mirror of the society from which it would pretend to remove itself. It is precisely not a matter of removing itself. What the unavowable community reveals to me in its unworkability, in the blanks and the rips and tears of daily communication, is the violent dissymmetry of my presence to an Other, to an Other [*Autrui*] who, as Levinas reminds us, is closer to God than to myself. The community is the only place where the *infinity* of alterity responds to the call of *finitude.* Solitude—is it necessary to recall this?—is never experienced alone.

—Translated from the French by Thomas Pepper

II. In Time, Among Contemporaries

DOMINIQUE RABATÉ

The Critical Turn: Blanchot Reads des Forêts

In the critical work of Maurice Blanchot, in his reflection on literature, certain texts, certain authors occupy a choice place, forming the benchmarks and the points of reference that constitute the sites of interrogation or of the return of a demanding thought, of a demand of thought that returns us to these texts by a movement of repetition and making deeper, a movement that accompanies them indefatigably. No last word [*mot*] but an utterance [*parole*] that returns upon the enigma and the secret of works that call forth and relaunch an open meditation through their questioning. It seems that one might thus trace the space of these texts, draw the figure that Blanchot's oeuvre has helped to make appear, to the point that this space must end up being indistinguishable from the "literary space" of one of his titles. The names of Flaubert, Kafka, Proust, Mallarmé, Rilke, Sade, or Lautréamont would be indispensable scansions, to evoke only some of the writers of the past toward whom reflection consistently turns. But certainly it is not a matter of drawing up a list, of classifying in some Pantheon, because Blanchot's questioning renders the very idea of such a Pantheon problematic. Meanwhile, we shall note that one of the primary original moments of criticism, according to Blanchot, occurs via the incessant movement of rereading, in the lack of satisfaction with the speech of commentary,—the word must be questioned—which approaches the work more than it actually claims to grasp it. For me, one of the first lessons such criticism provides is to open its reader to this particular dissatisfaction—composed of modesty and respect—that makes of the critical word—without certainty but not without affirmation—a worried discourse that must measure its achievements by a renewed expe-

YFS 93, *The Place of Maurice Blanchot,* ed. Thomas Pepper, © 1998 by Yale University.

rience of reading. In a certain way, thus, to learn to read is never to cease to reread, never to become a specialist of one author or another.

Furthermore, the above list would be incomplete because it is limited to authors of the past: for Blanchot's work is also decidedly marked—this would be its next original trait—by care for the contemporary. If the texts of Sade or of Kafka are important for us, it is because they bear witness to the movement of literature that bears them unto us. Thus we would have to double this first series with a second and just as significant one, of writers whose contemporary Blanchot remains, and whose works, commented upon at the moment of their appearance, permit the pursuit of the same fundamental interrogation. Camus, Paulhan, Bataille, Leiris, Beckett, Duras, along with many others, are thus the essential landmarks. For me there is something striking here in Blanchot: that an "oeuvre" (the quotation marks are of course necessary) could be constructed in several books, from the republication of texts originally published in journals—principally in the *Nouvelle revue française*—without the reader's ever having the impression of reading an ensemble of occasional pieces. This does not mean that these texts are not dated, that their moment of writing—which at the very least marks a capacity for reaction, the possibility of indicating the taking of a position from the first read—is indifferent; but their republication in book form grants them a new compass.

One would thus patiently have to follow the transformations from a journal version to a definitively published text in order to measure, each time, the effects and the displacements. Blanchot's critical activity is inscribed in this shuffling between a criticism of the current and a more durable meditation. And this is the place to reflect upon the role of journals in French literary and intellectual life since the forties, upon the place that they have occupied in a crucial way, at least until the seventies—even if it is true that they no longer fulfill the same function. Maurice Blanchot belongs to a generation of journal readers, a generation to whose sustenance and provocation he will have contributed; a generation for whom the critical act, understood more as discernment than as judgment, was capital. The task of distinguishing in the present the signs of a future or of a tension is imposed and necessitates the exercise of thought in a type of writing that has nothing of the journalistic. Participation in the collective work of a journal is one of the exemplary manifestations of the idea of community that animates Blanchot's thought. The plan for "La revue internationale" (for which *Lignes* has usefully furnished us the dossier) remains exemplary in this regard.[1] It relativizes the myth of an invisible Blanchot, in retreat from the world. Must it be recalled that Georges Bataille gives precisely the name *Critique* to the journal he founds in 1947, with the indispensible support of Blanchot and Eric Weil? And that such an enterprise manifests the intention not to dissociate political, philosophical, esthetic, and anthropological inquiries?[2]

This relation to the contemporary and to contemporaries is thus essential. It touches literature as much as philosophy and the human sciences, and evidently mobilizes a reflection on the time. I wish to broach this in a circumscribed manner, by evoking a particular case, by means of the texts Blanchot consecrates to one of these writers who undeniably count for him: I would like to speak of Louis-René des Forêts, whose discreet oeuvre Blanchot has not ceased to accompany. Furthermore, it is not an exaggeration to say that Blanchot has nourished des Forêts with readers for many years, readers who have been able to discover him through Blanchot's mediation. The celebrated postface to *Le bavard,* "La parole vaine," has done much for the justly-deserved fame of this story.[3] I emphasize this to mark what I will call the generosity of Blanchot, who, untiring and sensitive watchman, has welcomed and given a resonant place to the most singular works of his time.

1. THE DEBT

If "La parole vaine," published in 1963, is not, properly speaking, the first text Blanchot consecrates to des Forêts—I shall return to this—it is in any case the first systematic study in which the movement at work in *Le bavard* is measured. This postface (re)finds its place in *L'amitié*[4] in 1971, a book dedicated to Bataille. It is its natural place, one might add, because this "commentary" responds to a question asked by Bataille, shortly before his death, about des Forêts's story. Blanchot thus places his text into a shared speech, as the expression of a debt he would have contracted with his friend. The silence that had responded to Bataille's question (did Blanchot wish to speak of *Le*

1. See *Lignes* 11, devoted to Blanchot and to the dossier of "La revue internationale" (Paris: Librairie Séguier, September 1990).

2. In his introduction to the plan for "La revue internationale," Michel Surya recalls a conversation during which Bataille says that he would not have been able to realize *Critique* without the help of Blanchot and Weil (*Lignes* 11, 162).

3. Maurice Blanchot, "Le parole vaine," in Louis-René des Forêts, *Le bavard.* (Paris: Union Générale des Éditions, 1963).

4. Blanchot, *L'amitié* (Paris: Gallimard, 1971); henceforth *A.*

bavard?) is found to be changed into a request that this text thus must honor. Thus, it is not a question of a "work of criticism," nor of a "commentary," but rather of a discourse [*parole*] charged with the task of capturing the movement of the story. The temporal gap is thus significant in itself; Blanchot's study takes up this story on the occasion of its republication in a 10/18 paperback, seventeen years after the story's original appearance.[5] This lapse of time permits the essay to act in a subterranean fashion, and thus also to encounter the stories in *La chambre des enfants*.[6]

Thus placed under the sign of debt, "La parole vaine" seems to me to testify to a certain turn in the critical writing of Maurice Blanchot. This singular "I" will not be lacking in any of the texts devoted to des Forêts, this subject that speaks in its own name, that modestly affirms its engagement in a reading that holds itself back, and that does not wish to say everything about the text: "I shall not enter any further into the reading of *Le bavard*. Each must be able to pursue it on his own account and in taking from it the essential that is proper to it" (*A*, 147). Thus, this is not even a "commentary," but a careful effort to preserve an unsayable and singular relation to the text read. Even the enunciatory "we," so frequent in Blanchot's analyses, acquires a new value, that of a more perceptible weight, because it becomes common to both Blanchot and to Bataille. It seems to me that, starting from the beginning of the sixties, Blanchot's studies thus take on a more overtly personal accent, even if certainly it is a matter of personal relation to the impersonal—an accent that perhaps gives its specific tonality to the collection *L'amitié*, where Blanchot evokes Paulhan and Camus, his dead friends. The three texts gathered together in *Une voix venue d'ailleurs*,[7] and that address des Forêts's "poems," do not belie this subjective implication. Perhaps it is expressed there with even more pathetic accents. The first text, which bears the title used for the book and which had first appeared in *La quinzaine littéraire*,[8] thus begins with the furtive evocation of an autobiographial memory of a stay at Eze. "Le blanc le noir" betrays a quite vivid literary sympathy concern-

5. 10/18 is the great collection founded by Christian Bourgois and published by the Union Générale des Editions. (Translator's note.)

6. Des Forêts, *La chambre des enfants* (Paris: Gallimard, 1960).

7. Blanchot, *Une voix venue d'ailleurs* (Dijon: Ulysse Fin de Siècle, 1992); henceforth *VV*.

8. Blanchot, "Une voix venue d'ailleurs," *La quinzaine littéraire* (1 July 1989).

ing the difficulty of the fragment: "I know from experience that nothing is more perilous than writing that lacks the continuity of narrative [*récit*] or the necessary movement of argumentation" (VV, 22).

2. "THE OBLIGATION OF VIGILANT FRIENDSHIP"

This expression, which is to be found in *Poèmes de Samuel Wood,*[9] is isolated by Blanchot in the article from *La quinzaine* (*VV,* 16). It is recalled in "Anacrouse" (*VV,* 37). These fairly brief texts are thus an echo chamber for this vigilance of friendship, which dictates our ethical "duty," duty of witness, duty to renounce speech struck with suspicion. What is not exactly a commentary must be understood as a response, an injunction not to shirk the emotion of the poem.

But this injunction must also be uttered in the reserve of the biographical secret: twice Blanchot alludes to a personal drama in the life of des Forêts, without saying anything about it, refusing to place himself in the space of anyone else's grief out of an obligation to decency. Friendship demands this neutrality. By the same token, Blanchot never evokes his personal ties with Louis-René des Forêts. I will recall them here in order to remark that this proximity does not authorize any invasion of the private domain, because this relation testifies once again to the role of friendship in philosophy and in Blanchot's ethical praxis.

The two writers become allied at the beginning of the fifties, when des Forêts comes back to live in Paris—the inevitable meeting in the midst of common friends: Bataille, Robert Antelme, Dionys Mascolo, among others. Moreover, Blanchot had signed an article on *Les mendiants,* in the *Journal des débats* of 29 September 1943. This article, in a more conventional journalistic format, has never been reprinted in a book. Under the title "L'influence du roman américain," Blanchot took notice of the formal necessity of des Forêts's first novel, which did not simply involve literary fashion, but also a vision proper to the novelist. The end of the article is nonetheless rather severe, in its noting that the different monologues that make up the book "are similar in tone and language." This monotony, certainly capable of bespeaking the unity of isolated but similar consciousnesses, is imputed to the "awkwardnesses of lyricism" of an author who does not dissociate himself enough from his characters.

9. Des Forêts, *Poèmes de Samuel Wood* (Montpellier: Fata Morgana, 1988).

The friendly relations are also reinforced because the political activity of Blanchot and des Forêts follows the same trajectory during the fifties and sixties: categorical opposition to de Gaulle's coming to power in 1958, signaled by collaboration on *Quatorze Juillet,* and the signature of the "manifesto of 121" in 1960. The only 1968 text by Louis-René des Forêts—"Notes éparses en mai," published in the journal *L'ephémère*—practically echoes—by the use of the word "refusal" in its very first line—the text written by Blanchot in October 1958 and reprinted in *L'amitié,* and where a note mentions the circumstances of its composition (*A,* 130–31). The two texts are very close, brought together by the same care, and the same celebration of a collective and anonymous voice that must be expressed. Thus this political engagement cannot be dissociated from a conception that we may only improperly call esthetic, and that concerns the status of the subject in the literary text as well as more generally.

The interview given by des Forêts to *Tel Quel* in 1962 repeatedly evokes the place of the psychological or narrative subject in novelistic fictions.[10] Des Forêts's answers are clearly quite close to formulations that might be those of Blanchot. For example: "the *I* that speaks in my stories is not a personal voice." The fundamental ambiguity of this subject is at the core of the work of the stories in *La chambre des enfants,* just as it is at the heart of Blanchot's literary reflection, which is always attentive to the effects of enunciation of a literary text. Des Forêts's oeuvre develops more on the side of fiction or of poetry; thus it includes openly theoretical considerations only marginally, in this one interview. In this way, it differs from oeuvres in which the critical portion accompanies the narrative work according to specific modalities, as is the case with Blanchot as well as with Bataille, but also with Sartre. But it is clear that this oeuvre cannot be read independently of the reflexive questioning it incorporates, so to speak, into its material, whether fictional—in the case of *La chambre des enfants*—or autobiographical—as in *Ostinato.*[11]

3. THE CRITICAL TURN

This proximity between the texts of Blanchot and des Forêts may also be marked by a questioning that holds the read text at the periphery of

10. Des Forêts, "La littérature aujourd'hui," *Tel Quel* 10 (Summer 1962), republished as *Voies et détours de la fiction* (Montpellier: Fata Morgana 1985).

11. Des Forêts, *Ostinato* (Paris: Mercure de France, 1997).

the theoretical progression, which nonetheless has magnetized it. Here I would like to evoke an example of these displacements between *NRF* versions and their rewrites for the books in which they find their places. In July 1960, Blanchot publishes, in the *NRF*, "La marche de l'écrevisse." This is an interview between two voices on the nature of inquiry [*recherche*], about the essential error to which searching is exposed from the moment it proceeds by way of words, from the moment it turns away from the gaze and from the relation to light. The first version ends thus:

> I would even say that every important literary oeuvre is even more important in as much as it puts this turn [*tournant*] directly and more purely to work, which sense, at the moment it is going to emerge, strangely makes the work waver.
> —For example?
> —Memorable example: Proust. More recent example: the stories of Louis-René des Forêts.[12]

Republished in *L'entretien infini*, this article changes its title in order to become "Parler, ce n'est pas voir."[13] In the one instance as in the other, the title is a citation from the dialogue; but the accent has shifted in order to underscore, no longer the paradox of this advance by detour [*tournant*] but the appearance of a new relation to truth, outside of distant visibility and close to seeing. This text, by its dialogical form (which exceeds Socratic dialectic in miming it), is integrated at a moment in the thinking deployed in this immense book, the most voluminous of all Blanchot has published. Thus it must efface its terminal references in order to remain in the generality of questioning, in order to evoke correctly "the absence of the oeuvre" that gives the article its new end. Thus we read, starting from the word turn [*tournant*]:

> . . . turning, which, at the moment the work [*oeuvre*] is going to emerge, leaves it hanging, the oeuvre where idleness [*désoeuvrement*] is held in reserve, as its always decentered center: the absence of the oeuvre.
> —The absence of the oeuvre which is the other name of madness.
> —The absence of oeuvre where discourse ceases so that the outside of speech, the outside of language, the movement of writing under the allure [*attrait*] of the outside may come. [*EI*, 45]

12. Blanchot, "La marche de l'écrevisse," *Nouvelle revue française* 91 (July 1960): 99.
13. Blanchot, "Parler ce n'est pas voir," in *L'entretien infini* (Paris: Gallimard, 1969); henceforth *EI*.

By this correction, the names of Proust and of des Forêts are effaced to the benefit of the "neutral," a horizon of thought where no specific work could be named any longer, even if it is a matter of the analysis of particular texts—most notably Proust, who is their keystone. Thus we might also think that Blanchot, having written "La parole vaine" in the meantime, was no longer capable of being satisfied by the allusive indication to the stories of *La chambre des enfants,* which had just been published by Gallimard in 1960. Two further points deserve to be specified concerning this example.

The first is that this correction indicates a potential relation between a text where it is a matter of reflective or philosophical movement and one where what is at issue is the "commentary" of a work [*oeuvre*]. Neither of these two forms—in as much as this word may be used here—exists separately in Blanchot's theoretical oeuvre, except perhaps in the first two critical collections, *Faux pas* (1943) and *La part du feu* (1949), which are of a more classical composition. Starting in the fifties, the blurring between reflective text, commentary, and philosophical discussion makes the generic status of Blanchot's text ever more uncertain. The "commentary" brings with it and calls for a meditation upon the whole group, which leads this meditation back to the "oeuvres" that had provoked it. This astonishing union, so singular in the conduct of Blanchot, is still to be found in "Anacrouse," where it is a matter "of understanding Lyotard's text entitled 'The Survivor,' while at the same time meditating on the poems published under the signature of Louis-René des Forêts" (*VV,* 29). The same relation—or more exactly the question of the relation to thinking—would be found yet again in the case of *La communauté inavouable,* between the texts of Jean-Luc Nancy and of Marguerite Duras.[14]

This coming-and-going brings me to the second remark. If these texts of Blanchot speak of literature, if they speak of always singular oeuvres, it is precisely in order to accompany or to prolong the "critical turn" of which *L'entretien infini* speaks. Thence comes without a doubt this curious impression that Blanchot's theoretical work [*oeuvre*] gives me: the most singular care for each text is deployed with an unmatched scrupulousness, and the critical word stays constantly within this concern for exactitude with respect to the movement proper to each text it comments. But it is borne by a rhythm and a phrasing proper to Blanchotian reflection. Blanchot's writing achieves

14. Blanchot, *La communauté inavouable* (Paris: Minuit, 1983).

this union with a secondary word that is yet primary, and achieves the restitution of that which is most alive and quickening, of that which touches us in each work [*oeuvre*], as if the dynamics of the text read infused that of the thought that traverses it—whence comes, I think, the fact that criticism, such as it is practiced by Blanchot, is more attentive to the project of the work [*oeuvre*], to its dynamic tensions, to its enunciatory paradoxes, than to its proper stylistic traits. Thus there is—but consubstantial with the particular idea of criticism according to Blanchot—an "insufficiency of commentary," which is not the least of his modesties!

4. "THE INSUFFICIENCY OF COMMENTARY"

The above heading obviously makes use of a citation from Blanchot himself, concerning des Forêts in fact, from the end of the text "Le blanc le noir." Here is the next to-last paragraph:

> In my turn, this is why I will remain silent, incapable of bearing the insufficiency of commentary and of reestablishing the guiding thread between the elements of a discourse that would attempt to make us understand the *ultima verba,* the intimacy of a definitive rupture. [*VV,* 24]

The weight of Blanchot's most recent texts, on *Poèmes de Samuel Wood* and *Ostinato,* echoes that of those that confront the test of mourning. They require a laconic utterance, which approaches the ineffableness of music. "Une voix venue d'ailleurs" opens with the evocation of the "Quartet for the End of Time"; "Le blanc le noir" recalls the obstinate motif that Berg heard in Schumann, and "L'anacrouse" is proposed as the rhythmic figure capable of doing justice to "the experience (the contretemps) of Louis-René des Forêts" (*VV,* 38). In these three texts, the insistent reference to music expresses the very same care that is found in the work of des Forêts, in an attempt to find in words the impossible equivalent of the lost chant: a beyond of language within language itself.

The "default" [*défaut*] of an adequate language[15] ("I think *Ostinato* must be spoken of, that one would have to speak of it, but deprived of words, in a language that obsesses me in its very defaulting": thus

15. Translator and editor's note: See here the final footnote to "Le problème de Wittgenstein," added between the first publication of the essay and its final housing (*EI,* 497).

begins "Le blanc le noir" [*VV*, 21]) ruins all mastery of commentary. It commands the text, which adopts in its turn the aspect of desolated fragments. It disjoins a discourse that refuses order, so as to open onto loss. In a very touching way, these three last texts return incisively to the more affirmed motif, developed already in "La parole vaine," precisely of the vanity of all utterance, thus *a fortiori* of all utterance that redoubles the tragic announcement of this vanity. But Blanchot's "commentary" remains, here again, faithful to the movement of des Forêts's oeuvre, which is invoked incidentally. The word of the Babbler [*Bavard*] becomes borrowed voice, that of Samuel Wood. "A vain voice?" Blanchot asks (*VV*, 16). "Perhaps," he answers. The question will remain unanswered. But, between the narrative written in 1946 and *Poems of Samuel Wood*, the meaning of the recourse to fiction, this detour by way of the mirages of beautiful language, has changed its value, if its very nature has not been truly altered.

I want to insist on this indecision, to render justice in the case of the trial to which Yves Bonnefoy subjects Blanchot—a little abusively, I think—concerning des Forêts. In *La vérité de parole*, Bonnefoy meditates at length on the adventure represented by des Forêts's texts.[16] He constructs his reflection against the version that would have been suggested by Blanchot, and thus makes of the *Bavard* a manifesto of nihilism, a triumph of the void, from the moment words are assigned only to grasping at fantasmatic prey. It seems to me that the consequences of this debate are entirely crucial; but I believe that Bonnefoy simplifies Blanchotian terms too much, transforming what is the assertion of a radical suspicion into a demand. In effect, Bonnefoy chooses to read des Forêts's entire oeuvre as a reconquest of presence, the insisting of the voice's desire to be, rather than as the victory of this negativity, which would only be a necessary and unhappy phase of contemporary literary consciousness. I cannot cover in detail here the lengthy analyses Bonnefoy conducts, nor account for their richness. But it seems to me simply that the polemical image against which this thesis is built deforms what it contests, and that Blanchot's discourse is more nuanced regarding the undeniable question of nihilism.

Let us remark first of all that the "infinite nihilism" of which Blanchot suspects *Le bavard* is not des Forêts's. It leans upon a work, or rather on a singular story, and no honest reading of the *Le bavard* can

16. Yves Bonnefoy, *La vérité de parole* (Paris: Mercure de France, 1988). See chapter 2, "Une écriture de notre temps," 115–259.

afford to get rid of this suspicion (from which Bonnefoy, furthermore, does not hold himself back). But this "nihilism" is not necessarily the last word, neither of the narrative nor of the oeuvre. Nevertheless, it introduces a certain insight [*prise de conscience*] which seems to me to be entirely essential, an awareness announced precisely in "La parole vaine." It is in this postface that Blanchot remarks with acuity that chatter [*bavardage*] is always stigmatized, and its very name is a reproach without appeal. He adds: "I have always been struck by the earnest and enchanted approbation given universally to Heidegger when he condemns inauthentic speech under the pretext of analysis and with the sober vigor proper to him" (*A*, 145). The stakes of the debate are to know whether such a standard (inauthentic speech) may serve as a measure. Heidegger would be joined here by Lacan, at least the Lacan of "Function and Field of Language in Psychoanalysis." In a similar way, poetry seems, for Bonnefoy, to be this possibility of rendering language to its authenticity. Blanchot's critical work—by which I mean his attentive reading of literature—makes such a dichotomy uncomfortable. Literature—which rejects no "ordinary" form of language—without a doubt would be conceived rather as the place of a putting of language to the test, rather than as the site of its purification.

Of course there remain song and music, which literature doesn't renounce the attempt to equal. But I do not believe them to have the status of authentic language in des Forêts; they figure a temptation as well as a horizon, the mirage of an immediacy that knows itself to be a dream, but a dream nonetheless impossible to abandon. Doubtless it is appropriate to hear here, with Jean Roudaut, the expression of an aggrieved hope, but whose place writing can compose.[17] As Blanchot indicates with the term "anacrouse," there remains a work about time—one that would be the particular work of writing. His studies of des Forêts's poems cite many times [*VV*, 37] the verses with which *Poems of Samuel Wood* simultaneously opens and is completed:

> If to make heard a voice come from elsewhere
> Inaccessible to time and to depletion [*usure*]
> Is revealed as no less illusory than a dream
> There is nonetheless within it something that lasts
> Even after its meaning has been lost

17. Here I refer to his beautiful book, *Louis-René des Forêts* (Paris: Seuil, Les Contemporains), 1995.

Its timbre yet vibrates in the distance like a storm
Of which one doesn't know if it's coming or going. [*VV*, 37]

The indecision of the oeuvre and the disquiet about its sense are formulated, in this poem, by the collision produced between the spaces and the syntax of the phrasing. This is precisely what the word of commentary must gather and allow to resonate. The rage of the Babbler and his hecatomb of words are no longer appropriate to this echo of a voice close to being distant; but the suspicion that the Babbler has bequeathed to des Forêts, as to his readers, is also what leads us upon the desolate and ravishing roads of poetry. Nihilism versus recovered presence? The terms of the debate are not so categorical. It is rather the presence made by absence, the undeniable trace of a voice in search of its utopian abode. A voice held to pursuing its quest by a moral obligation.

Not to evade its call, while knowing that silence would be its best receptacle as well as its most sure betrayal: it is in this paradoxical injunction that the life of speech is maintained. This paradoxical function, which appears in *Une voix venue d'ailleurs,* takes up once again that of des Forêts, and accompanies it in its difficult adventure. Thus it responds to the indestructible "obligation of vigilant friendship" of which it would already be something that it be given to us to share.

—Translated from the French by Thomas Pepper

MICHAEL SYROTINSKI

Noncoincidences: Blanchot Reading Paulhan*

> The encounter thus designates a new relationship, because at the point of coincidence—which is not a point, but a gap [*un écart*], noncoincidence intervenes (is affirmed in its coming-in-between [*s'affirme dans l'inter-venue*]).
>
> —Maurice Blanchot, *L'entretien infini*

> We will remember these days.
>
> —Letter from Jean Paulhan to Blanchot, May 1940

WHO SAID ANYTHING ABOUT TERROR?

How do we read the "encounter" in the 1940s between Jean Paulhan and Maurice Blanchot? Since Jeffrey Mehlman brought Blanchot's journalism of the 1930s out into the open,[1] the fate of the critical reception of Paulhan's *Les fleurs de Tarbes, ou la terreur dans les lettres* [The Flowers of Tarbes, or Terror in Literature] has become almost inseparably linked to Blanchot's reading of it, "How is Literature Possible?"[2] There is little doubt that the "encounter" between Blanchot and Paulhan was an extremely significant one. If Paulhan's book was recognized by Blanchot as one of this century's key texts of literary criticism, Blanchot's reading of it (coincidentally or not, and that is the question I would ultimately like to address) occupies a rather crucial place in the shift between Blanchot's career from being an apologist for a certain form of Right Wing nationalism in France during the 1930s to his more celebrated role as a fiction writer and literary critic from the 1940s onwards.

The question of the extent to which this encounter between Paul-

*Parts of this essay appear in slightly modified form in my *Defying Gravity: Jean Paulhan's Interventions in Twentieth-Century French Intellectual History* (Albany: State University of New York Press, 1998).

1. See Jeffrey Mehlman, "Blanchot and *Combat*," in *Legacies of Anti-Semitism in France* (Minneapolis: University of Minnesota Press, 1983).

2. Maurice Blanchot, "How is Literature Possible?," trans. Michael Syrotinski, in *A Blanchot Reader*, ed. Michael Holland (Oxford: Blackwell, 1995).

YFS 93, *The Place of Maurice Blanchot,* ed. Thomas Pepper, © 1998 by Yale University.

han and Blanchot allows us to interpret the transition and transformation of Blanchot's early writing career has been addressed in ways that have led to Paulhan's texts being appropriated and reinscribed for a number of different theoretical ends. Mehlman, for example, has attempted to link the timing of Blanchot's privileging of the essential silence or nothingness at the heart of the literary enterprise to Derrida's (and by extension deconstruction's) supposed evacuation of politics and history from literature, a conscious forgetting as a way of covering over its guilty origins, with Paulhan being described as one of the chief sources of this political "amnesia."[3] I would like to take a closer look at the "encounter" between Blanchot and Paulhan, which I take to be one of the crucial events of French twentieth-century intellectual history, and to broaden its historical frame of reference beyond Blanchot's reading of *Les fleurs de Tarbes,* to include Blanchot's later, and equally important essays, "Le mystère dans les lettres" [Mystery in Literature] and "La facilité de mourir" [The Ease of Dying].[4] In other words, I would like to *keep reading,* and this act of reading on produces a new twist to the questions with which both Paulhan and Blanchot engage: questions of history, of reading and writing, of their temporality, and of their occasions.

If *Les fleurs de Tarbes* can be said to have a historical context, then it is probably in its oblique intersection with several intellectual currents of the 1930s and 1940s in France. The concept of Terror had been revived in France in the 1930s, thanks mainly to Jean Hyppolite's

3. Mehlman, "Writing and Deference: The Politics of Literary Adulation," *Representations* 15 (Summer 1986). We in fact know very little of the empirical details of the relationship between Blanchot and Paulhan; and one could certainly not count Blanchot among Paulhan's vast circle of friends with whom he kept up long and unfailingly loyal correspondences. Furthermore, one of the main difficulties in writing about this encounter has come about as a direct consequence of Mehlman's intervention. His reading of Blanchot's career is based in part on a consultation of the correspondence between Paulhan and Blanchot. When Mehlman's article appeared in French in *Tel Quel* in 1983, Blanchot reacted by categorically denying Mehlman's claims, and forbade any further access to his correspondence with Paulhan. Although this puts any subsequent commentary somewhat at a disadvantage, it does not really alter the thrust of my own intervention.

4. Blanchot, "Le mystère dans les lettres," in *La part du feu* (Paris: Gallimard, 1949), 49–65; and "La facilité de mourir," *Nouvelle revue française* 197 (May 1969): 743–64; this essay was later published in *L'amitié* (Paris: Gallimard, 1971) in slightly modified form, and in English as "The Ease of Dying," trans. Christine Moneera Laennec and Michael Syrotinski in *Progress in Love on the Slow Side* (Lincoln: University of Nebraska Press, 1994), 122–42. All translations, here and throughout, are my own unless specified otherwise.

Genèse et structure de la Phénoménologie de l'esprit de Hegel [*Genesis and Structure of Hegel's Phenomenology of Spirit* (1946)] and Alexandre Kojève's *Introduction à la lecture de Hegel* [*Introduction to the Reading of Hegel* (1947)]. This French "discovery" of Hegel was largely due to the courses given by Kojève during the 1930s. His anthropologized version of *The Phenomenology of Spirit* followed a trajectory from the French Revolution to the First Empire, Napoleon's march into Jena being interpreted by Kojève as a literal "end of history." As Vincent Descombes puts it: "Kojève bequeathed to his listeners a *terrorist* conception of history."[5] This becomes an important motif in the philosophy of the period, and was carried over into the realm of literature. Queneau's novels of the 1930s and 1940s are clearly marked by Kojève's reading of Hegel, and Sartre gave an extensive analysis of the change in the relation of the writer to society after the French Revolution in *Qu'est-ce que la littérature?* [What is Literature?], in particular in the section entitled "Pour qui écrit-on?" [For Whom Does One Write?][6]

Blanchot's response to Sartre's text was "Literature and the Right to Death," which takes the form of an ironic commentary on Kojève's reading of Hegel, and at the same time is an implicit debate with Sartre on the question of what we might term the literariness of literature.[7] Sartre seems to ask the question "What is literature?" rhetorically, since he at any rate is very clear as to what literature is, or should be. It is certainly no accident that Blanchot should first take up the question, prior to Sartre's politicized promotion of committed literature, by way of Paulhan. Paulhan's entire oeuvre might be said to constitute an extended answer to this one question about the specificity of literature. Near the beginning of *Les fleurs de Tarbes*, Paulhan poses the question explicitly as "this childish question: 'What is literature?'—childish, but which we spend a lifetime avoiding."[8] The title of Blanchot's essay on Paulhan's book—"How is Literature Possible?"[9]—is, taken quite literally, a meditation on Paulhan's "childish" question.

5. Vincent Descombes, *Modern French Philosophy* (Cambridge: Cambridge University Press, 1980), 14.

6. Jean-Paul Sartre, "Pour qui écrit-on?" in *Qu'est-ce que la littérature* (Paris: Gallimard, 1948), 130–40.

7. Blanchot, "Literature and the Right to Death," in *The Gaze of Orpheus and Other Literary Essays*, trans. Lydia Davis (Tarrytown, New York: Station Hill Press, 1981).

8. Jean Paulhan, *Les fleurs de Tarbes, ou la terreur dans les lettres*, in *Oeuvres complètes* (Paris: Éditions du Cercle du livre précieux, 1966–70), vol. 3, 24.

9. Blanchot, "Comment la littérature est-elle possible," in *Faux pas* (this essay is

In terms of Paulhan's own work, *Les fleurs de Tarbes* represents his most sustained analysis of the critical terms one tends to associate with his name, that is, Terror and Rhetoric. His understanding of Rhetoric is, on the face of it, fairly traditional. Indeed, Rhetoric is for Paulhan necessarily on the side of tradition (he also refers to it as "la Maintenance" [*Fleurs,* 183]), and it goes hand in hand with a conviction that language is in no need of change. *Les fleurs de Tarbes,* however, presents itself on a first reading as an extensive survey of an opposing tendency within literature, which Paulhan calls *la Terreur* [Terror]. Terrorist writers, according to Paulhan, espouse continual change and renewal, and vigorously denounce Rhetoric's codification of language, its tendency to stultify the spirit and banalize human experience. *Les fleurs de Tarbes* appears to support, through a long series of proofs, the Terrorist conception of literature and language. The examples are drawn indiscriminately from ordinary language and from literature, with the central figure being Terror's own philosopher, Henri Bergson. The challenge to literature, spearheaded by Bergson, is described as "without a doubt the most serious reproach of our time: this is that the author of commonplaces gives in to the power of words, to verbalism, to the hold language has over it, and so on" (*Fleurs,* 30).

The opposition between Terror and Rhetoric appears to polarize two conflicting ideologies of expression: the aspiration toward originality on the one hand and, on the other, the attraction to the stability of the commonplace. Terror seems to stand not so much for the violent period of the French Revolution, to which it obliquely makes reference, but synecdochally for the Revolution, or rather for a decisive turning point in French history, and more specifically in French *literary* history. It underlines the shift Paulhan finds in French literature from pre-Revolutionary Classicism, when writers submitted happily to the various rules imposed by traditions of genre and rhetorical composition, to Romanticism and its successors, whose "terrorism" consisted in abandoning accepted literary form in search of a more authentic, original expressiveness. Terror is literature that rejects literary commonplaces and conventions in an attempt to accede to a pure,

subsequently referred to as *Faux pas* in the text). The essay was first published as a series of three review articles in the *Journal des débats:* "La terreur dans les lettres" (21 October 1941); "Comment la littérature est-elle possible?" (25 November 1941); and "Comment la littérature est-elle possible (2 December 1941); and then as a separate pamphlet published by José Corti in 1942. In 1943 it was included in *Faux pas,* which was Blanchot's first collection of literary articles.

authentic expression (Paulhan is fond of citing Rimbaud's rejection of the "poetic oldfashionedness" [*vieillerie poétique*] [*Fleurs,* 21] of his literary predecessors). As Blanchot correctly summarizes, the multitude of guises in which Terror appears in *Les fleurs de Tarbes* can be generally divided into two types: those that would like to bypass language altogether ("Art consequently has only one objective: to bring to light this inner world, while keeping it untouched by the crude and general illusions with which an imperfect language would dishonor it" [*Faux pas,* 95]) and those that are intent on cleansing language of its impure and worn-out expressions, "making sure that they rid language of everything which could make it look like ordinary language" (*Faux pas,* 95).

After spending the first half of *Les fleurs de Tarbes* confirming the validity of Terror's arguments, Paulhan unmasks their futility by showing that terrorists are the victims of an optical illusion ("we only enter into contact with literature, and language itself, nowadays . . . thanks to a series of errors and illusions, as common as an optical illusion might be" [*Fleurs,* 67]). Terrorist writers are in fact endlessly preoccupied with language, forever trying to bypass it, or rid it of its impurities:

> For Terror depends first of all on language in this general sense: that the writer is henceforth condemned only to express what a certain *state* of language leaves him free to express: restricted to the areas of feeling and thought in which language has not yet been overused. That's not all: no writer is more preoccupied with words than the one who is determined at every turn to get rid of them, to get away from them, or even to reinvent them. [*Fleurs,* 135–36]

If, according to Paulhan, both terrorists and rhetoricians are justified in their conceptions of literature, and therefore are both equally unjustified, *Les fleurs de Tarbes* seems to be in danger of becoming an endless exchange of reproaches and rebuttals, and the reader is liable to become dizzy watching what Michel Beaujour has referred to as "the whirligig of Rhetoric and Terror" [*le tourniquet de la Rhétorique et de la Terreur.*][10] The central enigma of *Les fleurs de Tarbes* is thus formulated as a certain form of undecidability: how can we tell whether an author intended his or her words to be read as commonplaces or as original expressions?

10. Michel Beaujour, "Jean Paulhan et la Terreur," in *Jean Paulhan le souterrain (Colloque de Cerisy)* (Paris: 10/18, 1976), 118–50.

Commonplaces become for Paulhan the locus of a deep-seated tension within language and literature. Far from being common, they are, as Blanchot rightly points out, "monsters of ambiguity" [*des monstres d'ambiguïté*] (*Faux pas,* 94). Paulhan apparently resolves the paradox by a revalorization (or a "reinvention") of Rhetoric. From the point of view of Rhetoric, the author is freed from a constant preoccupation with language precisely by submitting to the authority of commonplaces. In order to have a renewed contact with the "virgin newness of things" [*nouveauté vierge des choses*] (*Fleurs,* 92), writers should mutually agree to recognize clichés *as* clichés, and thereby institute a common, communally agreed-upon rhetoric as a means of resolving the perplexing ambiguity that characterizes commonplaces:

> Clichés will be allowed to become citizens of Literature again [*pourront retrouver droit de cité dans le Lettres*] the day they are at last deprived of their ambiguity, and their confusion. Now all it should require, since the confusion stems from a doubt as to their nature, is simply for us to *agree,* once and for all, to take them as clichés. In short, we just need to *make* commonplaces *common.* [*Fleurs,* 80]

The solution is a redoubled or, as Paulhan terms it, a "reinvented" Rhetoric. In his essay, Blanchot likens this reversal to a revolution that is both Copernican (since thought, in order to rediscover its authenticity, is made to revolve around and be dependent on the constant gravitational pull of language), and Kantian (since it involves an apperceptive awareness of the linguistic illusions according to which we are able to write). This granting of a "droit de *cité*" (my emphasis) to clichés makes them acceptable "citizens" of the realm of literature in that they become publicly quotable, marked by a communally recognized citationality.

This solution is itself framed by the allegorical narrative of the most common "place" of *Les fleurs de Tarbes,* that most communal of locations, the public garden of Tarbes. A notice [*écriteau*] at the entrance to the park reads something like a terrorist slogan: "IT IS FORBIDDEN TO ENTER THE PARK [*LE JARDIN*] CARRYING FLOWERS" (*Fleurs,* 24). As the story goes, the sign was erected by the keeper of the park (which is clearly intended to be the "garden of literature") to prevent people from taking the flowers (the flowers of rhetoric or literary commonplaces) and claiming they had brought them into the garden with them. But some visitors are determined to carry flowers and find several ways around this interdiction, and these ways correspond to the different "alibis" that authors give when confronted with the accusation of theft; for example, they carry ever more exotic flowers (the claim to a perpetual originality), or they say that the flowers just fell into their hair from the trees (the denial of authorial responsibility). The keeper's ban fails to solve the problem, and as Paulhan explains, it is merely compounded, since the continuous ingenuity of the visitors makes it increasingly difficult to determine whether the flowers are their own or are stolen public property (are they commonplaces or original thoughts?). The keeper's solution is consistent with Paulhan's reinvented rhetoric, and the allegory is concluded accordingly when the sign at the entrance is changed to: "IT IS FORBIDDEN TO ENTER THE PUBLIC PARK [*LE JARDIN PUBLIC*] WITHOUT FLOWERS IN YOUR HANDS" (165). The addition of "*public*" to "*jardin*" in the reworded sign underlines the common agreement to read commonplaces as commonplaces; it becomes a truly public park when the visitors, too burdened with their own flowers, will not even think of stealing the public ones. The allegory could thus be said adequately to frame the "apparent" version of *Les fleurs de Tarbes.* It follows the argument from Terror's denunciation of Rhetoric, through Rhetoric's exposure of Terror's illusions, to the reinvention of Rhetoric, which thus recovers literature's authenticity within its commonplaces. Yet this "solution" is not the end of the book, which in fact closes with an enigmatic retraction: "There are thus glimmers of light, visible to whoever sees them, hidden from whoever looks at them; gestures which cannot be performed without a certain negligence. . . . Let's just say I said nothing" (*Fleurs,* 94).

This seems at first to be just another example of the kind of modesty that is typical of Paulhan. However, if we look at it more closely, or at any rate read it more attentively, it is in fact a very troubling ending. How are we to read this disavowal? Is it intended to be taken literally, as an authentic expression of the author's feelings? But then how could the book be "nothing" since, if it were, we would not even be able to read this final sentence? Or is it to be read rhetorically as something that is just said, a cliché, a careless throwaway remark? But then was the entire book composed in an equally negligent fashion? What are we "seeing" or "reading" when we see or read this "nothing"? In Paulhan's own terms, this final sentence is strictly unreadable. He says earlier on in the book that "commonplaces can be intelligent or stupid, I don't know which, and I don't see any way ever of knowing it with any rigor" (*Fleurs,* 138–39). The book is thus a performance of the very radical ambiguity that it talks about, an ambiguity that is not simply an equivocation as to *what* the book is saying, but which suspends it between saying and doing, stating and performing, original and commonplace. As Blanchot says, "[Paulhan] factors in this equivocation, and does not attempt to dispel it" (*Faux pas*, 100). How can we read the "nothing" at the end of the book, since no sooner are the means given to us (the common agreement that allows us to read) than they are taken away again? The allegory of the public park is thus itself "framed" by the final retraction of the book. The frame of this book now requires an allegory that takes into account the failure of the apparent allegory. So that rather than the allegory being an allegory *of* the text, the text itself becomes an allegory of (the impossibility of) this allegory. In Paulhan's own terms, it is figured as being caught within the very illusion it believed it was catching out. The text is framed by what it was attempting to frame, so we can never tell whether we are inside or outside the frame, and we might well wonder if this could be said to be a "figure," since it involves the failure of figuration. The framing allegory of *Les fleurs de Tarbes*, far from defining literature by clearly demarcating the boundaries that surround the garden, makes it impossible for us to tell whether we are in the garden or not, since it is impossible to know whether we are carrying flowers or not.

In his essay "How is Literature Possible?" Blanchot is highly attentive to this "nothing" and to this radical unreadability. For him, the "nothing" is the reappearance and reaffirmation of the Terror that Paulhan's book had so painstakingly discredited. A "reinvented" Terror, to be sure, but one that testifies to the persistence of the claim of literature to authenticity and originality, despite the demonstrated impossibility of this claim (since it is always preempted by Rhetoric). Indeed, for Blanchot this impossible assertion of terrorist purity is no less than literature's "soul" (*Faux pas*, 97), and its very claim to exist. Blanchot's insistence on this "reinvention" of Terror takes us back to the beginning of his essay. He had started out by saying that it is possible to read *Les fleurs de Tarbes* as two books: an apparent one, and one that is hidden ironically by this apparent one. The second, secret book only begins to work on the reader once the "first" book has been finished, and according to Blanchot:

> It is only through the uneasiness and anxiety we feel that we are authorized to communicate with the larger questions he poses, and he is

> prepared to show us these questions only by their *absence.* [*Faux pas,* 92, emphasis mine]

Blanchot answers the question of the title of his essay at one level—the level of the "apparent" book—by saying that literature is possible by virtue of the illusions that allow Terror to assert itself despite its impossibility. At another level, the level that makes the reader dimly aware of the far deeper questions, literature is said to appear only through its absence. From the perspective of both Terror and Rhetoric, therefore, it is always already lost; we are left with a Terror that can only ever be reinvented, and a Rhetoric that never allows itself to be codified into any kind of literary convention. It is neither Terror nor Rhetoric, and yet it is both of them at the same time. Blanchot stresses that the duplicity of the two books cannot be overcome. The second book is only readable *after* the first book, thus confirming Paulhan's own observation in *Les fleurs de Tarbes:* "The reader places this extreme presence and this obsession with words at the *origin* of the incriminated phrase or passage, whereas it is in fact produced for him—as happened to us—at the *end* of his efforts" (65). In responding to the "hidden" book of *Les fleurs de Tarbes,* Blanchot truly implicates himself in the essential questions it raises, and begins to articulate concerns that will become major *topoi* in his later criticism.

The solution of the book *is* a necessary failure—"a sort of law of failure" as Paulhan calls it[11]—so that the "understanding" of this failure is not ultimately subsumed under the mastery of language, but through a kind of parody of understanding. This is how Paulhan describes it toward the end of the "Pages d'explication" [Some Explanations], where he makes the link between *Les fleurs de Tarbes* and another key theoretical text, *Clef de la poésie* [Key to Poetry]: "Do we need to look for even more rules in which the arbitrary predominates? This is the question addressed by *Clef de la poésie.*"[12] Blanchot himself begins his essay on *Clef de la poésie,* "Le mystère dans les lettres," (a title borrowed from Mallarmé's famous essay of the same name) by returning to *Les fleurs de Tarbes.* He calls the "nothing" at the end of the book a "strange, somewhat disorienting privilege," and clearly makes the link between the two texts by Paulhan ("Mystère," 65). The

11. In the 1936 versioin of *Les fleurs de Tarbes,* reprinted in *Les fleurs de Tarbes,* ed. Jean-Claude Zylberstein (Paris: Gallimard/Folio, 1990), 248.
12. Paulhan, *Clef de la poésie,* in *Oeuvres complètes,* vol. 2, 212.

figure of the unknowable, factored into the equation, becomes that of "poetic mystery" [*le mystère poétique*].

POETIC JUSTICE

Clef de la poésie is ostensibly a rather drily programmatic attempt to apply the rigor of logical thinking to the phenomenon of poetry, to submit it to some kind of law. Paulhan proposes to deduce such a law from what is common to all poetry, its lowest common denominator as it were. This common, unifying element or trait is that which makes poetry the *least* common of enterprises, what Paulhan terms "poetic mystery." Since what makes poetic mystery mysterious—and poetic—is that it is undefinable ("there is, at the heart of poetry, a properly unspeakable mystery [*un mystère proprement indicible*]" (*Clef*, 241), the project of *Clef de la poésie* is the difficult one of "finding a law whose legality is founded upon mystery [*dont la légalité soit celle du mystère*]," as Blanchot puts it in "Le mystère dans les lettres."

Such a project *appears* to be futile; but it is in fact precisely in terms of its appearances that poetic mystery allows itself to be approached. And this is achieved, Paulhan argues, by making the first (and only?) principle of the law of poetic mystery one of an absolute reversibility of terms, the same reversibility that is operative in *Les fleurs de Tarbes:*

> I'm thinking now of a poetic law such that, expressing a particular relationship of sounds to meanings, and of ideas to words, it is able, without thereby losing its validity or its verisimilitude, to stand seeing its terms inverted; to stand being inverted. [*Clef*, 241]

In submitting itself to its own poetic law ("it is able . . . to stand being inverted"), or in giving in, immediately, to poetry's demands, this law—which is still only, it should be remembered, a hypothesis—would be true to the inconceivability of poetic mystery:

> It is clear that such a law, whose formula would be double, would go further than verisimilitude [*vraisemblance*] to reach the truth. For want of rendering mystery directly—which is by definition impossible—it would in effect yield to this mystery: it would mime it, show it. [*Clef*, 242]

A little later on, in transferring this double schema to a metaphysical, then to a *political* domain, Paulhan finds that positions are switched with equal ease, so that he is led to conclude: "One suspects that the key, once discovered, would be valid also for domains other than literature or poetry" (*Clef*, 247). The apparent nonchalance with which each side betrays its position allows Paulhan to speculate that, as was suggested before, a form of betrayal is necessary in poetic mystery, and that this is even its most singular trait:

> We saw that there was a constant trait with poetry: it is the regular flaw [*défaut*] which each doctrine or reason betrays when dealing with it. . . . If I attempt less to explain this trait, or even to understand it, than to express it—to formulate it—it comes down to the following: that in poetry words and thoughts happen to be *indifferent.* [*Clef,* 249]

This formulation is an absolutely crucial one in Paulhan's essay. It gathers together in its conciseness all of the hypothetical speculation, and offers a first version of the law on which the essay will elaborate. We might feel that such a perfect formulation leaves no room for mystery, which seems itself to be betrayed, and that the effacement of differences leaves us with nothing, or with the flatness of a platitude. However—and here we can understand how such a formulation is possible—it never claimed to be anything other than a platitude, or rather, it only ever claimed to simulate poetic mystery ("In which we express mystery for lack of being able to think it" [*Clef,* 248]), to be only apparently true. It does not give us poetic mystery, which is not there to be given, but it allows it to insinuate itself as the invisible trait that only reveals itself in its appearances. It always appears as what it is not, and so the duplicity of its constant self-betrayal is the surest guarantee of its continuing effectiveness.

In a surprising move, Paulhan then goes on to pursue his argument by borrowing a system of expression from the field of mathematics, since he is concerned with satisfying both the scientific requirement of noncontradiction as well as (simultaneously) the poetic requirement of indifference. In fact, only by satisfying this double requirement will it be truly a law of poetic mystery. The mathematical formula he elaborates is as follows: since the sets of oppositions that govern any expression are not made up of isolated elements—that is to say, since there is always a more or less complex configuration of, for example, language and thought, sounds and meanings—Paulhan designates these sets by groups of symbols, calling them "functions." The necessarily double formula is thus:

> From F(abc) it follows that F′(ABC)
> From F(ABC) it follows that F′(abc). [*Clef,* 251]

How this is to be understood is that "a b c are words for classical poets and rhetoricians, and A B C thoughts. But that for romantic poets and terrorists a b c are on the contrary ideas and A B C words," (*Clef,* 251). Filling in the double equation we get:

> The function F(words) implies the function F′(ideas)
> [just as]
> The function F(ideas) implies the function F′(words).

The first half of the formula works like any scientific formula, and is even consistent with scientific precedent in assigning terms to something that is temporarily inconceivable. The second half, however, is of a different nature:

> The second test, which interests me, is particular to a poetic law: it is a question of knowing whether this law remains valid *despite* the mystery and the transmutation of its elements: if it is likely to resist this mystery and (so to speak) soak up the obstacle. [*Clef,* 252]

According to this double law, it makes absolutely no difference whether we go from cause to effect or from effect to cause, from thoughts to words or from words to thoughts. While the two directions are perfectly comprehensible in terms of scientific laws (the first is logical, the second is "simply" illogical), their simultaneous coexistence and interchangeability are not, and the formula thus fulfills the requirement of the law of poetic mystery.

Paulhan anticipates possible objections to his argument. And he does so by stating that the performance of the text has both "overtaken" his argument [*dépassé mon propos*], and in doing so has itself become an example of the law he is attempting to formulate: "I have proposed nothing that I have not undergone. . . . I was the very discovery that I was making" (*Clef,* 256). We might say that the text of *Clef de la poésie* is itself poetic to the extent that it obeys exactly the law of poetic mystery that it articulates; it functions on two registers, each absolutely distinct from the other, yet both interchangeable, self-betraying, and coexisting in a singular, indifferent relationship. *Clef de la poésie* is its own primary proof, precisely because it is a poetic "event" *as well as* a logical argument. But in declaring his text subject to its own law of poetic mystery, and to the illusions that always inform literary and critical endeavors, Paulhan seems to open and immediately close an interpretive circle. We are justified in asking whether in doing so, he does not forever foreclose the possibility of considering a generically circumscribed poetics. Is he being unduly naïve in forbidding himself access to an external, objective perspective?

According to Blanchot, Paulhan is the least self-deluded of critics precisely because of the rigor of his concentration on what appears simple and commonplace. Since literature always tends to produce the same division into Rhetoric and Terror, Paulhan's naïveté is, as Blanchot remarks, "the least unreflective possible" ("Mystère," 50). In subjecting his own texts to the same rigorous critical scrutiny he exercises in reading other texts, he is demonstrating that he is no less exempt from the same illusions as other writers. What is so difficult to grasp (for Paulhan too) is why he should find what is self-evident so perplexing. As Blanchot says of *Clef de la poésie:*

> The provocative nature of these remarks comes from their simplicity, and yet also from the impossibility of going beyond them. ["Mystère," 51]

Language is, according to Paulhan, always two-faced. In his essay on *Clef de la poésie,* Blanchot demonstrates how the metaphorical extension of this duplicity works. This division of the acts of reading and writing into two opposing and mutually exclusive camps is as illusory as the irreducibile separation of, say, words and thoughts; and Blanchot focuses on those rare moments of "short-circuiting" between the two. At such moments, Blanchot writes, both aspects appear simultaneously: "the whole of language, whose two sides we only make out otherwise when they are folded on top of one another, and hide one another" ("Mystère," 53). Blanchot pushes the logic of this play of appearance and disappearance to a point where a comparison between Paulhan and Mallarmé becomes possible, and this allows for a clarification of the distinction between "ordinary" language and poetry in *Clef de la poésie.* If, for Paulhan, words exist in an indifferent relationship with things, for example, then they have, as Blanchot says, a triple existence. They exist in order to make the thing appear (while themselves disappearing); they reappear as deictic signs showing the thing that only exists by virtue of being called forth by the words; and they again disappear to maintain the illusion of the thing existing independently of words. From the opposite perspective, the same "short-circuiting" takes place, but inversely. In defining the project of Mallarmé's poetics as the evocation, not of things, but of the *absence* of things,[13] Blanchot arrives at the following reformulation of Paulhan's law:

13. See, for example, Stéphane Mallarmé, "Crise de vers," "Quant au livre," and 'La musique et les lettres." Blanchot cites elliptically the famous passage concerning he "absent flower" from "Crise de vers" in *Literature and the Right to Death.*

> [W]ords vanish from the stage to usher in the thing, but as this thing is itself nothing more than an absence, what appears in this theater is an absence of words and an absence of things, a simultaneous void, nothing supported by nothing. ["Mystère," 55]

Thus, by very different routes, Paulhan and Mallarmé reach a strikingly similar conception of poetry, or of poetic mystery. Mallarmé's disappearing words and things leave us with an enigmatic emptiness that resembles the empty platitude of Paulhan's poetic law. Does this mean that poetry tends always toward the destruction of ordinary language? If so, we might feel doubly anxious: not only is poetry essentially empty, but once we reach this emptiness of poetry, there is no going back to "ordinary" language. This, however, is once more to presume that poetry is simply a particular form of language, and that it is accessible to cognition in the same way. Blanchot points out how absolutely different the dimensions of "poetry" and "ordinary language" are, and this radical incompatibility is itself irreducible to a logic of contradiction or paradox. In Blanchot's essay this produces a number of consequences that follow from this description of poetry: poetry can only *appear* as something *inapparent;* it renders language unworkable, yet it is the condition of possibility of language; and poetic mystery is absolutely hidden from sight, yet it is what illuminates everything.

In showing his essay to have been a poetic as well as a logical text, Paulhan does not simply reassert the supremacy of poetry over science. If we at first took the rather barren mathematical formula to be a subordination of poetry to the discourse of science, the moment of textual self-implication *makes* it a poetic event. In the text's own terms, it becomes a matter of indifference whether the text is a logical argument or a poetic event. In other words, we cannot tell whether poetry is subordinated to the discourse of science, or whether science is subordinated to poetry. Indeed, borrowing Paulhan's law of poetic mystery, we could express this opposition by the following double formula:

> From F (poetry) it follows that F′ (science)
> From F (science) it follows that F′ (poetry).

It is impossible to tell whether *Clef de la poésie,* which is the only evidence we have, the only place where the question can be decided, is a discourse of poetry or of science. As Blanchot puts it, Paulhan's text is "both a scientific and a nonscientific process, the disjunction as it were between the two, and the mind's hesitation between the latter and the former ("The Ease of Dying," 131). If *Clef de la poésie* and Blanchot's reading of it are in many ways important in understanding the relationship between Paulhan and Blanchot and in grasping Paulhan's subtle but telling impact on Blanchot's writing, the final critical essay Blanchot devoted to Paulhan, "The Ease of Dying," is perhaps the most crucial of all.

NOW I REMEMBER

"The Ease of Dying" was originally written for the 1969 issue of the *Nouvelle revue française* commemorating the death of Paulhan a year earlier, and is ostensibly concerned with Paulhan's *récits*, or short fictional narratives written for the most part around the time of the First World War. The significance of writing on the "occasion" of Paulhan's death is not lost on Blanchot, and he begins the essay recounting the story of their friendship, in what is, for Blanchot, an unusually anecdotal style.[14] As a story of friendship, however, it is presented in the barest of terms—as Blanchot says, it was a "relationship without anecdotes"—and its solemnity is accentuated by what he sees as its chance alignment with some of the watersheds of recent French history. Blanchot tells of their first encounter in May 1940; of how their relations were severed in 1958 over the question of Algerian Independence; and of how their planned reconciliation was thwarted by the events of May 1968.

As the essay develops, it calls to mind Blanchot's discussion of literature and revolution in "Literature and the Right to Death." Paulhan was, as Blanchot notes, a writer who had a marked tendency to publish during periods of great historical change (the First and Second World Wars), when the whole of history was being put into question. The historical vacuum thereby opened up (what Blanchot calls "a time outside of time") increases the chances of a kind of anonymity that is a requirement of the impersonal or neutral "rapport" about which Blanchot speaks:

> [G]reat historical changes are also destined, because of their burden of absolute visibility, and because they allow nothing but these changes themselves to be seen, to better free up the possibility of being under-

14. Blanchot's discussion in *The Unavowable Community* (trans. Pierre Joris [Tarrytown, New York: Station Hill Press, 1988]) of the "limit-experience" as one that involves the "death of the other" is particularly resonant here.

> stood or misunderstood intimately, and without having to spell things out, the private falling silent so that the public can speak, thus finding its voice. ["The Ease of Dying," 122]

This confusion of public and private is affirmed by Blanchot because of its potential to allow for the emergence of a different kind of intimacy that would neither be an anecdotal relationship nor one that is "without anecdotes." The "relationship" between Paulhan and Blanchot only begins here, it seems, after Paulhan's death. It is surely no coincidence that it is only once Paulhan has died that Blanchot is able to write: "I often observed that his *récits*—which touched me in a way I can better remember now . . ." ("Ease of Dying," 122). A few sentences earlier, quoting Paulhan's "prophetic" words in 1940—"We will remember these days"—Blanchot effectively transfers their relationship to a time that is a "time outside of time," one that would escape the double bind of an anecdotal or a nonanecdotal rapport, and one in which personal friendship would be subordinated to the "rapport," or "nonrapport," of reading and writing.

Elsewhere in the essay Blanchot makes the brilliantly simple remark that all of Paulhan's texts might be read as *récits*.[15] As he says: "It is through the movement of the *récit* (the discontinuity of the continuous *récit*) that we can perhaps best understand Jean Paulhan" ("Ease of Dying," 123). For Blanchot, the figure of this radical discontinuity (or irreversibility) is death, while the *récit*'s continuity is guaranteed, conversely, by the play of reversals of Paulhan's texts, which Blanchot names "illness." Thus "death" and "illness" become figures of irreversibility and reversibility respectively. It might appear that "death" carries the greater theoretical burden of the two terms. But the title of the essay, "The Ease of Dying," warns of a dangerous trap: nothing could be easier than "dying," in the sense that thinking and writing can easily recuperate and accommodate their own discontinuity. Reversibility—"illness"—thus becomes, in Paulhan's texts, a form of endless narrative vigilance and a paradoxical guarantee of irreversibility, or "death." What the *récit* names, therefore, in "The Ease of Dying" is a "reading-writing" that responds to its own essential condition, that is, an experience of radical incommensurability or noncoincidence. It is, in other words, very close to the symmetrical impossibility of writing and reading that Blanchot discusses at the beginning

15. The term *récit* is used increasingly by Blanchot during the 1950s to designate writing that engages with its own essential "exigency."

of *L'espace littéraire.*[16] The only place—or space, or occasion—for literature is a kind of "nonplace" [*non-lieu*]; this is the "place" that Blanchot, in "The Ease of Dying," accords to the *récit:* "The *récit* alone provides the space, while taking it away, for the experience which is contrary to itself" ("The Ease of Dying," 137).

If writing is necessarily its own impossible occasion, how can we understand the "occasion" of the "encounter" between Paulhan and Blanchot? We could see it as one in which the logic of the *récit* is *already* at work. If the *récit* names an essential noncoincidence between a text and itself ("writing"), then the critical response of Blanchot to Paulhan's *Fleurs de Tarbes* in 1941 is equally a form of reading that responds to the "unreadability" of Paulhan's text, its mysterious, inaccessible otherness. And the turn from political commentary to "reading-writing," in part occasioned by the reading of Paulhan's book, could be seen not as a forgetting of, or indifference to, the political circumstances of the time, but as the inauguration of a deeper questioning of the relationship between reading-writing and history. "Literature and the Right to Death" points the way toward an engagement with political questions that will be implicit or explicit in Blanchot's writing henceforth, an engagement that passes through precisely a critique of language's claims to immanence and transparency, and that includes a critique of forms of immanent (and potentially totalitarian) political ideology.[17]

So are we falling into the trap of a kind of immanent form of reading in proposing the relationship between Paulhan and Blanchot as a decisive and fully determined turning point in Blanchot's career? Yes and no. Shifting the focus to the *récit* allows us to see a logic of noncoincidence at work at the three levels of political writing (the noncoincidence of language and the world, or language as a fundamental negation of the world), literary act (writing is only truly writing if it responds to its own impossibility), and critical response (reading only occurs if it takes into account the fundamental unreadability of literature). Consequently we are "now" (in the "timeless" time of reading) in a better position to read Blanchot's opening remarks in "The Ease of Dying": ". . .[Paulhan's] *récits*—which touched me in a way I can better remember *now*—" (my emphasis). Consistent with the "after the fact" [*après-coup*] logic of the essay itself—or to quote from one of

16. Blanchot, *L'espace littéraire* (Paris: Gallimard, 1955); *The Space of Literature,* trans. Ann Smock (Lincoln: University of Nebraska Press, 1982).

17. See the opening pages of *The Unavowable Community.*

Paulhan's "causes célèbres," which Blanchot himself cites in "The Ease of Dying": "But how can we succeed in seeing at first sight things for the second time?" (137)—only "now" is Blanchot able to "read" Paulhan's *récits.* The essay itself replays the same logic of noncoincidence, both asking (again) the question of writing and its circumstances, and at the same time answering it in its very performance by narrating the impossibility of ever understanding the moment of their "encounter" as a "*rapport.*"

This is not to deny, of course, that there *was* an empirical relationship between Blanchot and Paulhan during the war, with its own history and anecdotes, a relationship that remains to be told. Although Paulhan's wartime activities were far more visible than Blanchot's, the latter's writings (critical, literary, and political) have tended to eclipse the former's. There can be no avoiding the *fact* of Blanchot's affiliation with fascist ideology in the 1930s, even if one seeks to palliate it by seeing it as a more mystical, less politically anchored form of nationalism.[18] But taking the *récit* as a medium of serious critical reflection allows us to better understand the *turn* in Blanchot's writing in the early 1940s, as a turning away from the politics with which he had been associated, but one that is not a turning away from politics and history, an averting of the gaze; rather it comes to assume the form of a reflection on the powerful fascination of the gaze itself. The *récit* will become, in Blanchot's later writing, the narrative logic, a logic anticipated by Paulhan, which names this contradictory process of turning itself: "that which turns itself away from thought returns to thought, a thought becomes its turning away."[19]

18. See Mike Holland and Patrick Rousseau, "Topographie-parcours d'une (contre-) révolution," *Gramma* 3 (1976): 8–41; and Patrick Rousseau, "Un écrivain de la transition" and Mike Holland, "Le hiatus theorique: le neutre," *Gramma* 4 (1976): 34–52 and 53–50, respectively.

19. Blanchot, *L'attente l'oubli* (Paris: Gallimard, 1962).

DENIS HOLLIER

Timeliness and Timelessness[1]

Take full advantage of radio's timeliness, write "the first alarm sounded half an hour ago," "the statement was released at the exact minute this program began," "a radio and press conference has been scheduled for 4 p.m., that's 17 minutes from now."
—Paul W. White, *Advice on Radio News Writing*

I

Last year I received a phone call that reminded me of the calls that typically wake up unemployed private eyes after the opening credits in a Raymond Chandler *film noir.* This scene, however, was not set in L.A. An editor who had heard I was in Paris for the year wanted to meet me. He had a proposition for me, but he couldn't tell me more until he saw me. It was all very mysterious. I went to our meeting point on rue de S. and he told me that the board had decided to offer me a contract for Blanchot's biography. What did I think? I was flattered, of course, a little. But also surprised, if only by the conspiratorial nature of the scene. Did they know something I didn't know? Were state secrets at play here? I thought of a title: *The Blanchot File.* Or, for the French version: *Dossier secret* (like the French version of *Mr. Arkadin*).

Why me? My first reaction, suspicion (what trap was being set for me?), made me realize to what extent, despite my resistance to some of the effects of a public acceptance of Blanchot that had grown rapidly over the last few years, I continued to move in a literary space that he had "formatted": a space that was too marked, too formatted by Blanchot for me to seriously imagine myself writing any biography, let alone his.

Once I had recovered from my surprise, I became superstitious. How old was he? I had forgotten when he was born. Would death force

1. A version of this essay was presented on the panel, "Hybrid Genres," organized by Susan R. Suleiman at the 1995 MLA Convention. The epigraph is from Paul W. White, *Advice on Radio News Writing* (New York: Harcourt Brace & Co., 1947), 79. All translations throughout this essay are by the translator unless specified otherwise.

on him what he had always refused to acknowledge in writing: a life? How many publishers were simultaneously betting on the likelihood of his impending entry into biographical space?

There were also practical questions: tracking down witnesses, mistresses, childhood friends, relatives, seducing them into the interviewing process, etc. Not to mention the problem of photographs. What would Blanchot leave behind? What would his *Nachlass* be made of? Was he himself preparing it? Would his death liberate suitcases full of papers?

What, for example, would be left of his correspondence, the primary material of any biography? There had been many rumors about Blanchot's letters, such as after Bataille's death in July 1962, Blanchot had destroyed all the letters he had received from his late friend.

This reminds me of the article Blanchot published in *Les lettres nouvelles* at the time. It was a strange obituary, a kind of mumbling requiem, solemn and reserved, almost anonymous, with Bataille's name appearing only once, in the middle of a clause, at the bottom of the second page. Instead of evoking the life of the man he'd been close to, Blanchot anticipated the world of rumor in which he would fade and be lost. His words stayed with me for a long time. They prophesied, with an oddly impotent sigh, the coming of the "complete works." I quote the paragraph in its entirety:

> The books themselves refer to an existence. That existence, because it is no longer a presence, is beginning to convert itself into history, and the worst of histories, literary history. An inquiring, meticulous history in constant search of documentation, it takes possession of a deceased will and transforms its own personal understanding of what has been left behind into knowledge. It is the time of complete works. We want to publish "everything," we want to tell "everything."[2]

Titled "L'amitié" ("Friendship"), the article, printed in italics, later served as a coda to the 1971 collection of essays to which it gave its title, most likely the last volume of literary criticism published by Blanchot.

The biographical void that Blanchot has been able to maintain around himself makes him one of the rare literary figures of this century to have acquired a truly legendary stature. With discreet effi-

2. Maurice Blanchot, *L'amitié* (Paris: Gallimard, 1971), 327. Blanchot's words were still in my mind when I chose "Georges Bataille, après tout" as a title for a conference organized to celebrate the actual completion of Bataille's complete works.

ciency, he has managed to elude all publicity traps. (Blanchot: "All that we say only veils the sole assertion: that everything must fade and that the only thing we can remain faithful to is the impulse that erases, to which something in us that rejects all memory already belongs" [*L'amitié*, 327]). A writer leaves no tracks. I am reminded again of the Orson Welles film in which Mr. Arkadin, amnesiac, hires a private investigator to reconstruct his past, and then destroys, one after the other, the surviving witnesses that the biographer-for-hire manages to flush out.

Blanchot continues his requiem by reworking, once more, the motif around which his literary reflections had been organized since their inception, twenty years earlier: the status of the first person. The three volumes that make up Bataille's *Somme athéologique* (*L'expérience intérieure, Le coupable, Sur Nietzsche*) are pieced together from notebooks Bataille kept during the Second World War. Most of their entries are written in the first person. But, says Blanchot, it is enough for the word "I" to be uttered by Bataille for the first person pronoun to cease to be really personal; carried away by the impersonal energy of the writing impulse, it is constantly on the verge of becoming no one's pronoun. Bataille's "I," he claims, is never really an "I," an "ego"; it has the indeterminacy of an interrogative "Who?" or of a "Who is this me that I am?" or of a "Who am I?"

In one of Derrida's essays on Blanchot, one of the voices wonders whether he/she would use the informal "you" (*tu*) with Blanchot. How could one address as "you" someone who refuses to say "I," someone whose entire body of nonfictional writing has been driven by the strategic avoidance of the first person, by the quest for a language capable of diverting, of eluding the identifications, the appropriation and centralization of the first person? Someone whose inventions are all geared toward undoing the grammatical personalization of language? Literary space is an Arcadia without ego, a space that cannot be entered in the first person. It surfaces at the very moment that the first person sinks and no one is left to keep the ship's log. Call me Ishmael, he says.

II

Will Blanchot's editors or biographers one day discover a personal handwritten diary? A log written in the first person, with daily entries relating events and memories, what happened to him, what thoughts crossed his mind? It is unlikely. It would be surprising. It is not impossible.

The literary space, Blanchot has always said, is generated through a kind of Copernican revolution, a pronominal decentering that turns sentences written in the first person into sentences in the impersonal third, converting "I" into "He" or "It" (which is the ground of what Blanchot called the right to die). At a time when linguistics was focusing more and more on what Benveniste calls "Man within language," Blanchot, under the aegis of literary space, contrived a strange linguistic desert, a space of uninhabited language, of language without speech, a language man cannot enter. It evokes the strangely selective aphasias that, according to Jakobson, deprive the schizophrenic speaker of a single function: the use of the first person. The birth of literature is correlative to a linguistic disengagement, a withdrawal, a subtraction (defacement) of man from language.

Accordingly, the personal diary, like letter writing for that matter, is not a literary genre. It is, at best, an exercise in resistance to literature: a means of binding writing to external time, of imposing on it the measure of time, of tying it to both a chronometry and a chronology, a means, that is, of writing without facing the risks associated with writing. For it is important here not to misunderstand what Proust meant by "*temps retrouvé*": what is recaptured is not the common time, the shared time of historical "*lieux de mémoire.*" Proust's project, according to Blanchot, exemplifies the radical incompatibility of the writing of the novel and that of the diary: "There is no writer more removed from the daily recording of his life." Or, as he says in reference to Benjamin Constant's *Adolphe,* the novel begins by taking one far from the "movement of hours."[3] Or again, in reference to Mallarmé: "The work must embody the awareness of the conflict between 'the time' (*l'heure*) and the literary game" (*LàV,* 282).

Thus, keeping a personal diary very well, to use Blanchot's condescending expression, can provide its keeper with the "illusion of writing." But it is only an illusion. Its writing is illusory to the precise extent that it is written in real time: the calendar spares its keeper the test of the right to die, it allows him even to fantasize that writing could end up providing a right to live. Even when the diarist feels lonely, even when he has no one to talk to, he can still say "dear Diary." His solitude is no longer essential solitude. "Clearly, the diary works as a safeguard against the dangers of writing" (*LàV,* 227). Or: "The diary

3. Blanchot, *Le livre à venir* (Paris: Gallimard, 1959), 226. Hereafter referred to as *LàV* in the body of the text.

roots the writing impulse in time, in the humility of the quotidian, which is dated and preserved by its date. . . . The date marked is that of common time where what happens really happens."[4]

From this follows the idea that writing in real time is unreal writing. The time "where what happens really happens" can do no more than give the illusion of writing. One must, thus, choose between two truths, that of writing and that of the event; one must choose between living for real and writing for real, between participating in things that really happen and "really" writing, that is, producing writing that is inspired by things that never happen in reality.

III

I would like to stay a little longer at the border of this space without borders, to prolong my reverie as to what Maurice Blanchot's diary would consist of, a diary in which Blanchot would have inscribed, daily, in accordance with the dating of calendar time, what, because it happened in shared, common time, really happened.

What could it contain?

What, according to Blanchot, really happens when a writer decides to go on board? To board real time? What events are recorded in these logs when a writer, terrified of the prospect of literary shipwreck, decides to climb aboard and be part of the action?

The diary question never stops coming back in Blanchot's critical writings. But its most striking aspect is the way, each time, Blanchot reduces what supposedly really happens to nothing. The diarist, one would think, abandons his creative writing in order to give events a chance. Blanchot, however, seems to be committed to preventing such an outcome at any cost. By giving up the novel for the diary, the writer passes from a space where nothing really happens to a time where nothing really happens. Whether it's Maurice de Guérin, or Amiel, or Joubert, what happens, at least according to Blanchot, when a writer starts keeping a diary is that the world freezes, everything stops happening. Their diaries record lives caught between two fears, the fear of writing and the fear of living; they compulsively perform infinite variations on the theme of nothing to report. The diarist, Blanchot com-

4. Blanchot, *L'espace littéraire* (Paris: Gallimard, 1955), 21. These sentences apply, beyond the limits of the diary, to any form of dated personal writing, correspondence included: "Similarly, Van Gogh has his letters and a brother to write them to" (*Le livre à venir*, 227).

ments, "lets himself be distracted from writing by the futilities of the day, savors his trivia in order to retell it" (*LàV*, 227). Blanchot's uncompromising resistance to the idea that something could really happen to a diarist becomes particularly clear when we realize that, contrary to what I said too hastily in my book on Sartre, when Blanchot uses the word "*journal,*" he is thinking exclusively of personal, intimate journals. The word in French, however, has another meaning. The daily recording of events is not primarily ascribed to domestic space. There is the *journal* (diary) that one writes, but there is also the *journal* (newspaper) that one reads. And it can happen that the two overlap.

IV

Let's return once more to Blanchot's claim: a diary is the record of a common time when what happens really happens. In the middle of her memoir, *La force de l'âge,* something, says Simone de Beauvoir, *happens.* (She uses the same verb as Blanchot.) The scene is set in the late summer of 1939. "Then one morning it happened. It was now, in an agony of loneliness, that I began to keep a diary. Its entries strike me as more vivid and accurate than any narrative I could piece together out of them, so I give them here: . . . . "[5] Colon. Followed by some hundred pages of the diary she kept continuously over the course of about a year. The first entry is dated 1 September 1939. This date refers to a common time, where what happens really happened. France and England have just declared war on Nazi Germany. This dramatic rupture in daily life changes her writing routine:

> September 1
> 10 A.M.: the papers print Hitler's demands, without comment. The disturbing nature of the news is not overemphasized, but no one any longer takes a hopeful line, either. I go to the Dôme, unsettled and at loose ends. Not many people there. Have hardly ordered a coffee before a waiter announces: "They've declared war on Poland." A customer inside has a copy of *Paris-Midi.* Others make a rush for him, and also for nearby newsstands, but *Paris-Midi* hasn't come in. I get up and go back to my hotel. People in the street don't know anything yet, they are still as cheerful as they were a while ago. One or two people along the Avenue du Maine are carrying copies of *Paris-Midi,* and passersby stop them to read the headlines. I find Sartre. . . .

5. Simone de Beauvoir, *The Prime of Life,* trans. Peter Green (New York: Paragon House, 1992), 302–3.

Simone de Beauvoir, in the middle of writing *L'invitée,* puts her novel aside. The declaration of war having deprived her of the freedom of mind she needs to write a fiction, for the first time in her life, she starts to keep a diary. But the impulse here owes nothing to the motives Blanchot discusses. She is not defending herself against the totalitarianism of fiction, nor does she fall back on the trivia thanks to which life can be everyday. There is no withdrawal into a morose and analytical celebration of the futility of real life. Simone de Beauvoir is very far from Amiel. Indeed, she is not threatened by writing; it's her writing that is threatened by history. What happened to her, one among millions of other individuals, on 1 September 1939 shows that, at certain times in history, a writer can become submerged by something other than writing.

In Simone de Beauvoir's life and memoirs, 1 September 1939 is the prototype of an impressive series of narrative interruptions. First, the composition of *L'invitée* is interrupted when the war causes her to put the novel aside and keep a diary instead. Then, some twenty years later, in *La force de l'âge,* she suspends the retrospective narrative of her memoirs to quote directly from her 1939 diary. But then the composition of *La force de l'âge* itself, which took place around 1958, is interrupted in its turn by a new French political crisis, a crisis almost as serious as the one in 1939. Simone de Beauvoir will evoke it in the following volume, which covers the period of the cold war and of decolonization, *La force des choses.* When her narrative arrives at the coup in Algiers, the memoirist becomes a diarist for the second time. In terms of the event as well as of the writing, May 1958 repeats September 1939. Beauvoir herself presents it that way. "My state of idleness," she writes, "and the general anxiety led me, as in September 1940 [*sic:* she is confusing 1939 and 1940], to start writing my diary again. . . . I shall transcribe it here, as I have done before: . . ." And the diary begins: "May 26. Strange days, in which we listen hour after hour to the radio and INF. 1, and buy every edition of the newspapers."[6]

Can we call this a personal diary?

One could say (without necessarily diminishing the historical importance of these events) that, in a way, the diaristic impulse was part and parcel of what "happened" to a lot of people during the course of those days. Simone de Beauvoir was certainly not alone. Sartre, for one,

6. Beauvoir, *The Autobiography of Simone de Beauvoir: Hard Times, Force of Circumstance, II,* trans. Richard Howard (New York: Paragon House, 1992), 112.

also began keeping a diary in September 1939 (which became his *Carnets de la drôle de guerre*). One could make a list of the diaries that begin on 1 September 1939: There's Guéhenno's *Journal des années noires,* Bataille's *Le coupable,* Lise Deharme's diary, Drieu la Rochelle's, Fabre-Luce's, Braibant's, Ramuz's, etc. The diaristic impulse was itself a fundamental dimension of the events of the time. What "happened" was not only the events recorded in the diaries, but also the impulse that drove novelists to transform themselves into diarists in order to record them.

But this diaristic impulse is one that no longer obeys the separation of private and public that is essential to Blanchot's definition of the genre. Not only does September 1939 mark the first time that Simone de Beauvoir has kept a diary. It also marks the first time in her life, or at least in the narrative of her life as told in her memoirs, that she has shown enough interest in the news to mention waiting for the newspapers, or buying them, let alone reading them or listening to the news on the radio. In these two instances, in 1939 and 1958, the journal space is doubled. Her personal entrance into the space of the diary is at the same time the entrance of the collective diary into her private space, the inscription of the quotidian that is read within the quotidian that is written; the invasion of outside events into Simone de Beauvoir's inner life. The indexical sign always rings twice: the writing of the "*journal*" (private diary) is prompted by the reading of the "*journal*" (public diary).

This connection is all the more striking given that, as I said, outside events had never previously captured de Beauvoir's attention. History, she writes, never interested her until it was already over, until it had become historical, until it was History. "I wasn't interested in events until they were already a year old," she writes (171). And, speaking of Sartre and herself: "Public affairs bored us" (*The Prime of Life,* 19). A truly dutiful daughter does not read the papers. With only two exceptions: she tells how at one time, during the '30s, she spent several days reading newspapers in the public library in Rouen, but those newspapers were already ten years old, she had to research the '20s for the novel she was then writing. The other exception: she confesses to a weakness for *Détective,* but this tabloid magazine specialized exclusively in crimes, especially the gorier ones. "While books and entertainments meant a good deal to us, public events touched us scarcely at all" (*The Prime of Life,* 45)

The repeated narrative structure, chapter after chapter, throughout de Beauvoir's memoirs, is dictated by the partition between private life and public space, by the segregation of the individual and the collective, of the psychological and the political. Because nothing affecting the collective fate penetrated Mademoiselle de Beauvoir's existence, the history-in-the-making of the early '30s left no trace in her memory. She is incapable of speaking of it in the first person. Chapter after chapter opens with a brief, objective, historical reconstruction of events she paid no attention to at the time. Once this backdrop has been set, she enters the stage and then moves on to the scenes of personal memory: her hopes, her joys, her life, her self. But the background never encroaches on the personally experienced, the heroine pays no attention to the decor in which her existence is taking shape. Collective history and individual psychology are separate acts, set on different stages.

At least until September 1939, when the declaration of war, changing her narrative routine, ends their separation. Until this date, world history alternated with the life of Simone de Beauvoir, parallel yet independent. Suddenly, they collide ("History burst over me," she writes). The diary is witness to this collision, in both its form and its content. It is both its index and its icon, both its effect and its recounting, which is why it cannot be called a personal diary. What triggers it is precisely the historical violation of the personal, the violent intrusion of history into subjectivity.

The 1938–1940 crisis induced a change in Blanchot as well. It triggered Sartre's and Simone de Beauvoir's conversion to newspaper-reading and diary-writing. For Blanchot, it triggered the opposite conversion. It made him move away from newspapers into literature, drift out of common time where the things that happen really happen. Opposite journeys: at the very moment Sartre and de Beauvoir discover the world of newspapers, Blanchot begins to detach himself from it.[7]

Blanchot, who may or may not have kept a diary at some point, returned again and again, in his critical writings, to the literary status of diaries. Curiously, his active career as a full-time journalist in the extreme-right newspapers of the '30s never led him to ask similar questions about a writer's involvement with nonprivate diaries. This notwithstanding, it was clearly on this activity—which was Blanchot's

7. As many critics have pointed out, *L'arrêt de mort* opens with the Munich crisis (date in text: Wednesday, 13 October 1938). It is the only Blanchot narrative in which the "action" is "dated."

before he entered the space of literature, before he moved from "I" to "He," before he abandoned the timeliness of hours and days for the timelessness of the literary space—it was on this still little explored activity as a journalist that an editor was betting, as he tried to launch the production of a book that would go so definitely against the grain of its subject matter as would a biography of Blanchot.

V

In *Après coup* (1983), one of the few texts in which he allows himself to look back and reminisce about the period before the war, Blanchot contends that, while a professional journalist, he was, to quote Paul Auster's translation, "astonishingly cut off from the literature of the time."[8]

How to characterize this literature? I would like to evoke briefly experiments that were carried out by the avant-garde of the '20s and '30s and which probably never figured in Blanchot's literary horizons; when he was a journalist, he did not pay any attention to them, and later, his rejection of journalism would have excluded them from the literary field in any case.

Simone de Beauvoir's grafting, on the occasion of the onset of the war, of her diary, and through it, of newspapers, onto the narrative fabric of *La force de l'âge* evokes, if in a toned-down form, various experimentations with the hybridization of the novelistic and journalistic narrative that were carried out not only by the militant members of the proletarian avant-garde of the '20s and '30s (from Dos Passos to Ehrenburg via Döblin et al.), but also by the surrealists (Breton in *Nadja* or Aragon in *Le paysan de Paris*). These experiments were meant to blur the border between narration and information. The press was a key factor in the nineteenth-century redistribution of the relationships between the real and the imaginary. The worldwide commodification of information required a narrative code of ethics that would allow the reader to distinguish reality from fiction.

These experiments are the literary equivalent of the collage in the visual arts, sharing with it a taste for the newspaper's headlines-and-columns layouts, to the point of reproducing them in facsimile. They test the possibility of shifting, within the framework of a single work of art, from a space of iconic representation to that of indexical happen-

8. Blanchot, "After the Fact," in *Vicious Circles*, trans. Paul Auster (New York: Station Hill Press, 1985), 64.

ing, of shifting from the space of signs to the space of events. How can a newspaper break into the space of the work (how can one expose the work of art to a truth that is not, as in René Girard, novelistic, but journalistic, the journalistic truth in painting)? How can one incorporate an event, a real event, into a novel? And make that novel not merely the narration of an event, but an event in itself? All these experiments are supported by a profoundly anti-Proustian inspiration: they aim at reintroducing *"le temps perdu"* (lost time) back into *"le temps retrouvé"* (time recaptured). This operation requires a sharpening of the heterogeneity of the two narrative media involved, the metonymical, transgressive contact between high and low, lost and found, sign and event, icon and index.

VII

Pervasive in Blanchot's critical work is a philosophy of the history of literature. Like all philosophies of history, his is teleological: literature aims toward its end. It reaches this end with Mallarmé. According to Marx, the history of man is that of class struggle, and man would cease to be historical when Communism had instituted a classless society. Similarly, Blanchot's history of literature, coextensive to the division between prose and poetry, will last as long as this difference does. It will reach its conclusion on the day that the (internal) difference between verse and prose is overthrown by the (external) difference between literature and nonliterature. Which is Mallarmé's message when he announces: There is no prose. There is no prose, that is, unless we move prose out of literature, unless we decide to call prose what belongs in reality no longer to literature but to universal reportage. In other words, framed between a restricted poetry and a generalized textuality, Blanchot's literary space is not a space without external borders. Literature is not a space without exterior. There remains one boundary, and it separates the novel and journalism.

Blanchot, thus, reshuffles the Mallarméan legacy. The first post-symbolist generation (that of Valéry), as a defense reaction to the contamination of literature by journalism and politics, fell back on poetry, abandoning the novel, in its retreat, to the indistinct realm of what Mallarmé called universal reportage. As if poets, having secured their hold on words, let the novelists deal with things. With his famous sarcastic comment about a genre that tries to interest the reader in "the fact that the marquise went out at five o'clock," Valéry was the spokesperson for this generation. According to him, there is no common ground between the poem, which is driven by internal necessity, and the novel, which relies on an anecdotal exterior. Why did the marquise have to go out? And why at five o'clock instead of five past five, seven past five, or five thirty? If she had been unable to go out, would anything have been different?

But Blanchot finds Valéry's interpretation of Mallarmé's lesson too narrow. Mallarmé did not speak only for poets. Moreover, poetry does not have a monopoly on obscurity and the signifier any more than the novel has to make do with transparency and the signified, or, even worse, the referent. There is no ground for a division of labor that requires a poem to put us in touch with words while a novel must put us in touch with things. The novel, like poetry, begins where language ceases to be everyday, where what is called common language loses its common usage, where everyday words become unusual, untimely, timeless. What a mistake, Blanchot would say, what a mistake to think that Mallarmé could have thought for a second of abandoning the novel to journalists! On the other hand, it is true that novelists should once and for all forget the marquises and their schedules and explore what one could call, after the manifesto-like articles Blanchot collected in *Faux pas*,[9] "a Mallarméan novel." The literary partition no longer separates poetry and prose, poetry and the novel, but two types of narration: *le roman* (the novel) and *le récit* (the narrative) or, to use Benjamin's terms, narration and information, one of which belongs to literature while the other does not. A Mallarméan novel will no longer be defined by its subject, it will no longer call on reality for help. "How strange," thinks Blanchot, "that in order to justify the novel's necessity we invoke the fact that it reproduces events, which are themselves unnecessary, the outcome of a confused and impenetrable system of chance and happenstance."[10] Moreover, is there anything more antiesthetic than "making the necessity of the work depend on its subject rather than on the work itself?"

> How to save from chance a work in which sentences follow each other for no particular reason, where almost all the words could be replaced by others without harm, which is not more than a combination of details and episodes fortuitously assembled? It is only too natural for the writer to justify himself with this answer: My novel, which is

9. Blanchot, *Faux pas* (Paris: Gallimard, 1943).
10. Blanchot, "L'enigme du roman," in *Faux pas*, 224.

made of an uncertain sequence of words and a problematic series of facts in which consequently nothing seems justified, is justified after all by the image of life it presents; it enjoys a certain necessity to the extent that it appears to be the narrative of events that have taken place or could have taken place.[11]

One last word on the subject of chance and necessity, which will take us back to the diary, a form (or a practice) that is, even more radically than the novel, unable to escape the aleatory nature of the worldly referent. Given its fundamental heteronomy, given its generic availability for the hazards of the law of the day, for the accidents of history and the random events of daily life, *le journal,* diary or newspaper, is the literary form, or lack of form, that most radically resists the Mallarméan redemptive formatting. If, following both Mallarmé and Blanchot, we identify the Book with the esthetic abolition of chance, the diary is the literary form that cannot be converted into a book. The small amount of necessity it can claim will always come from life, never from art; it is, by definition, a form of writing that lacks any internal necessity, that is subject throughout to the heteronomy of current events, to the follies of the day, or even of the hour.

VIII

I must conclude. I will do so by trying to retrace what I see as the curve of Blanchot's work.

To whom should one attribute the lines from *Faux pas* that I just quoted? Who is pronouncing these judgments on the novel? A critic? A theoretician of the work of art? One cannot exclude any of these voices, but Blanchot's Mallarméan definition of the novel is first of all a novelist's definition. It is the novelist, even more than the critic, who is speaking when Blanchot invokes Mallarmé to shield the novel from the folly of the day and from journalism. It is the novelist and not the critic who encourages novelists to follow Mallarmé's example rather than Zola's.

Unlike the great critics of the French tradition, from Sainte-Beuve to Barthes, whose work is haunted by the ghost of a storyteller whose reality they will never be quite sure of, Blanchot is a writer, perhaps the only one to have practiced with equal strength two genres, the author not of "critical fiction," to use a term that was fashionable a few years

11. Blanchot, "Le jeune roman," in *Faux pas,* 218.

ago, but of fiction and of criticism. These simultaneous but distinct discourses are inseparable. They constitute, in their duality, a unique device.

This device gives its structure to what Blanchot called literary space. If, sometime around 1940, he ceased to be a journalist, he did not do so in order to become a novelist or a critic. He did so in order to become both one and the other, one through the other. He left journalism in order (both as a novelist and as a critic) to force the novel to follow him out of timeliness.

Twenty years later, however, somewhere between *Le livre à venir* (1959) and *L'attente l'oubli* (1962), this bifocal device constitutive of the literary space fell apart. More or less simultaneously, Blanchot stopped both writing narratives and writing on the narrative. The contract between criticism and fiction broke down. Writing passed from the "book to come" to the "absence of the book." And this rupture took place, to give it a symbolic date, in May 1958.

This date is important, doubly important, because of the events that took place at the time, and also because those events, it seems, forced Blanchot's writing back into the common calendar, the collective datebook, shared time, the follies of the day.

In 1939, Simone de Beauvoir wrote the date in the diary that the ongoing events had inspired her to keep. In 1958, Blanchot did something similar.

L'amitié, published in 1971, gathers together essays that Blanchot had previously published in various periodicals. They are republished without mention of the date and place of their first publication, with one exception: the article entitled "Le refus" ("The Refusal"). Blanchot adds a footnote at the bottom of the page. It reads: "As an exception, I will note when and where this little text was published for the first time: in October 1958, in *14 juillet,* number 2. It was written a few days after General de Gaulle returned to power, brought there this time, not by the Résistance, but by mercenaries" (131).

As I have said, soon after, it seems that, at the same time, Blanchot stopped writing narratives and only very occasionally did he go back to what can be called, in the limited sense of the phrase, literary criticism.

I will not dwell on what could have made "Le refus" the occasion of such an interruption. I would like simply to point out the extent of the redistribution of discourses that accompanied this return of the date Its obliteration around 1938, we recall, is what led to the formation of

Blanchot's solid, bifocal but undivided literary space. In the name of Mallarmé, the border between verse and prose disappeared, the new frontier lying between literature and nonliterature, between literary language and common language. The return of the date in 1958 marked the collapse of this second border. What disappeared then was not, as in 1940, an internal distinction, but the external difference of literature. Literature has ceased to distinguish itself from its opposite.

Now, literature follows in the Marquise's footsteps. It's literature's turn to go out—it's five o'clock:

> It is irritating to see, in the place of so-called literary works, an ever-increasing mass of texts that, under the heading of documents, testimonials, almost raw speech, seem to ignore every intention of literature. We say: this has nothing to do with the creation of objects of art; we say: these are witnesses to a false realism. But what do we know? . . . Why couldn't these anonymous, authorless voices, which do not assume the form of books, which are temporary and want to be temporary, be alerting us to something important that what we call literature could also wish to tell us? [*LàV*, 242]

—Translated from the French by Deborah Treisman.

SIMON CRITCHLEY

Who Speaks in the Work of Samuel Beckett?

> We *have* to talk, whether we have something to say or not; and the less we want to say and want to hear the more willfully we talk and are subjected to talk. How did Pascal put it? "All the evil in the world comes from our inability to sit quietly in a room." To keep still.
>
> —Stanley Cavell

STORYTIME, TIME OF DEATH (*MOLLOY, MALONE DIES*)

In Beckett's *Trilogy,*[1] there is a relentless pursuit, across and by means of narrative, of that which narration cannot capture, namely the radical unrepresentability of death. Yet—and this is the paradox upon which, arguably, the entirety of Beckett's fiction turns—to convey this radical unrepresentability, the *Trilogy* must represent the unrepresentable. That is to say, it must construct a series of representations, a litany of voices, names, and figures, "a gallery of moribunds" (*T,* 126), that revolve or "wheel" (*T,* 270) around a narrative voice or protagonist, passing in succession. These wheeling figures, these "delegates" (*T,* 272), have names that have long become familiar: Molloy (but also Dan [*T,* 18], Mellose and Mollose (*T,* 103]), Jacques Moran,[2] Malone, Mahood (but also "Basil and his gang" [*T,* 278; 283], the billy-in-the-bowl), and Worm. But, in the *Trilogy* we also find earlier delegates recalled: Murphy (*T,* 268) and the pseudo-couple Mercier-Camier (*T,* 272), a mini-library of Anglo-Gallo-Hiberno-nyms, a series of "M" names (forget-

1. Throughout, I use the abbreviation *T* to refer to Samuel Beckett, *The Beckett Trilogy* (*Molloy; Malone Dies; The Unnamable*) (London: Picador, 1979).

2. And how does one pronounce these names? Are they to be spoken *à la française,* in British English, ,or Irish English? To take the example of Moran, is this to be pronounced with the stress on the first syllable, as in Irish English, on the second syllable, as in British English, or with equal stress on both syllables, as in French?

YFS 93, *The Place of Maurice Blanchot,* ed. Thomas Pepper, © 1998 by Yale University

ting Watt for a moment) which is completed by a "W," an inverted "M," where Worm "is the first of his kind" (*T*, 310).[3]

The dramatic tension of the *Trilogy*, to my mind, is found in the disjunction that opens up between the time of narrative, the chain of increasingly untellable and untenable stories, and the nonnarratable time of the narrative voice, which I have elsewhere described in detail as the time of dying.[4] In Blanchot's terms this is the disjunction between the impossible temporality of *le mourir* and *la mort*, the time of the possible. The double bind within which the *Trilogy* wriggles, and out of which it is written, is that between the impossibility of narration or representation, and its necessity. The development of the *Trilogy*, to speak provisionally in a quasi-teleological vocabulary, is one where the experience of disjunction between these two temporal orders becomes increasingly acute, where the order of the work (narrative, representation, and storytelling) breaks down or opens into the experience of *désoeuvrement*, a worklessness that should not be confused with formlessness. Blanchot summarizes his reading of the *Trilogy* as follows:

> Aesthetic sentiments are out of place here. Perhaps we are not in the presence of a book but perhaps it is a question of much more than a book: the pure approach of a movement from whence all books come, from this original point where doubtless the work is lost, which always ruins the work, which restores endless worklessness in the work, but with which an ever more primal relationship has to be maintained, on pain of being nothing.[5]

This disjunction between the time of narrative and the time of dying can be traced in *Molloy* by considering the symmetries and disymmetries between the two parts of the novel. Initially, at least, the figures of Molloy and Moran—the latter being the agent given the assignment of finding the former, an encounter which never takes place—seem to be completely opposed. Moran, with his authoritarian relationship to his son who, like his father, is named Jacques, his dutiful relation to God, whether through the intermediary of Father Am-

3. On "M" and "W" as names in Beckett, see the following passage from the beautiful late prose piece *Company:* "Is there anything to add to this esquisse? His unnamability. Even M must go. So W reminds himself of his creature as so far created. W? But W too is a creature. Figment" (Beckett, *Nohow On* [London: Calder, 1992], 37).

4. I give a fuller discussion of Blanchot's and Beckett's work in *Very Little . . . Almost Nothing* (London: Routledge, 1996).

5. Maurice Blanchot, *Le livre à venir* (Paris: Gallimard, collection "Idées", 1959), 313; my translation

brose or the agency of Gaber (all too obviously the archangel Gabriel), and his possessive relation to self and to nature, is sharply distinct from Molloy, "the panting anti-self,"[6] with his expropriative relation to nature. To employ a psychoanalytic register, which much in the novel seems to encourage and which, I think, must be refused because it is so encouraged (for an example of a psychoanalytic red herring, see Moran's anagrammatic gift to Freudian readers, where "the Libido" becomes, somewhat clumsily, "the Obidil": "And with regard to the Obidil, of whom I have refrained from speaking until now, and whom I so longed to see face to face . . . " [*T*, 149]), the happily Oedipal Moran can be played off against the pre-Oedipal Molloy, with his failed quest for identification with his mother and his consequent abjection.

However, there is a progressive and deepening symmetry between the two parts of the novel, where, if you like, the authoritarian Oedipal subject becomes the pre-Oedipal abject self, what Moran calls "the disintegration of the father." Moran loses his faith, telling Father Ambrose "not to count on me any more" (*T*, 161), and the virile bourgeois subject undergoes "a crumbling, frenzied collapsing" (*T*, 137), through a syntax of weakness, through a poetics of increasing impotence: "I grew gradually weaker and weaker and more and more content" (*T*, 150); "on me so changed from what I was" (*T*, 136). On a more careful reading, the novel reveals what Molloy calls his "mania for symmetry" (*T*, 78),[7] where a chain of cumulating correspondences between Molloy and Moran can be detected: both hear a gong (*T*, 82; 106), both ride bicycles and end up on crutches (*T*, 60; 161) because of their painfully stiffening legs, both hear a strange voice offering succor (*T*, 84) or giving orders (*T*, 121; 156; 162), and both attain a point of stasis, with Molloy in his ditch ("Molloy could stay, where he happened to be" [*T*, 84]), and Moran in his shelter prior to the real or hallucinated arrival of Gaber ("I was all right where I was" [*T*, 151]).

However, more profoundly, the symmetry resides in the narrative form of both parts of the novel, where each protagonist writes from a position outside the events described in the narrative. Molloy writes at the behest of a man who gives him money in exchange for his pages (*T*, 9), Moran writes his "report" under the orders of Youdi (*T*, 84–85; 161).

6. See Declan Kiberd, "Beckett and the Life to Come," in *Beckett in Dublin* (Dublin: Liliput Press, 1992), 75–84; particularly 82.

7. On the figure of symmetry in Beckett, see J. M. Coetzee's "The Manuscript Revisions of Beckett's *Watt*," in *Doubling the Point. Essays and Interviews*, ed. David Attwell (Cambridge: Harvard University Press, 1992), 39–42.

Indeed, they both seem to be writing for the agent Gaber, Moran explicitly, Molloy implicitly insofar as "the queer one" who takes his pages, like Gaber, visits on Sunday and is always thirsty, usually for beer (*T*, 9; 86; 161).

What underpins the symmetry is the disinterestedness and disaffection of the relation each of the protagonists maintains to his writing, and it is here that the disjunction between the time of narrative and the time of dying can most clearly be seen. Molloy, finally in his mother's room, wants nothing more than to be left alone, to "finish dying" (*T*, 9), but "they do not want that." He is thus under an obligation or "remnants of a pensum" (*T*, 31) to write stories, although the origin of this obligation is unknown and the stories are incredible: "What I need now is stories, it took me a long time to know that, and I'm not certain of it" (*T*, 14). This situation produces a characteristically oxymoronic formulation of Beckett's writerly credo:

> Not to want to say, not to know what you want to say, not to be able to say what you think you want to say, and never to stop saying, or hardly ever, that is the thing to keep in mind, even in the heat of composition. [*T*, 27]

It is only when this is kept in mind that "the pages fill with true ciphers at last" (*T*, 60). Moran expresses a similarly disaffected attitude toward the writing of his "report," calling it "paltry scrivening" (*T*, 121), and noting toward the end that "it is not at this late stage of my relation that I intend to give way to literature" (*T*, 139):

> What a rabble in my head, what a gallery of moribunds. Murphy, Watt, Yerk, Mercier and all the others. I would never have believed that—yes, I believe it willingly. Stories, stories. I have not been able to tell them. I shall not be able to tell this one. [*T*, 126]

Moran tells untellable stories because he is following orders, although he admits that he is writing not out of fear, but rather out of the deadening force of habit, a habit whose implacable narrative drive opens onto the impossibility of that which the narrative voice cannot give itself, namely death.

In contradistinction to Moran's initial certainty about death, when he visits his little "plot in perpetuity" with its gravestone already in place (*T*, 124), Molloy writes:

> Death is a condition I have never been able to conceive to my satisfaction and which therefore cannot go down in the ledger of weal and woe. [*T*, 63]

This inconceivability of death is explored at length in *Malone Dies*, where the space of narrative is reduced from *Molloy*'s landscape of forest, seashore, and town—Turdy, Turdyba, Turdybaba, Bally, Ballyba, Ballybaba and Hole[8]—to a bed in a room where a figure, called Malone (who notes, without conviction, "since this is what I am called now" [*T*, 204], just as Moran noted, "This is the name I am known by" [*T*, 88]) lies dying. He is immobile except for a hand holding a pencil (a "Venus," which is later associated with "Cythera" [*T*, 192; 217]: morning star, evening star, source of venery)[9] that glides over the page of a child's exercise book. The third person present indicative of the book's title—*Malone meurt*—at the very least leaves it open as to whether Malone dies or not, as Christopher Ricks rightly points out: "*Malone Dies*: does he? In a first person narrative, you can never be sure."[10] In Heideggerian terms, the voice gives itself the possibility of death *as* possibility on the first page of the text—"I could die today, if I wished, merely by making a little effort"—only to deny this possibility: "But it is just as well to let myself die, quietly, without rushing things . . . I shall be neutral and inert . . . I shall die tepid, without enthusiasm" (*T*, 165). A little later, the voice runs through the same patterns of assertion and negation, articulating the whole gravity of the body, the fact of being riveted to oneself:

8. On this nomenclature, Martha Nussbaum claims (swallowing Beckett's psychoanalytic red herrings whole and with some sauce) that Moran's failure to get to Bally or to Hole "may suggest that he (i.e. Moran) is impotent as well as guilty." See "Narrative Emotions: Beckett's Genealogy of Love," in *Love's Knowledge* (New York: Oxford University Press, 1990), 301. Despite the undoubted felicities offered by a psychoanalytic interpretation of *Molloy*, I find Nussbaum's use of Kleinian categories a little too easy and fluent (the object of guilt is "parental sexual act" [298], the object of disgust is "above all the female body" [299]). What does it mean to employ such interpretative categories in relation to a literary text of such theoretical self-consciousness as Beckett's? There is, I feel, the danger of a *hermeneutic literalism* here, which is also revealed when Nussbaum claims, mysteriously, that Beckett identifies Moran as the writer of all the novels in the *Trilogy* ("he [i.e. Moran] identifies himself as the author of this entire novel and of Beckett's other novels" [303; the claim is repeated on 308]); a claim that can be refuted with reference to *T*, 299, "I am neither, I needn't say, Murphy, nor Watt, nor—no, I can't even bring myself to name them." For a more extended critique of Nussbaum's reading of Beckett, see Lecture Three in *Very Little . . . Almost Nothing*,

9. This might be connected with the opening lines of the late prose piece *Ill Seen Ill Said*: "From where she lies she sees Venus rise" (*Nohow On*, 7). A possible source for the reference to Cythera might be Baudelaire's dystopic vision in "Un voyage à Cythère," in *Les fleurs du mal* in *Œuvres complètes*, vol. 1 (Paris: Gallimard, 1975), 117–19.

10. Christopher Ricks, *Beckett's Dying Words* (Oxford: Oxford University Press, 1993), 115.

> If I had the use of my body I would throw it out of the window. But perhaps it is the knowledge of my impotence that emboldens me to that thought. All hangs together, I am in chains. [*T,* 201]

Thus *Malone Dies* takes place in the impossible time of dying, and it is into this ungraspable temporal stretch that the voice gives itself the possibility of telling stories: "while waiting I shall tell myself stories, if I can" (*T,* 115). Thus, Malone is an identity minimally held together by a series of stories—of Saposcat or Sapo, the Lamberts, Macmann, Moll, Hairy Mac, Sucky Moll, Quin, Lemuel and Lady Pedal—but these stories are no longer credible. The tales are like the teller, "almost lifeless," "all my stories are in vain" (*T,* 214). Each of the stories breaks down into tedium—"this is awful" (*T,* 175), "what tedium" (*T,* 174; 198; 201). The reader is continually referred back from the time of narrative to the time of mortality, to "mortal tedium" (*T,* 200), the time of dying. The time of narrative and possibility, where the voice is able to lay hold of time and invent, continually breaks down into an unnarratable impossibility, a pattern typified by Beckett's syntax of weakness that can be found in a whole series of self-undoing phrases in the *Trilogy:* "Live and invent. I have tried, Invent. It is not the word. Neither is live. No matter. I have tried" (*T,* 179).

A similar disjunction between the time of narrative and the time of dying can be illustrated with a couple of examples from *Endgame.* First, Nagg is unable to tell the rather hackneyed Jewish joke about the Englishman, the tailor, and a pair of trousers, and this inability is marked textually with a series of stage directions, where Nagg moves between the voices of the Englishman, the tailor, the raconteur, and his normal voice: "I never told it worse. (*Pause. Gloomy.*) I tell this story worse and worse."[11] However, this disjunction can be seen even more clearly in the central speech of *Endgame,* Hamm's ham-fisted soliloquy where he tries to tell the story of how Clov came into Hamm's service, what Adorno neatly calls "an interpolated aria without music."[12] Once again, Beckett marks the disjunction in stage directions by calling for a shift between "narrative tone" and "normal tone":

> Enough of that, it's storytime, where was I? (*Pause. Narrative tone.*) The man came crawling towards me, on his belly. Pale, wonderfully pale and thin, he seemed on the point of—(*Pause. Normal tone.*) No,

11. Beckett, *Endgame* (London: Faber, 1958), 21.
12. Theodor W. Adorno, "Trying to Understand *Endgame,*" trans. S. W. Nicholsen, in *Notes to Literature,* vol. 1 (New York: Columbia University Press, 1991), 267.

> I've done that bit. (*Pause. Narrative tone.*) I calmly filled my pipe—the meerschaum, lit it with . . . let us say a vesta, drew a few puffs. Aah! (*Pause.*) Well, what is it *you* want? (*Pause.*) [*Endgame,* 35]

Blanchot asks, "Why these vain stories?" and responds that it is in order to people the emptiness of death into which Malone and the whole gallery of moribunds feel they are falling, "through anxiety for this empty time that is going to become the infinite time of death" (*Le livre à venir,* 310). Stories both try to conceal the failure of narrative identity by drawing the self together into some sort of unity while, at the same time, Malone's transcendent sarcasm (For example: "A stream at long intervals bestrid—but to hell with all this fucking scenery" [*T,* 254]) is directed toward trying to disengage the time of narrative from the time of dying. Malone tries to silence the emptiness by telling stories but only succeeds in letting the emptiness speak as the stories break down into mortal tedium. Thus, stories are a deception, but a necessary deception: we cannot face the emptiness of death with them or without them. They return us insistently to the passivity, ungraspability, and impossibility of our dying: "with practice I might be able to produce a groan before I die" (*T,* 232). Beckett is often given to the phrase "come and go," and it provided the title for a 1965 dramaticule.[13] Malone writes: "Because in order not to die you must come and go, come and go" (*T,* 213). Stories enable one to come and go, come and go, "incessant comings and goings" (*T,* 268), until one dies and "the others go on, as if nothing had happened" (*T,* 214). On.

MY OLD APORETICS: THE SYNTAX OF WEAKNESS (*THE UNNAMABLE*)

This experience of disjunction between the time of narrative and the time of dying is pushed even further in *The Unnamable,* a book Adorno describes as Beckett's "wahrhaft ungeheuerlicher Roman" (truly monstrous or genuinely colossal novel),[14] in comparison to which, and in opposition to both Sartre and Lukács, the "official works of committed art look like children's games." The opening pages of *The Unnamable* are the methodologically most self-conscious part of the *Trilogy,* where

13. In Beckett's *The Complete Dramatic Works* (London: Faber, 1986), 351–57, the phrase can be found on *T,* 168; 170; 176; 178; 201; 231; 214; 218; 226; 229; 254; 268; 353.

14. *Notes to Literature,* vol. 2 (New York: Columbia University Press, 1992), 90.

the narrative voice gives the faintest sketch of the method to be followed in the text: an *aporetics.*[15]

> What am I to do, what shall I do, what should I do, in my situation, how proceed? By aporia pure and simple? Or by affirmations and negations invalidated as uttered, or sooner or later. Generally speaking. There must be other shifts. Otherwise it would be quite hopeless. But it is quite hopeless. I should mention without going any further that I say aporia without knowing what it means. Can one be ephectic otherwise than unawares? I don't know. [*T,* 267]

This echoes a line from early in *Malone Dies:* "There I am back at my old aporetics. Is that the word? I don't know" (*T,* 166).

Of course, these phrases are performative enactments of the very method being described. They are aporetic descriptions of aporia, suspensions of judgment (hence "ephectic") on the possibility of a self-conscious suspension of judgment: "I don't know." We proceed by aporia, that is, the path to be followed is a pathless path, which means that we do not proceed, but stay on the same spot, even if we are not quite at a standstill, although this is the voice's desire: "the bliss of coma" (*T,* 298); "the rapture, the letting go, the fall, the gulf, the relapse to darkness" (*T,* 179). As a consequence, we wheel about as if with one foot nailed to the floor.

Although *The Unnamable* is hardly a discourse on method, the word "aporia" reappears at several key moments in the text,[16] and Beckett's aporetics are a performative and quasi-methodological expression of what we saw above as the impossibility and necessity of narration: we have to go on and yet we can't go on (and yet we can't not go on). This technique—and it is a question of technique here, of a quite rigorous rhetorical procedure at work in Beckett's writing—might be characterized in terms of what Adorno rightly calls, with reference to *Endgame,* a technique of reversal:

> Where they come closest to the truth, they sense, with double comedy, that their consciousness is false: that is how a situation that can no longer be reached by reflection is reflected. But the whole play is constructed by this technique of reversal. [*Notes to Literature,* vol. 1, 274]

15. On the figure of aporia in Beckett, see Leslie Hill, *Beckett's Fiction* (Cambridge: Cambridge University Press, 1990), 63–64.

16. *T,* 274; 278; 318; 321; 334; 338.

It is in terms of this technique of reversal that I would understand Beckett's remark, cited above, about "affirmations and negations invalidated as uttered." As Stanley Cavell points out, this can be seen as an almost spiritual exercise in logic, where statements are made, inferences derived, negations of inferences produced, and these negations are, in turn, negated.[17] The language of *The Unnamable* is an endlessly elaborating series of antitheses, of imploding oxymorons, paradoxes, and contradictions, a "frenzy of utterance" (*T*, 275), where a coherent and perhaps even formalizable technique of repetition is employed to give the appearance of randomness and chaos.[18] Some examples: "I, say I. Unbelieving. . . . It, say it, not knowing what. . . . So I have no cause for anxiety. And yet I am anxious. . . . Perhaps it's springtime, violets, no, that's autumn. . . . Perhaps it's all a dream, all a dream, that would surprise me" (*T*, 267; 276; 376; 381). Or a longer passage:

> These things I say, and shall say, if I can, are no longer, or are not yet, or never were, or never will be, or if they were, if they are, if they will be, were not here, are not here, will not be here, but elsewhere. But I am here. So I am obliged to add this. I who am here, who cannot speak, cannot think, and who must speak, and therefore perhaps think a little, cannot in relation only to me who am here, to here where I am, but can a little, sufficiently, I don't know how, unimportant, in relation to me who was elsewhere, who shall be elsewhere, and to those places when I was, where I shall be. [*T*, 276]

It is a question here of an uneasy and solitary inhabitation of the aporia between the inability to speak and the inability to be silent (*T*, 365). We cannot speak of that which we would like to speak—in my reading, the unrepresentability of death—and yet we cannot not speak, blissful though this might seem: "you must go on, I can't go on, I'll go on." There is only this voice, this meaningless voice "which prevents you

17. Stanley Cavell, *Must We Mean What We Say?* (Cambridge: Cambridge University Press, 1976), 126.

18. On repetition in the *Trilogy*, see the wonderfully detailed essay by Rubin Rabinowitz, "Repetition and Underlying Meanings in Samuel Beckett's Trilogy," in *Rethinking Beckett*, ed. L. St. John Butler and R. J. Davis (London: Macmillan, 1990), 31–67. See also Rabinowitz's *The Development of Samuel Beckett's Fiction* (Chicago: University of Illinois Press, 1984); Steven Connor, *Samuel Beckett: Repetition, Theory, and Text* (Oxford: Blackwell, 1988); *Becketts' Fiction*, 66–68. Repetition is obviously also central to Beckett's later fictions, in a text like *Lessness* (1969), which contains 1538 words, where words 770–1538 repeat, in a different variation, words 1–769. On precisely this point, see Coetzee's "Samuel Beckett and the Temptation of Style," in *Doubling the Point. Essays and Interviews*, 45; 49.

from being nothing" (*T,* 341), and all it has are words "and not many of them" (*T,* 381). And even when Malone writes, "I am lost, not a word" (*T,* 241) or Krapp—a later delegate—says "Nothing to say, not a squeak,"[19] this is not yet silence, it is yet a word, yet a squeak.

To return to my epigraph from Cavell, Beckett's work and perhaps—to generalize suddenly and rather violently—literature as such *is a long sin against silence* (*T,* 345) *that arises from our inability to sit quietly in a room.* The origin of the sin being unknown, we still sit in our thousand furnished rooms to read and even write books, which, of course, only produces inconstancy, boredom, anxiety, and the desire for movement—to come and go, to come and go.

The radicality of *The Unnamable* with respect to the earlier parts of the *Trilogy* is that the disjunction between the time of narrative and the time of dying takes place within the unit of the sentence itself, where each series of words seems to offer and deny "the resorts of fable" (*T,* 283). Of course, there are fables in *The Unnamable,* the quite hilarious story of Basil, arbitrarily renamed Mahood (*T,* 283), the billy-in-the-bowl, who completes the dwindling physicality of the "M" names, and Worm. What is one to say of Worm? First of his kind, "who hasn't the wit to make himself plain" (*T,* 310). Worm is unborn, unperceiving, unspeaking, uncreated, "nothing but a shapeless heap" (*T,* 328), a "tiny blur in the depths of the pit" (*T,* 329). And in this heap, a wild and equine eye cries without ceasing. He makes no noise apart from a whining, the noise of life "trying to get in" (*T,* 335)—a terrifying remark. With this last in the series of "bran-dips" (*T,* 359), the stakes have been raised once again: for if Mahood, like Malone, craved what he could not give himself, i.e. death, then Worm is not even born: "Come into the world unborn, abiding there unliving, with no hope of death" (*T,* 318). Worm is that which somehow *remains,* he is a remainder, what Blanchot calls "une survivance" (*Le livre à venir,* 312), outside of life and the possibility of death. Although he is the first of his kind, it is difficult to imagine how this series might continue and perhaps Worm is the end of the line.[20]

19. Beckett, *Krapp's Last Tape* (London: Faber, 1959), 18.

20. Perhaps. For nothing is the end of the line in Beckett, the line of writing stretches on interminably—*pour finir encore.* On this question of ending and beginning, one would need to read *The Unnamable* together with Beckett's final novel, *Comment c'est* (Paris: Gallimard, 1961), a title which, in French, is at least a possible quadruple pun (comment c'est [how it is], and the infinitive [*commencer*], the imperative [*commencez!*], and past participle [*commencé*]) of the verb "to begin." Thus, even at the end of *The Unnamable,* one re-commences with a further dissolution of narrative form in

However, despite such fables, which have to be tempered with familiar comments on the inadequacy of narrative—"this hell of stories" (*T*, 349)[21]—*The Unnamable* is made up of an endlessly proliferating and self-undoing series and sayings and unsayings, Beckett's syntax of weakness.[22] Some examples:

> I shall have to speak of things, of which I cannot speak, but also, which is even more interesting, but also that I, which is if possible even more interesting, that I shall have to, I forget, no matter. [*T*, 267]

And again,

> But my good-will at certain moments is such, and my longing to have floundered however briefly, however feebly, in the great life torrent streaming from the earliest protozoa to the very latest humans, that I, no, parenthesis unfinished. I'll begin again. My family. [*T*, 295]

And again,

> And would it not suffice, without any change in the structure of the thing as it now stands, as it always stood, without a mouth being opened at the place which even pain could never line, would it not suffice to, to what, the thread is lost, no matter, here's another. [*T*, 353]

And again,

> I resume, so long as, so long as, let me see, so long as one, so long as he, ah fuck all that, so long as this, then that, agreed, that's good enough, I nearly got stuck. [*T*, 367]

As Ricks rightly points out, this is a syntax of weakness not because the syntax is weak, but rather because it presses on, "unable to relinquish its perseverance and to arrive at severance" (*Beckett's Dying Words*, 83). Beckett's sentences are a series of *weak intensities* and *double inabilities:* unable to go on and unable not to go on. It is this double inability

the punctuationless prose blocks of *Comment c'est,* where a crouched figure murmurs in the mud, its tongue lolling out.

21. For other remarks on storytelling in *The Unnamable,* see *T*, 299; 354; 374; 381–82.

22. Although to qualify the implied teleology of my reading of Beckett here, I am not claiming that the syntax of weakness is absent from other parts of the *Trilogy,* only that it is presented in *The Unnamable* in a more extreme fashion. Indeed, if one rereads the opening pages of of *Molloy* in the light of the quasi-method of aporetics, it becomes increasingly difficult to sustain a simple teleological reading of the *Trilogy.* For example, the opening paragraph of *Molloy* contains four uses of "perhaps," five uses of "apparently," and six uses of "I don't know"!

that describes, I think, the weakness of our relation to finitude, the articulation of a physical feebleness, a dwindling, stiffening corporality, which is a recipe not for despair but for a kind of *rapture:* "There is rapture, or there should be, in the motion crutches give" (*T,* 60).

WHO SPEAKS? NOT I

Who speaks in the work of Samuel Beckett? Who is the indefatigable "I" who always seems to say the same thing? It is with these seemingly innocent questions that Blanchot begins both of his pieces on Beckett.[23] Yet with this question we brush against an (perhaps *the*) enigma.

The obvious response to the question, "who speaks?" is to tie the "I" to the narrative voice of the text and to identify that voice with the controlling intentionality of the author. Who speaks? Samuel Beckett speaks. Well, yes, this is doubtless correct, there existed a writer whose name was Samuel Barclay Beckett, who wrote the books we have read, played first class cricket for Trinity College Dublin, received the Croix de Guerre in 1945 and the Nobel Prize for literature in 1969, had terrible boils on his neck ("bristling with boils ever since I was a brat" [*T,* 75]), etc., etc., etc. There is an irreducible existential residuum of authorial experience in the creation of any text that we might call "literary."[24] But, to ascribe the voice that speaks in the work to the name Samuel Beckett, or to identify the narrative voice with a controlling consciousness that looks down upon the drama of Beckett's work like a transcendent spectator, is to fail to acknowledge the strangeness of the work under consideration and to read the work as an oblique confession or, worse still, a series of case studies in a reductive psychobiography. After remarking, "For if I am Mahood, I am Worm too, plop,"[25] the voice in *The Unnamable* continues:

23. "Où maintenant? Qui maintenant?," essentially a review of the *Trilogy,* first appeared in *La nouvelle revue française* 10 (1953): 678–86, and was reprinted in *Le livre à venir,* 308–13, with some significant but minor changes, mainly deletions. "Les paroles doivent cheminer longtemps," an *entretien* on Beckett's *Comment c'est,* first appeared under the title "Notre épopée," in *La nouvelle revue française* 100 (1961): 690–98, and was reprinted with very minor alterations in *L'entretien infini* (Paris: Gallimard, 1969), 478–86. *L'entretien infini* is translated as *The Infinite Conversation,* trans. Susan Hanson (Minneapolis: University of Minnesota Press, 1993).

24. Obviously, in Beckett's case, this residuum has been decisively documented by Deirdre Bair in *Samuel Beckett: A Biography* (London: Jonathan Cape, 1978).

25. On the possible significance of terms such as "plop" and "ping" in Beckett, see Coetzee's "Samuel Beckett and the Temptations of Style," 43–49. Coetzee reads these terms as an "editorial metalanguage . . . that repeatedly fractures the surface of the fiction," and that has "evacuated itself of lexical content" (45). This partially confirms

> Or is one to postulate a tertius gaudens, meaning myself, responsible for the double failure? [i.e. of Mahood and Worm] Shall I come upon my true countenance at last, bathing in a smile? I have the feeling I shall be spared this spectacle. At no moment do I know what I'm talking about, nor of whom. [*T,* 310–11]

If one is to be capable of listening to the voices that speak from the pages of the *Trilogy,* then it is at the very least necessary to suspend the hypothesis identifying the narrative voice of Beckett's work with the smiling third party of a controlling pure consciousness and ascribing the latter to Samuel Beckett. As Blanchot writes—rightly—"in literature there is no direct speech" (*The Infinite Conversation,* 327). That is—and this is Blanchot's hypothesis—in Beckett's work we approach an experience, a *literary* experience, that speaks to us in a voice that can be described as impersonal, neutral, or indifferent: an incessant, interminable, and indeterminable voice that reverberates outside of all intimacy, dispossessing the "I" and delivering it over to a nameless outside. Beckett's work draws the reader into a space—the space of literature—where a voice intones obscurely, drawn on by a speaking that does not begin and does not finish, that cannot speak and cannot but speak, that leads language toward what Blanchot calls with reference to *Comment c'est* "an unqualifiable murmur,"[26] what I will describe presently as a buzzing, *the tinnitus of existence.* As Blanchot writes, this is "strange, strange" (*The Infinite Conversation,* 330).

Blanchot's point about the narrative voice can be restated by following a crucial feature of Beckett's prose in the *Trilogy.* On three occasions in the second part of *Molloy* (*T,* 115; 128; 152), we come across the words "Not I," employed in a seemingly innocent way during Moran's monologue. However, this phrase comes to pervade *The Unnamable* in a number of crucial passages, not all of which can be cited, and which begin to be repeated with ever-increasing frequency—mania even—toward the end of the text.[27] About a third of the way into *The Unnamable,* the voice writes:

his otherwise contestable thesis that, in Beckett's later fictions such as *Ping* and *Lessness,* Beckett marches "with eyes open into the prison of style" (49). But why should style be a prison? If style is redescribed in terms of worklessness, then might it not, on the contrary, be some strange kind of liberation, however workless?

26. Although the main reference is to "the murmur in the mud" in *Comment c'est* references to murmuring can already be found in *The Unnamable,* initially to describe the voiceless noise emitted by Worm (*T,* 310; 323; 351; 375; 376; 381).

27. See *T,* 292; 315; 319; 326; 355; 369; 370; 371–72; 373; 374; 375; 380; 381.

> But enough of this cursed first person, it is really too red a herring, I'll get out of my depth if I'm not careful. But what then is the subject? Mahood? No, not yet. Worm? Even less. [*T*, 315]

Slightly further on, we read:

> I shall not say I again, ever again, it's too farcical. I shall put in its place, whenever I hear it, the third person, if I think of it. [*T*, 315]

Unsurprisingly enough, and in accord with the aporetic method sketched above, the voice does not always "think of it" and persistently falls back into the first person. However, the point here is that the voice is attempting to move from the first person to the third person, from "I" to "s/he/it" (a Beckettesque pun of questionable taste offers itself here, but I will resist). The voice insists that "it's not I speaking," but another, a more impersonal and neutral voice. In this way we can begin to make sense of the first line of *The Unnamable*, "I, say I. Unbelieving" (*T*, 267), and the almost mantric phrase that is repeated obsessively toward the end of the text, "It's not I, that's all I know" (*T*, 380). But the crucial passage in this regard is the following; I quote it in full:

> It's always he who speaks, Mercier never spoke, Moran never spoke, I never spoke, I seem to speak, that's because he says I as if he were I, I nearly believed him, do you hear him, as if he were I, I am far, who can't move, can't be found, but neither can he, he can only talk, if that much, perhaps it's not he, perhaps it's a multitude, one after another, what confusion, someone mentions confusion, is it a sin, all here is a sin, you don't know why, you don't know whose, you don't know against whom, someone says you, it's the fault of the pronouns, there is no name, for me, no pronoun for me, all the trouble comes from that, it's a kind of pronoun too, it isn't that either, I'm not that either, let us leave all that, forget about all that, it's not difficult. [*T*, 371–72]

There is no name for the voice that speaks in *The Unnamable*. Whoever speaks in Beckett's work, it is not "I," it is rather "he" (although this is still a pronoun, and that's the trouble), the third person or the impersonal neutrality of language. The neutral character of the third person is what Blanchot refers to as "the narrative voice," and, for him (thinking of Kafka rather than Beckett),[28] to write is to pass from

28. There is an almost amusing moment in Blanchot's obituary for Beckett in "Oh tout finir" (*Critique* 46/519–20 [August/September 1990]: 635–37), when he writes, "In the eulogies that have been respectfully delivered in order to mark his (i.e. Beckett's)

the "I" to the "he" (*The Infinite Conversation,* 380). In literature—and this is the defining quality of the literary for Blanchot—I do not speak, it speaks. In relation to Beckett, Blanchot writes of "a soft specter of speech" (*The Infinite Conversation,* 331), the unqualifiable murmur at the back of our words. The narrative voice is like some specter that lingers in the background of our everyday identity, disturbing the persistent "I" of our monologues and dialogues, denying the "daydream gratification of fiction"[29] and reappearing at nightfall, a kind of void that opens up in the work and into which the work evaporates in a movement of worklessness. There is an irreducible logic of spectrality at work in literature, the night of ghosts, that denies us the sleep of the just in the name of justice. This is perhaps why Blanchot defines the writer as "the insomniac of the day."[30]

Who speaks? Not I. On this point an interesting connection can be made between *The Unnamable* and the extraordinary 1973 dramatic piece *Not I,* a piece that I would want to see as a distilled redrafting of *The Unnamable,* and that employs a very similar, apparently manic, pattern of repetition and breathless phrasing as in the final pages of the latter.[31] On five occasions in the ten-minute dramaticule, the Mouth cries "what? . . . who? . . . no! . . . she!" As Beckett laconically points out in the only note to *Not I,* the Mouth is engaged in a "vehement refusal to relinquish third person." It should be noted that this third person is "she" rather than "he," (played in the original production by the sublime Billie Whitelaw), and it is here that one might want to raise the question of gender and challenge the alleged neutrality of the narrative voice.

passing, the great works of the age have been evoked, Proust, Joyce, Musil, and even Kafka. . . . " For readers of Blanchot, this "and even Kafka" is so revealing.

29. Coetzee, "Samuel Beckett and the Temptations of Style," 49.

30. Blanchot, *L'écriture du désastre* (Paris: Gallimard, 1980), 185. On the themes of insomnia, sleep, and the night in Beckett and Blanchot, see Deleuze's reading of Beckett; he writes, "In the insomniac dream, it is not a question of realizing the impossible, but of exhausting the possible" ("L'épuisé," in *Quad et autres pièces pour la télévision* [Paris: Minuit, 1992], 100–01).

31. *The Complete Dramatic Works,* 373–83. Possible precursors for the two characters in the cast of *Not I*—"Auditor" and "Mouth"—might be found in *Malone Dies:* "the raising of the arms and going down, without further splash, even though it may annoy the bathers" (*T,* 254); and in *The Unnamable:* "Evoke at painful junctures, when discouragement threatens to raise its head, the image of a vast mouth, red, blubber and slobbering, in solitary confinement, extruding indefatigably, with a noise of wet kisses the washing in a tub, the words that obstruct it" (*T,* 359). On the connection between *Not I* and *The Unnamable,* see James Knowlson and John Pilling, *Frescoes of the Skull* (London: Calder, 1979), 197.

On several occasions, the Mouth speaks of a buzzing in the ears: "for she could still hear the buzzing . . . so-called . . . in the ears . . . the buzzing? . . . yes . . . all the time the buzzing . . . so-called. in the ears." This buzzing is described as "a dull roar in the skull . . . dull roar like falls," which can be linked both to what was said above about murmuring and to references to "the noise" in the *Trilogy*.[32] For example, Malone notes:

> What I mean is possibly this, that the noises of the world, so various in themselves and which I used to be so clever at distinguishing from one another, had been dinning at me for so long, always the same old noises, as gradually to have merged into a single noise, so that all I heard was one vast continuous buzzing. [*T*, 190]

Who speaks in the work of Samuel Beckett? It is not the "I" of the author or a controlling consciousness, but rather the "Not I" of the insomniac narrative voice that opens like a void in the experience of literature, *as* the experience that literature approaches: *le neutre, le dehors, désastre, l'espace littéraire* [the neutral, the outside, the disaster, the literary space]. Beckett's work leaves us "open to the void" (*T*, 377), and this void is not the ultramarine blue of Yves Klein or Derek Jarman, but a more sombre monochrome; not the Mediterranean, but the Black Sea:

> These creatures have never been, only I and this black void have ever been. And the sounds? No, all is silent. And the lights, on which I had set such store, must they too go out? Yes, out with them, there is no light. No grey either, black is what I should have said. Nothing then but me, of which I know nothing, and this black, of which I know nothing except that it is black and empty. That then is what, since I have to speak, I shall speak of, until I need speak no more. [*T*, 278]

The narrative voice approaches a void that speaks as one vast, continuous buzzing, a dull roar in the skull like falls, an unqualifiable murmur, an impersonal whining, the vibration of the tympanum (*T*, 352). This is what I mean by the tinnitus of existence. It is, I believe, this condition that the voice in Beckett's work is trying to approach. It is this *truth* with which Beckett's frenzy of utterance is concerned (*T*, 275). Of course, there is *only* the approach, because the voice cannot grant itself the possibility of its own disappearance into the void—death is impossible. Thus, we resort to fables: "To tell the truth—no,

32. See *T*, 189; 190; 325; 332; 345; 357.

first the story" (*T*, 300). That is just how it is. And that is how I read a phrase near the end of the 1981 text *Ill Seen Ill Said:* "Absence supreme good and yet."[33] It is this "and yet" that is so determinate for Beckett's art, this holding back from the bliss of absence, this qualification of the rapture of annihilation in a syntax of weakness.

33. *Ill Seen Ill Said,* in *Nohow On,* 58.

III. Voices, Persons

ANN BANFIELD

The Name of the Subject: The "il"?[1]

> What is strange in the Cartesian certitude "I think, therefore I am," is that it only presented itself by speaking, and that speech, precisely, caused it to disappear, suspending the *ego* of the *cogito*, consigning thought to anonymity without any subject.[2]

It is a truth not universally acknowledged that the name assigned the subject is not, contrary to common sense expectations, the pronoun "ego" or "I." But ordinary language does not supply a name for the subject. Indeed, the nearest formulation for subjectivity has the grammatical form not of a noun phrase, a name, but of a sentence, one with specific grammatical properties: "cogito." The Cartesian concept of subjectivity is thus not equivalent to either the sense or the reference of the first person pronoun.

How does the grammar of the "cogito" define subjectivity? For it is through a grammatical analysis of the sentence "I am thinking" that the notion of the subject can be isolated. That analysis will reveal that the Cartesian subject is something less, something more "neutral" than the "I." Grammar also will make precise what is meant by "neutrality"—*le neutre* is indeed already a grammatical term. I choose the French term because it contains within it two grammatical notions not normally associated in English—the neuter gender and the

1. The following texts by Bertrand Russell are cited and abbreviated as follows: *The Analysis of Mind* (London: George Allen & Unwin, 1921), hereafter *Mind; Logic and Knowledge: Essays 1901–1950* (New York: Macmillan, 1956), hereafter *LK; Mysticism and Logic* (Garden City, New York: Doubleday, [1917] 1957), hereafter *ML; An Outline of Philosophy* (Cleveland & New York: [1927], 1960), hereafter *OP; Philosophical Essays* (New York: Simon & Schuster, 1966), hereafter *PE; The Problems of Philosophy* (London: Oxford University Press, [1912], 1959), hereafter *PP; An Outline of Philosophy* (Cleveland & New York: [1927], 1960), hereafter *OP; Theory of Knowledge: the 1913 Manuscript, The Collected Papers of Bertrand Russell,* Vol. 7, ed. Elizabeth Ramsden Eames (in collaboration with Kenneth Blackwell) (London: George Allen & Unwin, 1984), hereafter *TK.*

2. Maurice Blanchot, *The Writing of the Disaster,* trans. Ann Smock (Lincoln: University of Nebraska Press, 1995), 54; hereafter *WD.*

YFS 93, *The Place of Maurice Blanchot,* ed. Thomas Pepper, © 1998 by Yale University.

impersonal construction. "Neutrality" is also a term that comes up in the philosophical tradition: as "neutral monism." It is not neutral monism *per se* that will interest us, but the idea of something neutral between subject and object that the term stands for. For one direction of philosophical commentary on the "cogito" has thought the neutral notion of subjectivity with recourse to those grammatical notions. In examining that commentary, our argument will add an unexpected third party to the conjunction of linguistics and philosophy. It will find in literary language, specifically, in that of the novel, the closest equivalent to the neutral pronoun, which, if it existed in ordinary language, would designate the subject more accurately than "I." Here is the special importance of Maurice Blanchot for our inquiry. As both novelist and theorist of literature, Blanchot has placed at the center of these two activities what he calls *"le neutre."* Blanchot explicitly refers to both the grammatical "neuter" and "impersonal."[3] *Thomas the Obscure,* moreover, presents its own "neutralization" of the "cogito," isolating something caught between "an already dead man or a man yet to be born," "that which could bear no name," "the indiscernible nullity which I nevertheless coupled with the name Thomas."[4] Elsewhere, the "I think" is linked to "I write (I pronounce)," as Blanchot opens the essay "The Narrative Voice."[5] Are we justified in designating this "unnamable"[6] thing with the written "il" that Blanchot discovers in "the narrative voice" and taking it as the name of the subject? To answer this question, I beg the patience of the reader. For our analysis of the "cogito" will not proceed via a reading of Blanchot himself. The "morceaux choisis" from Blanchot that punctuate this text will establish the pertinent connections. Our central argument will be offered as one possible understanding of what was at stake for Blanchot in the *neutre.*

3. Blanchot includes other grammatical notions besides the neuter and the impersonal under the term "neutre"—the plural, for instance. These will not concern us here.

4. Blanchot, *Thomas the Obscure,* trans. Robert Lamberton (New York: David Lewis, 1973), 112; 97; hereafter *TO.*

5. Blanchot, *The Infinite Conversation,* trans. Susan Hanson (Minneapolis: University of Minnesota Press, 1993), 379; hereafter *IC.*

6. There is a tradition that treats the first person itself as "unnamable." It underlies Beckett's use of the term, as in "Unnamable. Last Person. I" (*Company* [New York: Grove Press, 1980], 24). And Roland Barthes speaks of "I" as "still the form which expresses anonymity most faithfully" (Barthes, *Writing Degree Zero,* trans. Anette Lavers and Colin Smith [New York: Hill and Wang, 1968], 36).

THE GRAMMAR OF THE COGITO

> [T]he madness of the taciturn thinker appeared before me and unintelligible words rung in my ears while I wrote on the wall these sweet words: "I think, therefore I am not." [*TO*, 99]

The "cogito" represents the point of cessation of doubt; "je pense" states all and only those things that can be said and hence known with certainty. What will define the object of our investigation are the grammatical properties of the sentence "cogito" that give it its indubitability. These properties link indubitability with linguistic subjectivity. In order for the statement on which Descartes's argument depends to represent certain knowledge, it must have the following features: 1) its grammatical subject is obligatorily first person; 2) its tense is obligatorily present; and 3) its verb is one of a class of psychological verbs with animate subjects.

Its subject must be first person, because statements such as "(s)he is thinking" are subject to doubt; they raise the problem of "other minds." Its tense must be present because "I was thinking" is subject to doubt. Indeed, its tense must be a true present—in English, a progressive, a condition that can be made explicit if we require that it be cotemporal with *now*. Thus, I translate "cogito" or "je pense," following the linguist John Lyons, not as "I think" but as "I am thinking," in conformity with the general translation of the Latin or French present tense in such nongeneric, nonstative contexts.[7] The English intransitive sentence "I think," in its normal, generic reading—one that can be qualified by the temporal adverbials like "every day" or "all the time" that modify habituals in general—is subject to doubt. In asserting "I think all the time" or even "I think," I may be mistaken. But not in stating "I am now thinking."[8] Finally, "I am walking," to borrow an example from Descartes's reply to Gassendi on the *Second Meditation*, does not possess the indubitability of "I am thinking." The verb *cogitare* is not narrowly restricted to rational thought—Descartes is explicit about it. As Bernard Williams comments, "'cogito' is not just one peculiar item, but rather the representative of a large class of different propositions." Rather, "a *cogitatio* or a *pensée* is any sort of

7. John Lyons, "Deixis and Subjectivity: *Loquor, ergo Sum?*" in *Speech, Place and Action: Studies in Deixis and Related Topics*, ed. Robert J. Jarvella and Wolfgang Klein (Chichester: John Wiley & Sons Ltd, 1982), 101–24. See also Russell *PP*, 19 and *OP*, 21.

8. Simple presents with psychological verbs in the first person can be indubitable, if the statement is modifiable by the deictic *now*—"I now think it possible that over 250,000 Iraquis were killed in the bombing."

conscious state or activity whatsoever; it can as well be a sensation (at least in its purely psychological aspect) or an act of will, as judgment or belief or intellectual questioning."[9] So, from "I am seeing a table" or "I am doubting my senses," I can conclude "ergo sum," but "you have no right to make the inference: *I walk* [i.e., "I am walking"], *hence I exist*" of a "motion of the body" but only of my "awareness of walking" as "a thought."[10] It is as one of a class of verbs sharing a feature Descartes names "thought" that "to doubt" or "to see" is equivalent to *cogitare;* the certainty resides in that minimal feature and does not extend to the difference between these modes of thought.[11]

As a sentence, the "cogito" consists of nothing more than the convergence of these three grammatical factors, and, insofar as it formulates the core of subjectivity, it thereby defines it as both more and less than the "ego" of "cogito." The Cartesian subject it makes the ground of certainty is not the "I" but the I-who-am-thinking, as opposed to the one who is walking or who was thinking.

THE REDUCTION TO A PARSIMONIOUS COGITO

> [O]ne can recognize in the entire history of philosophy an effort either to acclimatize or to domesticate the neuter by substituting for it the law of the impersonal and the reign of the universal, or an effort to challenge it by affirming the ethical primacy of the Self-Subject, the mystical aspiration to the singular Unique. The neutral is thus constantly expelled from our languages and our truths. [*IC,* 299]

> Unless the "il," specified as an indeterminate term in order for the "I" in its turn to be determined as the major determinant, the never subjected subject, if not the relation even of one to the other. . . . A word perhaps, nothing but a word, but a surplus word, one word too many which for that reason is always lacking.[12]

9. Bernard Williams, *Descartes: the Project of Pure Enquiry* (Atlantic Highlands, New Jersey: Humanities Press, 1978), 78; hereafter *DP.*

10. René Descartes, *The Philosophical Works of Descartes,* trans. Elizabeth S. Haldane and G. R. T. Ross (Cambridge: Cambridge University Press, 1967), vol. 2, 207. Descartes continues: "It is of this alone that the inference holds good, not of the motion of the body, which sometimes does not exist, as in dreams, when nevertheless I appear to walk."

11. See Jean-Claude Milner on the "modalities" of thought. *L'oeuvre claire. Lacan, la science, la philosophie* (Paris: Seuil, 1995), 72 n.9.

12. Blanchot, *Le pas au-delà* (Paris: Gallimard, 1973), 12–13, my translation.

In fact, there is a tradition that claims that Descartes's "I am thinking" is not an adequate rendering of the minimal subjectivity needed for certainty because it is not entirely impervious to doubt. It takes its inspiration from the eighteenth-century German physicist and aphorist Georg Lichtenberg. Its objection to Descartes's "cogito" is what Williams has described, in taking issue with it, as "[t]he objection . . . that in saying 'I am thinking' Descartes is saying too much" (*DP*, 95): "The most that Descartes could claim was 'cogitatur,' 'there is some thinking going on'—like, in Lichtenberg's own comparison, 'there is lightening'" (*DP*, 95). Williams locates an espousal of Lichtenberg's "cogitatur" within modern empiricism (*DP*, 95), particularly its logico-empiricist form, from Vienna to Cambridge, singling out Ernst Mach, perhaps the first of the Viennese positivists to revive Lichtenberg's version of the "cogito."[13] Russell, who calls Mach's *The Analysis of Sensations* "a book of fundamental importance,"[14] may very well have had in mind, in *The Problems of Philosophy*, the passage in which Mach cites Lichtenberg when he cautions that "some care is needed in using Descartes' argument," because:

> "I think, therefore I am" says rather more than is strictly certain. It might seem as though we were quite sure of being the same person today as we were yesterday. . . . But the real Self . . . does not seem to have that absolute, convincing certainty that belongs to particular experiences. When I look at my table and see a certain brown colour, what is quite certain at once is not "I am seeing a brown colour," but rather, "a brown colour is being seen." This . . . does not of itself involve the more or less permanent person whom we call "I." . . . Thus it is our particular thoughts and feelings that have primitive certainty. [*PP*, 19]

It is via Ludwig Wittgenstein that Lichtenberg's hypothesis entered later British philosophy. According to G. E. Moore, Wittgenstein "quoted, with apparent approval, Lichtenberg's saying 'Instead of "I think" we ought to say "It thinks"' ("it" being used, as he said, as 'Es' is

13. In *Wittgenstein's Vienna* (New York: Simon and Schuster, 1973), Allan Janik and Stephen Toulmin assert that "Mach was, in fact, the first man to draw attention to the philosophical significance of Lichtenberg, whose writings soon became popular and influential in the artistic and intellectual circles of Vienna" (134; see also 176). See Ernst Mach, *Contributions to the Analysis of Sensations* (La Salle, Illinois: Open Court, 1890 and 1896), 22.

14. See G. N. A. Vesey, "Self-Acquaintance and the Meaning of 'I,'" in *Bertrand Russell Memorial Volume*, ed. George W. Roberts (London: George Allen & Unwin; New York: Humanities Press, 1979), 342.

used in 'Es blitzet')".[15] We recognize Lichtenberg's influence when Peter Geach, imagining Descartes's "saying 'I'm getting into an awful muddle,'" asks "but who then is this 'I' who is getting into a muddle?" For "in this context the word 'I' is idle, superfluous"; Descartes, Geach claims, "could quite well have expressed himself without saying the first person pronoun at all; he could have said: 'This is really a dreadful muddle!' where 'This' would refer back to his previous meditations."[16] The interpretation of "cogito" that Lichtenberg's position entails is also known in the rationalist tradition, as we shall see.

The Lichtenbergian project, it should now be clear, is to subject the "cogito" to Occam's razor. It finds in the statement "I am thinking" something in excess of strict indubitability. What all the versions of "cogitatur" have eliminated from the "cogito" should be apparent: "it is thought" retains the present tense and the psychological verb "cogitare," "to think," but the first person disappears. "What Descartes really felt sure about was a certain occurrence," Russell says, but "the words 'I think' . . . were not quite an accurate representation of the occurrence," in particular, "he was not justified in bringing in the word 'I' in describing this occurrence" (*OP*, 172).

In eliminating the first person, the most obvious candidate for the name of the subject has been eliminated. A strange operation that would have subjectivity represented by everything but the first person! Indeed, Descartes's own formulations already half eliminated it: the Latin is not "ego Cogito" nor is the French "Moi, je pense"—what Russell recognizes in insisting that the English translation cannot have a contrastively stressed subject. This is perhaps another interpretation of Geach's claim that in "cogito," "I" is "superfluous." The agentless passive only goes a step further. Yet how can the remaining "cogitatur," or rather, the "it is being thought," have the requisite indubitability that "I am thinking" has, since we saw that "(s)he is thinking" does not? In other words, how can the statement minus the first person remain subjective? There must be something more to Lichtenberg's proposal than simply replacing a first person statement by a third person statement. To discover what is at stake in the grammar of the "cogito," we have to separate, in the various properties of the first person, what is essential to indubitability—tantamount, we saw, to linguistic subjectivity—from what is subject to doubt. Does

15. G. E. Moore, *Philosophical Papers* (London: George Allen & Unwin), 309.

16. Peter Geach, *Mental Acts: Their Content and Their Objects* (London: Routledge & Kegan Paul, 1957, 1971), 118; hereafter *PG*.

grammar give us any hint as to what "thing" from a lingustic point of view Descartes calls the "res cogitans" and why the first person is not its appropriate name?

THE FIRST PERSON AS SPEAKER

> *However, the neuter, or neutral, is not simply a grammatical gender—or as a gender and a category . . . let us say that the one who does not enter into what he says is neutral; just as speech can be held to be neutral when it pronounces without taking into account either itself or the one who pronounces it.* (*IC*, 303)

> [T]he writer who consents to sustain writing's essence loses the power to say "I."[17]

The first person pronoun, by all traditional accounts, designates the sentence's speaker. It is not, however, the "I"'s speakerhood that is essential to Descartes's argument, but something of which speakerhood is only an accidental adjunct. This can be demonstrated by experimentally eliminating all but the pure producer of speech. Bede Rundle observes:

> We, anticipated by Descartes, are struck by the fact that someone's utterance of "I" cannot but identify the speaker, but we had to suppose that there was a speaker—a person to whom the utterance could be referred and a person making a genuine use of language. Without this assumption the utterance would have not have had the same significance: "I" somehow produced from the mouth of a dead man or by an electronic device is not the basis for any such inference.[18]

The conclusion to draw from Rundle's observation is that it is not the speaker *qua* speaker to whom the utterance must be referred. A recording "saying" "I am thinking" does not proffer an indubitable statement. If, upon hearing a recording of my own voice, I comment "I am thinking," it functions much as "I am walking"; it becomes, as Descartes says of the latter, "a motion of the body," and hence is not indubitable. I might have mistaken my sister's voice for my own, for instance. Finally, "dead to myself," I might utter "I am thinking" in my sleep without being in a state to be certain of its truth.

17. Blanchot, *The Space of Literature*, trans. Ann Smock (Lincoln: University of Nebraska Press, 1982), 17; hereafter *SL*.

18. Bede Rundle, *Grammar in Philosophy* (Oxford: Clarendon Press, 1979), 46; hereafter *BR*.

The assumption that speakerhood is essential to the "cogito" is entailed, however, by Jaakko Hintikka's treatment of the "cogito" under the heading of Austin's category of performative utterances, which, to quote Williams, "cover certain uses of language by which the very act of uttering a sentence, in a correct context, constitutes the act to which the sentence refers: 'I hereby warn you . . . ,' 'I bid . . . ,' 'I promise . . . ,' are well-known examples" (*DP,* 75). The sentence "cogito" does share certain superficial syntactic properties with performatives, namely their first person, present-tense form. Austin's performative is obligatorily first person and present tense. We can treat both as members of a larger class of sentences with properties in common without making them dependent on the speaker's role in a speech act. For Hintikka's argument misleadingly suggests that it is as a speech act that the "cogito" is crucial to Descartes's argument. Performatives can fulfill the requirements for their "felicitous" accomplishment even if the speaker does not understand the words—a priest might validly pronounce someone man and wife in Latin without understanding that language or simultaneously thinking of its meaning—whereas if a speaker said "cogito" in Latin without understanding its meaning, it could not be taken to be indubitable. If "cogito" is understood as performative, Williams says, "[t]his might suggest . . . that the peculiar certainty that the thinker possesses about the proposition is the product of the fact that he has made it true" (*DP,* 75).

Indeed, the difference between the "cogito" and the performative is grammaticalized. The progressive aspect of the present we found appropriate to the "cogito" contrasts with the simple present of the performative, which signals the act that "makes it true." The sentence "I am thinking" does not perform the thinking; it gives linguistic form to a proposition itself standing for something not linguistic—a thought in the process of being thought; it *need* not take linguistic form, however, to figure in Descartes's argument. For a sentence itself is not necessarily a speech act. This is essentially Geach's argument that "[t]he use of 'I' in . . . soliloquies" of which "I am thinking" is one example "is derivative from, parasitic upon, its use in talking to others; when there are no others, 'I' is redundant and has no special reference" (*PG,* 120).

THE FIRST PERSON AS AGENT

The narrative "he" or "it" unseats every subject just as it disappropriates all transitive action and all objective possibility. This takes two

> forms: (1) [T]he speech of the narrative always lets us feel that what is being recounted is not being recounted by anyone: it speaks in the neutral; (2) in the neutral space of the narrative, the bearers of speech, the subjects of action—those who once stood in the place of the characters—fall into a relation of self-nonidentification. Something happens to them that they can only recapture by relinquishing their power to say "I." [*IC,* 384–5]

The first person as speaker is then in excess of indubitability and so falls to Occam's razor. In determining what else is too much for certainty, the syntax of the various rewritings of the "I am thinking" are suggestive. The Latin "cogitatur," which Lichtenberg translates by an impersonal construction, makes use of the passive, as do Russell's examples. It is Nietzsche who makes explicit what is eliminated by the passive: the *I*'s agenthood. Certainly we hear Lichtenberg echoed in the assertion in *The Will to Power* "that there must be something 'that thinks' when we think, is merely a formulation of a grammatical custom which sets an agent to every action."[19] The objection that "I" as the agent of an act of thinking is not part of what can be asserted with certainty also subtends Russell's criticism of Meinong's claim that the act is contained in the thought. "We say: '*I* think so-and-so,' and this word 'I' suggests that thinking is the act of a person. Meinong's 'act' is the ghost of the subject, or what was once the full-blooded soul" (*Mind,* 17–18).

For Nietzsche it is "grammatical custom" that adds a thinker to thought. But grammar itself does not seem to require it, as Russell's perfectly well-formed agentless passive replacement for "I see a trian-

19. Friedrich Nietzsche, *The Complete Works of Nietzsche,* ed. Anthony M. Ludovici and Oscar Levy (Edinburgh and London: T. N. Foulis, 1913), vol. 15, Book 3, 14. Russell's statement that Descartes "would say that thoughts imply a thinker" as "there could not be motion unless something moved" derives from the assumption "that the categories of grammar are also the categories of reality" (*OP,* 171) surely echoes Nietzsche.

Perhaps it is via Nietzsche that Lichtenberg's proposal entered French political discourse in the wake of the Dreyfus affair. Maurice Barrès writes in his 1897 novel *Les déracinés:* "What a paltry thing, at the very surface of ourselves, intelligence is. Certain Germans don't say 'I think,' but 'it thinks in me'" (cited in Jeffrey Mehlman, "1898: The Dreyfus Affair," in *A New History of French Literature,* ed. Denis Hollier [Cambridge MA.: Harvard University Press, 1989], 827). Lichtenberg is made to counter Cartesian universalism with a collective, national, or racial unconscious. Alain Finkielkraut comments on the same passage: "Barrès peut ainsi exhorter ses compatriotes à se détourner des grands mots d'éternel ou de toujours, et . . . , à la place de 'je pense,' laisse la possibilité de dire: *Es denkt in mir,* 'ça pense en moi'" (Alain Finkielkraut, *La défaite de la pensée* [Paris: Gallimard, 1989], 65.

gle"—"A triangle is being seen" (*OP*, 215)—attests: it contains no *by*-phrase. Moreover, because "I am thinking" is intransitive, its passive resembles an impersonal, since its subject is an "expletive *'it.'*" The construction "it is thought that . . . " in English is generally analyzed as an impersonal.[20]

Jerrold Katz invokes agency to dispute Geach's claim that "the 'I' of the cogito and other soliloquy uses has no sense,"[21] i.e., is superfluous:

> There is a very straightforward reply to Geach, namely, neither introspection nor metaphysics is needed to "give the 'I' a special sense" because the pronoun has a sense in the language already. Roughly speaking, this sense is the concept of being the agent of the action expressed by the verb whose subject is the pronoun. [*JK*, 119]

But "I"'s agenthood is not sufficient to distinguish it from the third person in "he is thinking," which lacks the required indubitability of the first person sentence. This is why the Lichtenbergian revision is "cogitatur" and not "cogitat." Moreover, constructions like "it occurs to me that" and "it seems to me that" represent variants of "cogito," yet in them the first person would be assigned another thematic relation than that of agent: that of "experiencer," i.e., the psychological location. Agency may well be involved in some uses of the first person, but that is not what is essential to the "cogito"; it too must be dispensed with.[22]

THE FIRST PERSON AS EGO

> *The neutral, the neutral, how strangely this sounds to* me. [Nietzsche, cited in *IC*, xxi]

Another thing the first person must not be understood to designate Russell calls "the meaning of 'the ego,'" with which "the meaning of the word 'I' must not be confused"; "'[t]he ego' has a meaning which is universal," what "makes each one of us call himself 'I.'" But "I" names "not a universal" but a particular:

20. See Noam Chomsky, *Lectures on Government and Binding* (Foris: Dordrecht, 1981).

21. Jerrold Katz, *Cogitations: A Study of the Cogito in Relation to the Philosophy of Logic and Language and a Study of Them in Relation to the Cogito* (New York: Oxford University Press, 1986), 119; hereafter *JK*.

22. As further confirmation, Henry Le Roy Finch characterizes the Lichtenbergian position that Wittgenstein adopts as what has "been called the 'no agent' view of thinking" (*Wittgenstein—The Early Philosophy: an Exposition of the Tractatus* [New York: Humanities Press, 1971], 153).

> [O]n each occasion of its use, there is only one person who is I, though this person differs according to the speaker. It is more nearly correct to describe "I" as an ambiguous proper name than to describe it as a universal. [*TK*, 36][23]

Here Russell's position approaches Jean Laporte's, who holds that the "cogito" cannot be "*[t]hought*, restricted to itself, [which] remains something abstract."[24] Russell's making "I" a particular is part of his general position on the class of words including the demonstratives that "I" is assigned and that linguists call "deictics" or "indexicals." The position is his rejection of the Hegelian one set forth in the opening of *The Phenomenology of Mind* and adopted by British Idealism: As Richard Wollheim writes: "There is a traditional view, prevalent amongst empiricist logicians, according to which demonstratives [e.g., 'this,' 'that,' 'here'] function unlike the expressions that have hitherto been considered, and are really verbal equivalences of pointing at a particular thing or place. . . . This view Bradley rejects. All demonstratives are universals: '"This," "now," and "mine" are all universals.'"[25] Russell objects: "The word 'this' is always a proper name, in the sense that it applies directly to just one object" (*TK*, 39). By "proper name" Russell means not the ordinary proper name like "Scott," but what he calls the "logically proper name," which is for him the name of a particular. Insofar as it is akin to "this," "I" is thus for Russell a "logically proper name." Its particularity in "cogito" is the counterpart of the nongeneric present progressive tense of the verb. For speaking about universals is done in the "generic" present. "The sum of the angles of a triangle is two right angles" is the appropriate form of an axiomatic statement and not "The sum is being. . . . " "Early to bed, early to rise, makes (not 'is making') a man healthy, wealthy and wise" but "is making me healthy, wealthy and wise."

23. Possibly some such considerations led James Strachey, like Russell a Cambridge Apostle, to choose the translation "ego," which Bruno Bettelheim found so objectionable, for Freud's "das Ich."

24. Jean Laporte, "L'idée de liaison nécessaire," in *Actes du Congrès Descartes* (Paris, 1937), vol. 2, 14. Translation cited in Martial Gueroult, *Descartes' Philosophy Interpreted According to the Order of Reasons: I: The Soul and God*, trans. Roger Ariew et al. (Minneapolis: University of Minnesota Press, 1984), 288 n. 8; hereafter *MG*.

25. Richard Wollheim, *F. H. Bradley* (Harmondsworth, Middlesex: Penguin, 1959), 55. For Hegel on "this," see *The Phenomenology of Mind*, trans. J. B. Baillie (New York: Harper & Row, 1967), 149–50.

THE FIRST PERSON AS PERSON AND NAME OF A PERSON

> The third person substituting for the "I": such is the solitude that comes to the writer on account of the work. . . . The third person is myself become no one, my interlocutor turned alien; it is my no longer being able, where I am, to address myself and the inability of whoever addresses me to say "I"; it is his not being himself. [*SL,* 28]

Particulars are neither permanent nor personal. The two notions are distinct but they intersect: the concept of the person involves the idea of persistence or "survival" over time[26] and of identity. Russell sees the first person as denoting this persisting entity in speaking of "the more or less permanent person whom we call 'I.'" Yet if "I" belongs to the class of words that name particulars, it cannot designate the permanent person, which is not indubitable; only a "momentary" subject can be asserted with certainty. Thus one reason he gives for substituting "cogitatur" for "cogito" is that "I" in "I see a triangle" "take[s] us beyond what the momentary event reveals." It "means the person who had certain remembered experiences and is expected to have certain future experiences." Hence, "'I see a triangle now and I saw a square a moment ago'" is a possible sentence in which "[t]he word 'I' has exactly the same meaning in its two occurrences." Yet Descartes's concern is "the contribution to your knowledge which is made by seeing the triangle at the moment." Russell's conclusion is that "since the word 'I' takes you beyond this contribution, we must cut it out if we want to find a correct verbal expression for what is added to our knowledge by seeing the triangle. We will say 'A triangle is being seen'" (*OP,* 215). We might compare this point to the "imaginative tour de force on the part of Locke" by which, in G.E.M. Anscombe's words, he "detached the identity of the self or 'person' from the identity even of the thinking being which does the actual thinking of the I-thoughts."[27] So also in *Theory of Knowledge,* it is the "permanent person" Russell explicitly wishes to eliminate:

26. See David Lewis, "Survival and Identity," in *The Identities of Persons,* ed. Amélie Oksenberg Rorty (Berkeley: University of California Press, 1976), 17–40.

27. G. E. M. Anscombe, "The First Person," in *Demonstratives,* ed. Palle Yourgrau (Oxford: Oxford University Press, 1990), 141; hereafter *GA.* Anscombe paraphrases Locke thus: "Might not the thinking substance which thought the thought 'I did it'—the genuine thought of agent-memory—nevertheless be a different thinking substance from the one that could have had the thought 'I am doing it' when the act was done?"

> [I]t is necessary to pare away from 'I' a great deal that is usually included—not only the body [the body is eliminated by the psychological verb—AB], but also the past and future in so far as they may possibly not belong to the subject of the present experience. It is obvious that all these are obtained by an extension from the present subject, and that the essential problem is concerned with our consciousness of the present subject. [*TK*, 36]

Martial Gueroult also insists on the separation of the "personal concrete self" from the Cartesian subject; otherwise, "one is forced to establish a modal distinction between substance and its principal attribute, in opposition to what Descartes teaches." Gueroult clearly places the issue in the context of the Lichtenbergian critique: "J. Laporte adds that, by opposing '*thought* as impersonal attribute with a *personal* subject' we went against Descartes's language, which says *Cogito* (*my* thought) and not *Cogitatur*. However, in this case we were aiming at Laporte's expressions, and not Descartes's . . . '" (*MC*, 288 n. 8). Gueroult is not willing to substitute "cogitatur" for "cogito," but we will see that this requires reading "I" in the latter as a reduced version of "I" in its normal uses.

There must be words that, unlike particulars, name persons with persisting identities and allow the different experiences of one individual to be connected. It is apparent that Russell connects the person to the (ordinary) proper name:

> It is supposed that thoughts cannot just come and go, but need a person to think them. Now, of course it is true that thoughts can be collected into bundles, so that one bundle is my thoughts, another is your thoughts, and a third is the thoughts of Mr. Jones. But I think the person is not an ingredient in the single thought: he is rather constituted by relations of the thoughts to each other and to the body. . . . [T]he grammatical forms "I think," "you think," and "Mr. Jones thinks," are misleading if regarded as indicating an analysis of a single thought. It would be better to say "it thinks in me," like "it rains here"; or better still, "there is a thought in me." [*Mind*, 18]

The proper name denotes the single, identifiable, persisting individual; to it are attached free-floating "bundles" of thoughts it thereby ties down to a permanently fixed designator. Note that "I" (and "you") are treated by Russell along with the proper name "Mr. Jones." Certainly the ordinary, as opposed to the "logically" proper name, is such a label for a person. The question not yet settled is whether "I" *is*, as Russell assumes here. Descartes clearly took what the proper name refers to as subject to doubt, by contrast with the referent of the "I," as Gueroult's commentary makes clear, for I can be deceived as to my identity and name:

> What do I know if I am not deceived when I believe myself to be Descartes? Do not madmen believe themselves to be gourds, Louis XIII, or the Cardinal? . . . But in order to be deceived in this case, I must at least be thinking. . . . In brief, in order to be deceived about myself, it is not necessary that I be Socius, Descartes, the Cardinal, nor any such individual or a person in general, but simply that I be 'a thinking thing,' meaning a self. [*MG*, 288 n. 8]

I may not know I am René Descartes, so the sentence with the proper name "I am René Descartes" is not indubitable; but I cannot not know I'm me.

The question then is whether "I" is the name of a particular or of a person. All the commentators on Descartes we have been considering are agreed that the proper formulation requires the name of a particular. Is "I"'s insertion in the subject position of a present-tense verb of consciousness, as in ". . . am thinking," sufficient to limit it to "momentariness"? Such was our analysis of the difference in certitude between "I am thinking" and "I was thinking." Gueroult in effect thinks "I" is not an ordinary name but the name of a particular. This is also Wittgenstein's position:

> "When I say 'I am in pain,' I do not point to a person who is in pain. . . . I did not say that such-and-such a person was in pain, but 'I am . . . . . ' Now in saying this I don't name any person. Just as I don't name anyone when I *groan* with pain."[28] [First ellipsis mine; second ellipsis Wittgenstein's]

Saul Kripke, in his commentary on Wittgenstein's private-language argument, concludes that "the first person pronoun, for Wittgenstein, is to be assimilated neither to a name nor to a definite description referring to any particular person or entity."[29] Russell, however, despite his including "I" with the other deictics, clearly understands it to refer to the person and therefore adopts the Lichtenbergian position. This leads him in *An Inquiry Into Meaning and Truth* to resort to a

28. Ludwig Wittgenstein, *Philosophical Investigations*, The English Text of the Third Edition, trans. G.E.M. Anscombe (Oxford: Basil Blackwell, 1958; New York: Macmillan, 1953), 404.

29. Saul Kripke, *Wittgenstein: On Rules and Private Language* (Cambridge, Massachusetts: Harvard University Press, 1982), 144; hereafter *SKW*.

neologism, the "I-now,"[30] to avoid the implication of a persisting person in "I am thinking."

THE FIRST PERSON AS CONSCIOUSNESS

[T]he neutrality of a featureless third person. [*SL*, 30]

Russell's "I-now" and Gueroult's "thinking subject" can be considered to interpret the subject of "am thinking" similarly. It yields the first positive result of the reduction of the "cogito": the self as consciousness, as bare point of awareness, what *Theory of Knowledge* calls "the bare subject" (*TK*, 37). The bare subject operates as a momentary point of attachment for free-floating thoughts. For Russell, it becomes the end point of the reduction with some hesitation, however. The hesitation arises from the controversy over "consciousness of self" argued by a number of Descartes's critics.[31] In the passage of *The Problems of Philosophy* that first raises the issue, the question is whether the momentary subject is, like the sense-datum, an object of the immediate knowledge Russell calls "acquaintance," which contrasts with "knowledge by description" in the important Russellian distinction.

But is *I* both subject and object of acquaintance? For "acquaintance with the contents of our minds" is "self-consciousness" but not "consciousness of our self: it is consciousness of particular thoughts and feelings." It is less certain "we are also acquainted with our bare selves." "When we try to look into ourselves we always seem to come upon some particular thought and feeling, and not upon the 'I' which has the thought or feeling." But Russell concedes "some reasons for thinking that we are acquainted with the 'I.'" Distinguishing in my acquaintance with an acquaintance, e.g., "with 'my seeing the sun'" "the sense-datum which represents the sun to me" from "that which sees this sense-datum" and finding acquaintance consists of "a relation between the person acquainted and the object with which the person is acquainted" and "the person acquainted is myself," he concludes that "the whole fact with which I am acquainted is 'Self-acquainted-with-sense-datum.'" Since "we know the truth 'I am acquainted with this sense-datum,'" it seems plausible we are "ac-

30. Russell, *An Inquiry Into Meaning and Truth* (Harmondsworth: Penguin, 1962), 102.

31. Jean-Paul Sartre's notion of the "pre-reflective cogito" in *Being and Nothingness* is one attempt to avoid implying that "I am thinking" means I am conscious of myself thinking.

quainted with something which we call 'I,'" not necessarily the "more or less permanent person, the same today as yesterday" but "that thing, whatever its nature, which sees the sun and has acquaintance with sense-data" (*PP*, 50–51). The subject is "that which is aware of things or has desires towards things" (*PP*, 51), "the two words 'acquaintance' and 'awareness'" being used synonymously (*TK*, 35). Acquaintance is modeled on perception, for Russell draws the analogy between "acquaintance in sensation with the data of the outer senses, and in introspection with the data of what may be called the inner sense—thoughts, feelings, desires, etc.; we have acquaintance in memory with things which have been data either of the outer or of the inner sense" (*PP*, 51).

In the later *Theory of Knowledge*, the referent of "I" is no longer a possible object of acquaintance but only the subject of the relation to the object of acquaintance: "We will define a 'subject' as any entity which is acquainted with something, i.e., 'subjects' are the domain of the relation 'acquaintance'" (*TK*, 35). "Let it therefore be assumed, in this discussion, that 'I' means the subject of the experience which I am now having (the vicious circle here is important to observe), and that we have to ask ourselves whether 'I' in this sense is something with which we are acquainted" (*TK*, 36). If "an experiencing, as opposed to the mere object experienced, seems, empirically, not as a matter of a priori necessity, to be only capable of being experienced by one person" (*TK*, 34), the privacy of experience does not entail, for Russell, the equivalence of this privacy with self-reflection. The subject of consciousness can never be its object: "We can easily become aware of our own experiences, but we never seem to become aware of the subject itself" (*TK*, 36). The locus of an indubitable "knowledge" (acquaintance), it cannot be acquainted with what nevertheless makes acquaintance possible. In this sense, having acquaintance with the subject is making the subject an object. Having acquaintance with the subject seems almost to be logically impossible, since acquaintance "consists in a relation between the mind and something other than the mind" (*PP*, 42) and hence implies the at least partial independence of the object.

Behind Russell's attack on consciousness of self is Hume's "notorious" rejection of Descartes's claim "that the one entity of whose existence I may be certain . . . is myself" or "my own mind," as Kripke puts it (*SKW*, 121). Kripke links it to Lichtenberg, although Lichtenberg "wrote independently of Hume" (*SKW*, 123 n. 7). He quotes this celebrated passage from Hume:

> There are some philosophers, who imagine we are intimately conscious of what we call our SELF; that we feel its existence and its continuance in existence. . . . Unluckily all these positive assertions are contrary to that very experience, which is pleaded for them, nor have we any idea of *self*, after the manner it is here explain'd. . . . For my part, when I enter most intimately into what I call *myself*, I always stumble on some particular impression or other, of heat or cold, light or shade, love or hatred, pain or pleasure. I never can catch *myself* at any time without a perception, and never can observe any thing but the perception. [David Hume, *A Treatise of Human Nature*, Book I, Part 4, Section 6 ("Of Personal Identity"), cited in *SKW*, 121–22]

Hume's formulation returns us to the "cogito" as a particular thought—Russell's word "bundles" was an obvious allusion to Hume. Even the bare self would seem almost too much. So we reach two end points of the process of radical doubt which the Lichtenbergian project aims to carry beyond Descartes. One is the momentary subject, bare point of attachment for a thinking; the other is the unattached single thought. Is the one significantly different from the other? The momentary subject, not an object of acquaintance and thus, also, not "an ingredient of a single thought," is like the subject of the *Tractatus*[32] which "does not belong to the world" but is its "limit" and "shrinks to an extensionless point" (5.632; 5.64) as the eye is not in the field of sight (5.633; 5.6331); Moore interprets Wittgenstein's invocation of Lichtenberg (cited in note 15 above) as meaning "something similar to what he said of 'the eye of the visual field'" (*PP*, 309). Not identifiable but a nameless, faceless nonperson, the subject is a seeing that cannot be seen by the seeing, like Mach's drawing of the subject that has no face. This no doubt is why Descartes referred to it by the word "res"—it is a thing, albeit a thinking thing. *Tractatus* 5.633 includes the statement "And from nothing *in the field of sight* can it be concluded that it is seen from the eye." Similarly, the *Investigations* claims that nothing in the groan allows us to posit the person uttering it. Kripke finds that Wittgenstein's position there anticipates Hector-Neri Castañeda's account of "the problem of 'self-consciousness,'" apparent in the fact that "'Jones said that he was hungry' does *not* mean 'Jones said that Jones was hungry,' for Jones need not realize that he is Jones" (*SKW*, 144).

32. Wittgenstein, *Tractatus Logico-Philosophicus*, trans. C. K. Ogden (New York: Harcourt, Brace, 1922).

To decide whether there are different empirical consequences of the bare-subject and the single-thought theories or whether they are only notational variants, we must now consider whether the two positions would require different reformulations of "cogito." That will also lead us to decide whether "cogitatur" is a sufficient linguistic representation of the speakerless, agentless, personless, "cogito." The process will establish the link between the two positions on Cartesian privacy that separate the early Wittgenstein, whose thinking developed in intense interaction with Russell, from the later Wittgenstein. "In the *Tractatus,*" Kripke claims, "Wittgenstein bases his account of the self on the Hume-Lichtenberg thought experiment. . . . In the *Investigations,* the special character of the self, as something not to be identified with any entity picked out in any ordinary manner, survives, but it is thought of as deriving from a 'grammatical' peculiarity of the first person pronoun, not from any metaphysical mystery" (*SKW,* 144–45). "Privacy" there is attributed to language, hence the "private language" argument. But our task has been to bring the one to bear on the other, to analyze "cogito" as a sentence in the light of the Lichtenbergian critique in order to discover what grammatical properties are necessary and sufficient for the cessation of doubt. Our analysis has brought us to the "'grammatical' peculiarity" of the first-person pronoun as the source of the problem. We will discover that it divides into something that leads Russell to treat it as the name of a person and something that leads the later Wittgenstein to say that it doesn't "name any person." The first makes it unsuitable to name Cartesian privacy; the second cannot be eliminated from the "cogito" without eliminating its certainty. "Clearly much more needs to be said here: a few sketchy and allusive remarks on the analogy between 'I am in pain' and a groan hardly give a complete theory, or even a satisfying picture of our talk of ourselves," Kripke concludes (*SKW,* 145). As a step in the direction of such a theory, we propose to isolate the grammatical property required to capture "the elusiveness of the subject in introspection" (*TK,* 36) contained in "I" but not equivalent to it.

RENDERING "COGITATUR" INDUBITABLE

> I think, it said, I bring together all that which is light without heat, rays without brilliance, unrefined products; I brew them together and conjugate them, and, in a primary absence of myself, I discover myself as a perfect unity at the point of greatest intensity. I think, it said, I am subject and object of an all-powerful radiation; a sun using all its energy

> to make itself night, as well as to make itself sun. I think: there at the point where thought joins with me I am able to subtract myself from being, without diminishing, without changing, by means of a metamorphosis which saves me for myself, beyond any point of reference from which I might be seized. [*TO*, 99]

The problem is that the various reductions of the "cogito," in eliminating what is in excess of complete certainty in the "I," have also eliminated the markers of subjectivity, so none seems to possess the requisite indubitability we equate with linguistic subjectivity. "In the Lichtenbergian jargon, 'there is pain' *always* means that *I* feel pain," Kripke says (*SKW*, 129). But our concern is to determine if that "jargon," like Descartes's use of the "I," is in conformity with natural language. Making explicit in what linguistic property subjectivity lies is the required step. It will reveal if restoring to the various Lichtenbergian revisions their now missing indubitability requires restoring the "I." Consider the various alternatives. The sentence as Mach quotes it from Lichtenberg (this is of course a translation of Mach) is "it thinks," on the analogy with an impersonal like "it lightenings," with an "expletive" or so-called "weather 'it'," or rather, because this shows the same mistake in translation that "I think" does, "it is lightening" or "it is raining." Williams gives the existential sentence "There is some thinking going on" on the analogy with "there is lightening," translating the same German sentence "Es blitzet." Russell's versions, which use a sensation verb as their psychological verb (as Descartes allows), include the passive—"a brown colour is being seen"—as well as, like Williams's, the existential sentence—e.g., "There is a triangle." We list the options (note that both the impersonal and the existential have an expletive subject, "it" or "there," grammatically in subject position, but they are semantically empty, "dummy" subjects):[33]

(1)	Impersonal:	It is thinking.
	Existential:	There is some thinking going on, there is a triangle.
	Passive:	It is being thought, a brown colour is being seen.

From the linguistic point of view nothing in these constructions confers on them the indubitability that Descartes argued "I am think-

33. Katz sees the Lichtenbergian "view" to mean "that the 'I' in 'I am thinking' is what grammarians call an 'expletive word.'" Again, he concludes, this entails that "there would be no agent place in the semantic structure of 'think'" (118–19). See also *JK*, 194 n.18.

ing" has. Russell's analysis of "I see a triangle," by contrast with "there is a triangle," draws that conclusion, so we return to it. Searching for the difference "between the propositions 'There is a triangle' and 'I see a triangle,'" Russell at first pronounces that "[b]oth these statements seem as certain as any statement can be," although "we are quite certain of something, but not quite certain what it is that we are certain of" (*OP,* 214). But, "on the assumption that we should not say 'There is a black dot' when we see a black dot which we attribute to eye trouble" (*OP,* 215), the assertion with "there is" turns out to be "a stronger assertion than when you say 'I see a black dot'" (*OP,* 214). It takes us "far beyond the region of immediate certainty"; "stating an event in the world, supposed to be equally discoverable by other people," it "makes inferences to something public, and thus goes beyond the bare datum." So Russell returns to "I see a triangle" as coming "nearest to expressing the fact of which we are immediately certain" (*OP,* 215). But the Lichtenbergian critique that Russell accepted was that the linguistic form of statements like "I am thinking" and "I see a triangle" asserted something not completely indubitable. "I" "depends on memory and expectation" (*OP,* 215). The quandary then is that both "I see a triangle" and "there is a triangle," "cogito" and "cogitatur," go beyond absolute certainty. Surely there is more to Lichtenberg's claim than the substitution of one doubtful statement for another.

Russell's substitution of the agentless passive "'A triangle is being seen'" for the active, the momentary sensation for "I," as "one step nearer to what we are seeking," encounters the further objection that the "causal word" "seen" in the passive is "dependent on the eyes" (*OP,* 215). He proposes "[T]here is a visual triangle," as not "logically dependent upon experience" (*OP,* 216). While it does not involve "previous experience" (*OP,* 215), presumably the word "visual" adds to "There is a triangle" the missing element of "immediate experience" (*OP,* 216), of privacy, which is required for certainty. The problem is that the adjective "visual" is not *grammatically* subjective or private, as the first person pronoun was felt to be. What is to prevent the reading that the triangle is being seen by another mind, a third person? This possibility Russell does not consider.

A more suggestive direction of inquiry is opened up by Russell's discovery that "in English the words 'there is' are ambiguous. When I used them before, saying 'There is a triangle,' I meant them in the sense of 'voilà' or 'da ist.' Now I mean them in the sense of 'il y a' or 'es giebt' [sic]" (*OP,* 216). As translations of "there is," "voilà" and "il y a" divide the ambiguous English phrase into a private and a public statement, respectively. "Il y a" contains the impersonal "il" of "il pleut." "Voilà," by contrast, functions as a demonstrative by virtue of the deictic adverb "là" it contains. Russell could have found an English equivalent of "voilà" that captures its subjectivity—"Here is a triangle" or "There is a triangle!" for instance, where "there" is the demonstrative and not the expletive "there." ("There" is the name of a place in private space, so Russell can speak of "dream-objects being 'there'" [*ML*, 168].) It is the presence of the deictic word "here" that renders the statement grammatically private; it is the presence of the deictic present progressive and not the word "visual" in "A visual triangle is occurring" that should be the basis of Russell's conclusion that "we have arrived at what is indubitable and intrinsic in the addition to your knowledge derived from a visual datum" (*OP*, 216).

Does this mean that with "here is a triangle" or "a triangle is occurring" we have a grammatical equivalent for the reduced "cogito"? Russell seems to claim the contrary, for he states that with "[t]here is a triangle" he meant "voilà un triangle," whereas with "there is a visual triangle" he means "il y a un triangle [visuel]." One would have anticipated that if the statement "there is a black dot" is not appropriate for dots caused by fatigue or if "there is a triangle" can be used "if you had seen it a moment ago but now had your eyes shut" (*OP*, 214), "there is" in these cases is to be disambiguated in the direction of "voilà." The difference between the "existential" statement "there is a table in the room," by contrast with "this is the table" or "here is the table," is that the referent of "the table" in the existential is a physical object unavailable to immediate apprehension, while in the examples with deictics it is a sensible (visual) table. "Il y a un triangle" and "voilà un triangle," and their English counterparts, are evidence, then, of a dualism within language, dual systems of reference that presuppose, on the one hand, a dualist ontology, a theory of "what there is," and, on the other hand, an accompanying theory of knowledge. The aim of Russell's reduction of "I see a triangle" is the elimination or, rather, the neutralization of dualism. This is because the "occurrence" it registers "has no duality" and represents "a datum equally for physics and for psychology . . . neither mental nor physical" (*OP*, 217). Here Russell specifically invokes the theory of "neutral monism," but even where he does not explicitly embrace that position, it is a minimal neutrality between subject and object, his "physical subjectivity" and its linguistic representation he is after. At this point, we have arrived at the dualism of "there is." Our expectations select its disambiguation as "voilà" for the neutralized "cogito"; Russell seems to choose the other reading.

THE GRAMMAR OF PERSISTING THINGS AND THE GRAMMAR OF A MOMENTARY SUBJECTIVITY

> Between the two falsely interrogative propositions—why is there something rather than nothing? and why is there evil rather than good?—I do not recognize the difference which is supposed to be discernible, for both are sustained by a "there is" [*un "il y a"*] which is neither being nor nothingness, neither good nor evil, and without which the whole discussion collapses. [*WD*, 65]

The universe of referents conjured up by language thus follows the epistemological division between persisting physical objects existing in physical time and space and subjective, momentary "particulars." Particulars, unlike physical objects, can be known by "acquaintance"; physical objects, on the other hand, are known "by description." Russell's terminology makes it clear that his theory of knowledge is to be mapped into his theory of descriptions: definite descriptions denote permanent physical objects with which acquaintance is not possible. The person will then fall into the class of physical objects and the self into that of momentary particulars. Both the ordinary proper name "Scott" (which Russell analyzes as a disguised description) and the definite description "the author of *Waverly*" name a "more or less permanent person." Indeed, the paradigmatic referring expressions treated by all the classic theories of reference by their nature refer to things that are not momentary. This is clearly the case as well for what Kripke has called "rigid designators."[34] We can take them as the paradigm of reference to persisting objects. For in Kripke's account, proper names and uniquely referring common nouns that are names of natural kinds refer "rigidly" in the sense that they refer to objects or persons with a "trans-world identity." The theory employs the idea of possible worlds, for which the primary evidence is the behavior of such designators in counterfactuals—e.g., "Nixon might not have won the election." One case of trans-world identity is the persisting identity of a referent at different moments.

There are also, we saw, "names" that refer to nonpersisting things, the "logically proper names," the demonstratives "this," "that,"

34. Kripke, "Naming and Necessity," in *Semantics of Natural Language*, ed. Donald Davidson and Gilbert Harman (Dordrecht: Reidel, 1972), 253–355.

"these," and "those." The referent of "this" is a particular—a sense-datum or a thought. Demonstratives, we saw, are part of the larger class of "deictics," which includes the first and second person pronouns, a set of time adverbs like "today," "five days ago," and "at this time," a set of locatives such as "in this place," "over yonder," "to the right," the nonliterary and the nongeneric tenses, and certain verbs like "come" and "bring." Certain deictics are derivative of others, which furnish the purely deictic element. These pure deictics we can consider "now," "here," "this," and the present tense, leaving aside for the moment the status of "I," which is the subject of our inquiry. The other temporal deictics can all be treated as containing "now." Thus, "today" is the day which is "now"; "tomorrow" is the day after that day. Unlike "today," the pure deictic "now" has no more lexical content than its deictic temporality, whereas "today" can be considered to incorporate a deictic element with some lexical semantic content. In like fashion, the deictic locatives are all analyzable as containing the pure element "here."

The pure deictics are all circularly defined—"now" is the moment in which "I" am speaking, "here" is the place where "I" am speaking, etc.; they show "the vicious circle" Russell pointed to in defining "I" as "the subject of the experience which I am now having" (*TK,* 36). It is these circularly defined "names" for momentary things to which our inquiry into the grammar of "cogito" has led us. At the start, we equated the sentence's indubitability with its subjectivity. That coincidence of certainty and subjectivity we can thus locate in the circularity of the deictic. Let us now try to define, first, the nature of their certainty and then the nature of their subjectivity.

Deictic certainty is bound up with the fact that this class of words is a form of linguistic pointing, as the etymology of the terms "demonstrative" and "deictic" or "indexical" suggests. That is, their referent can be shown; unlike the physical object, known by description, it is necessarily present and knowable by acquaintance. As Gareth Evans observes, "Russell introduced us to the idea that demonstrative identification is a mode of identification quite unlike descriptive identification."[35] The paradigm case of the referent of a demonstrative is a sense-datum. Since deictic reference points to a sense-datum or other object of acquaintance, it cannot show "failure of reference"; skepti-

35. Gareth Evans, *The Varieties of Reference,* ed. John McDowell (Oxford: Clarendon Press, 1982), 143.

cism can never arise: "we can never point to an object and say: 'This lies outside my present experience'" (*TK*, 10).[36] Russell's claim here amounts to syntactic evidence. That is, sentences like Russell's are not acceptable sentences containing "this" or certain other deictics, as can be seen in the list below:

(2) This is not here.
I am not here.
I can't find this.

The certainty of deictic reference is hence a factor of its circularity: "this" is what "I" have "here" "now." "'This is here,' said Jinny, 'this is now. . . . This is only here; this is only now.'"[37] For this reason, Russell treats the "datum" it provides as "giv[ing] rise to knowledge" but itself not knowledge—precisely because it "has no duality" (*OP*, 217). By contrast, "knowledge of physical objects, as opposed to sense-data, is only obtained by an inference, and . . . they are not things with which we are acquainted. Hence we can never know any proposition of the form 'this is a physical object,' where 'this' is something immediately known" (*PP*, 108–9). "This is a physical object" is thus not a neutralized "cogito" but a kind of logical impossibility.

Deictic certainty has thus the elusiveness of the subject. It is reflected in the other grammatical peculiarity of deictics: their ability to shift their referent from utterance to utterance, giving rise to an alternate term for them, Roman Jakobson's "shifters."[38] It refers to the fact that deictic pronouns do not rigidly designate the same object each time they are used: "a [logically] proper name . . . seldom means the same thing two moments running" (*LK*, 201). This nonrigidity of deictic reference is what Russell treats as "ambiguity." His "pronouns" and "proper names" clearly intend the deictics, because they include "now":

> Pronouns stand for particulars, but are ambiguous: it is only by the context or the circumstances that we know what particulars they stand for. The word "now" stands for a particular, namely the present mo-

36. Anscombe claims that "there exist counterexamples which show that 'this' may fail to refer." Her example—where a speaker who thinks an empty box contains ashes says "[t]his is all that is left of poor Jones"—only fails to refer if the referent must be a physical object. If, as with one of her options, it is "an optical presentation" (*GA*, 143), "this" cannot fail to refer to the visible box.

37. Virginia Woolf, *The Waves* (Harcourt Brace Jovanovich, 1931), 23; hereafter *W.*

38. See Roman Jakobson, "Two Aspects of Language and Two Types of Aphasic Disturbances," in his *Fundamentals of Language* (The Hague: Mouton, 1956), 55–82.

ment; but like pronouns, it stands for an ambiguous particular, because the present is always changing. [*PP*, 93]

Unlike "June 14, 1991," which designates the same moment every time it is used, the referent of "now" does not refer to a fixed moment independent of its use. "But when used," as Russell says of "I," it "is not in the least ambiguous" (*TK*, 36). This is made apparent by marking each instance of a deictic with a different "coreferential index" indicating its noncoreferentiality:

(3) this_i is white. This_j is white, too.
Now_i you see it. Now_j you don't.
You_i stay here. You_j come with me.

". . .and now_i a bird was dashed against the pane, and now_j there was a clap of thunder. . . ."[39]

"Now_i where are we, she said to herself. Where is the train at this moment? Now_j she murmured, shutting her eyes, we are passing the white house on the hill; now_k we are going through the tunnel; now_l we are crossing the bridge over the river. . . ."[40]

"The Old Kent Road was very crowded on Thursday, 11 October 1928. People spilt off the pavement. There were women with shopping bags. Children ran out. . . . Here_i was a market. Here_j a funeral. Here_k a procession with banners." [*O* 216–17]

In (3), the referent of the deictic term shifts with each new complete, independent, or conjoined sentence. It is true that certain of the deictics shift more frequently—notably "this":

(4) You can fix this_i with this_j.
Take this_i and this_j and this_k.

Such sentence-internal shifting is also possible for the spatial deictics, but, in that case, their interpretation implies that the speaker is moving. Witness the following:

(5) Move this chair here_i to about here_j.

Move this chair from here to there.

The shifting of "now," by contrast, is typically limited to the introduction of a new, nonsubordinate sentence. Ignoring the greater frequency

39. Woolf, *Orlando* (Harmondsworth: Penguin), 184; hereafter *O*.
40. Woolf, *The Years* (London: Hogarth Press, 1937), 271; hereafter *Y*.

with which the demonstratives shift, we will say that all deictics are referred to the space and duration of "here-now" defined by the sentence. In "I was here yesterday," for instance, we conclude that I am here now and that that is what is certain.

We have available a more precise grammatical explanation of this property of the deictic than ambiguity. Grammatically, deictics refer "nonrigidly," i.e., unlike Kripke's [nonlogically] proper names. Jean-Claude Milner has proposed a linguistic basis for Kripke's notion of rigid designation in the idea of lexical reference, in which, "the logical notion of a designator coincides with the linguistic notion of a lexically specified N" [i.e., N-Double-Bar or Noun Phrase, AB]:[41]

> Indeed, from a linguistic point of view, the characteristic feature of rigid designators is that their reference is fixed independently of the particular proposition in which they appear. That is why the fixed reference never varies and is not affected by the particular proposition in which the rigid designator is used. [*PC,* 60]

If rigid reference is determined lexically, nonrigid reference, in Milner's analysis, is determined by the grammar:

> [T]he reference of rigid designators is fixed in a way that is entirely independent of the linguistic properties of the proposition in which it appears; the reference of a non-rigid designator is fixed in a way that depends entirely on the linguistic structure of the proposition in which it appears. Accordingly, if the speaking subject does not know what object is designated by a rigid designator, the linguistic form of the sentence does not help him: linguistic rules in that case are neither necessary nor sufficient; on the contrary, the linguistic form of the sentence, as analyzed by linguistic rules (such as Principles of binding, rules of LF etc.) and linguistic knowledge in general are both necessary and sufficient to determine the referential interpretation of a non-rigid designator. [*PC,* 59]

When he concludes that "[t]he fixing of reference in a proposition appears then to be a discourse operation, that somehow resembles the operation described in terms of *shifters*" (*PC,* 59), he makes the deictics paradigms of nonrigid reference. But how precisely does the grammar assign deictic reference? We saw above that the domain of the

41. Jean-Claude Milner, "Some Remarks on Principle C," in *Binding in Romance: Essays in Honour of Judith McA'Nulty,* ed. Anne-Marie Di Sciullo and Anne Rochette (Ottawa: Special Publication of the Canadian Linguistic Association, 1990), 59; hereafter *PC.*

space-time deictics is the "highest," or nonsubordinate sentence. In *Unspeakable Sentences,* I treated the peculiar shifting of the temporal deictic with each new independent sentence by a principle, "1 E/1 Now," which introduces a nonrecursive symbol E(xpression) to replace S, the initial syntactic unit or highest node in the tree.[42] This was implicitly generalized so as to include the entire class of shifters. It is with respect to the node E, as well, that nonrigid reference is assigned in Milner's account: "The reference of a rigid designator is fixed independently of the E that dominates it; the reference of a nonrigid designator is fixed by the E that dominates it" (*PC,* 60).

We conclude that the linguistic subjectivity that lends indubitability to some statements lies in the unfixed or shifting reference of certain of their terms. The Lichtenbergian "cogitatur" acquires indubitability only with such a term: "there is some thinking" must be replaced by "here is some thinking." Why does the criticism of the "cogito" not treat the first person as another such term when the nondeictic third person prevents "(s)he is thinking" from being indubitable?

THE EXCEPTIONAL STATUS OF THE FIRST PERSON

> But if so-called subjectivity is the other *in place* of me, it is no more subjective than objective; the other is without interiority. Anonymity is the name, and outside is the thought of the other . . . , just as the neutrality and passivity of dying would be his life. [*WD,* 28]

In most accounts, the shifting property of deictic reference is defined with respect to the speech act. Thus, the first person is defined as the speaker of the speech act, "now" as the time of the speech act, "here," the place of the speech act, and so on.[43] We can call the traditional speech-act centered account "egocentric," borrowing the other term Russell used in 1940 for deictics, "egocentric particulars."[44] (*Theory of Knowledge* uses "emphatic particulars" [40]). Its effect is to make the first person the paradigmatic "shifter"—we saw that he treated " 'I' as an ambiguous proper name" rather than "as a universal." The fact that,

42. Ann Banfield, *Unspeakable Sentences* (London: Routledge & Kegan Paul, 1982). See also my "Narrative Style and the Grammar of Direct and Indirect Speech," *Foundations of Language* 10 (1973): 1–39.

43. See, for instance, Bernard Comrie, *Tense* (Cambridge: Cambridge University Press, 1985), 14; and Rundle, 43.

44. See Russell, *An Inquiry into Meaning and Truth,* chapter 7.

as we have already concluded, the "cogito" is not properly treated as a speech act suggests that the egocentric account of these shifting terms should be revised. And indeed, the behavior of the first person is unique among deictics in not shifting from E(xpression) to E, as Russell himself points out, while still insisting "I" is ambiguous. "We might say 'I see a triangle now and I saw a square a moment ago,'" he writes (*OP*, 215). Russell's example, in fact, constitutes syntactic evidence, if it is revised. "1 E/1 Now" clearly applies to the entire conjoined sentence; it is a single E and a single "Now," a reading the "a moment ago" makes explicit, even if the past tense suggests that "I" refers to a persisting person. But note that in the series of Es in (6), where there is a shift to a new "now," the "I" does not likewise shift its referent:

(6) I_i see a triangle now. Now I_i (not: I_j) see a square.

The idiosyncratic behavior of the first person among the deictics or shifters is observable elsewhere, namely in a certain principle of the written language. It requires all instances of the first person to be interpreted as coreferential in any sequence of related Es, i.e., a sequence understood to form a unit. Let us call such a unit a "Text." This difference of the first person is captured in *Unspeakable Sentences* by the principle of "Concordance of Person," which states the condition "1 Text/1 Speaker [I]."[45] In fact, the coreferentiality of all first persons is one of the features that defines which of these sequences constitute units, i.e., Texts. A sequence of linguistic examples, for instance, would not form such a unit, nor would a dialogue. (One consequence is that direct speech constitutes a shift to a new Text because the referent of the first person may then and only then shift.)[46]

The principles of "1 E/1 Here-Now" and "1 Text/1 Speaker" make the exceptional status of the first person as a shifter a function of the level at which its referent is fixed: at the level of the Text but not at the

45. In "Anaphor Binding and Narrative Point of View: English Reflexive Pronouns in Sentence and Discourse" (*Language* 65/4 [1989]: 695–727), Anne Zribi-Hertz proposes "a Domain of Point of View (DPV)," i.e., "a portion of discourse which . . . may not include a switch of narrative viewpoint" (713). Within the framework of *Unspeakable Sentences*, E is the domain of "Self" or point of view. That in practice it may extend over a series of Es is already accounted for by the general rules for third-person pronoun coreference. Whether there is any need for a "DPV" is a question that takes us beyond the limits of this essay. But see Milner, *Introduction à une science du langage* (Paris Seuil, 1989), 482 n.14.

46. See Chapter 1 of *Unspeakable Sentences.*

level of the E. This then is what makes it unsuitable as the "name" of the momentary subject. The fact that this status is not generally recognized explains the debate over the proper analysis of the "cogito," one position understanding it as an E-level shifter and the other objecting to it as a Text-level shifter. The confusion arises because "I" is not a lexically fixed, rigid designator either, as Russell's sometime treament of it as the name of a persisting person might suggest. Herein lies the "grammatical peculiarity" of the first person about which Kripke insists "much more needs to be said." The Lichtenbergian position in general and Russell in particular object to it as a Text-level shifter. Gueroult's analysis—as well as that of the Wittgenstein of the *Investigations*—accepts it, contra grammar, as an E-level shifter; Anscombe's argument that "'I' is neither a name nor another kind of expression whose logical role is to make a reference, *at all*" (*GA*, 148)—where "reference" is understood as rigid and not E-level, like a deictic—wishes similarly to deny it artificially its Text-level shiftingness: "*if* 'I' is treated as a referring expression," the consequence is that Descartes's "position has . . . the intolerable difficulty of requiring an identification of the same referent in different 'I'-thoughts. (This led Russell at one point to speak of 'short-term selves')" (*GA*, 146–47). In other words, either it must be eliminated or it cannot be permitted its normal usage in the "cogito."

The source of Descartes's "difficulty" is the apparent absence of any E-level pronoun to refer to the short-term self without referring to the long-term person. Russell's "short-term selves" are in grammatical terms "E-level" selves. Descartes's "saying too much" in saying "I" is then naming something whose proper interpretation requires going beyond the bounds of the E. The shifters other than "I" are E-level terms, but the versions of the "cogitatur" using them—Geach's "This is really a dreadful muddle!" for instance—opt to represent the single thought as the minimum of subjectivity required, since the privacy of these statements is contained in words that cannot be said to designate a subject. Russell's "it thinks in me" on the analogy with "it rains here" can be rewritten to avoid the first person altogether but retain a shifter as in "it is thinking here" (on the analogy with "it is raining here") or "there is thinking here," where not only is "the person . . . not an ingredient in the single thought," as Russell says, but neither is the momentary subject. The resources of language seem to force us to accept the Humean position.

THE THIRD PERSON PRONOUN OF THE NARRATIVE VOICE

> To write . . . is to pass from the first to the third person, so that what happens to me happens to no one, is anonymous insofar as it concerns me, repeats itself in an infinite dispersal. [*SL*, 33]

Is there then no way to represent the short-term self, what Anscombe calls "this self," as not anything more than the emitter of a cry or groan accompanying a gesture, the "eureka!" "There!" or "Here!"? The only shifters apart from "I" or "you" that could designate a subject are the pronouns "he" and "she" used demonstratively, typically with contrastive stress. But "*she* is thinking" is just as uncertain as the unstressed version. In fact, a candidate for such a pronoun can be found in a surprising source—in the "il" of that "narrative voice" whose peculiarity Blanchot so emphasizes. This is the third-person self of what is known in French as *le style indirect libre* and which I call "represented thought." It is illustrated in (7):

(7) But whose foot was he thinking of and in what garden did all this happen?[47]

She was thinking how all those paths and the lawn, thick and knotted with the lives they had lived there, were gone: were rubbed out; were past; were unreal, and now this was real; the boat and the sail with its patch; Macalister with his earring; the noise of the waves—all this was real. [*TL*, 248–49]

[F]or she was thinking, as the boat sailed on, how her father's anger about the points of the compass, James's obstinacy about the compact, and her own anguish, all had slipped, all had passed, all had streamed away. What then came next? Where were they going? [*TL*, 280]

This "Self" of the E is its unique center of subjectivity, a fact captured by the principle "1 E/1 Self," analogous to "1 E/1 Now," both independently required to account for the novelistic language of subjectivity. "1 E/1 Self" assigns each E a unique subjective center that operates as the reference point to which subjective elements like deictics and exclamations are referred for interpretation. It is the syntactically justified category E that provides the domain for the application of the combined "1 E/1 Self and Now." Another principle, "Priority of Speaker," obligatorily interprets the Self as coreferential with any first

47. Woolf, *To The Lighthouse* (Harcourt Brace, 1927), 275; hereafter *TL*.

person present in the E. Hence, the third-person pronoun is interpretable as the designator of the Self only in those written contexts without a first person. In the absence of "I," "(s)he" becomes a shifter, a role it normally plays only when contrastively stressed and used demonstratively. Deixis, in the language of the non-first-person novel, if no longer egocentric, continues to be organized around subjective centers.

The third-person pronoun of represented thought can thus be taken to stand for the minimal subject of the Lichtenbergian "cogito." It is less than a speaker and a person; its momentariness is bound up with its attachment to the E. In the examples of (7), the pronoun is the grammatical subject of the verb "think." It need not appear as the subject of "think," however; it may be the subject of another psychological verb or verb "of consciousness" or even without any such verb, as the examples in (8) illustrate. In "[t]here it was before her—life" (*TL*, 91), for instance, the pronoun "her," the complement of a preposition, refers to the Self, in a position that could not easily receive the contrastive stress Russell gave "I" in "I am thinking." Or the pronoun might appear in a separate E, as with "She could not see" (conjoined sentences are treated as separate Es).

(8) Which was their house? She could not see it. [*TL*, 2]

Turning, she looked across the bay, and there, sure enough, coming regularly across the waves first two quick strokes and then one long steady stroke, was the light of the Lighthouse. [*TL*, 94]

[F]or she was absorbed by what they were saying. So he had actually heard from her this evening! (*TL*, 131–32]

Here he sat drumming his fingers on the table-cloth when he might have been—he took a flashing bird's-eye view of his work. What a waste of time it all was to be sure! [*TL*, 134]

But the language of the novel also shows sentences representing subjectivity with no pronoun referring deictically to the momentary subject, as in (9):

(9) But how extraordinarily his note had changed! [*TL*, 52]
Was everybody dining out, then?[48]
Here was that woman moving—actually going to get up—confound her![49]

48. Woolf, *Mrs. Dalloway* (Harcourt, Brace & World, 1925), 249; hereafter *MrsD*.
49. Woolf, *Jacob's Room* (Harcourt Brace, 1922), 8; hereafter *JR*.

In "So he had actually heard from her this evening!"; "there, sure enough . . . was the light of the Lighthouse"; and "What a waste of time it all was to be sure!" in (8) as well, there is no pronoun referring to the self. Each E represents what Russell calls "a single thought"; the thought need not contain any explicit reference to the thinker. These Es, indeed, resemble Geach's revision of "cogito": "This is really a dreadful muddle!", save for their past tense. The object of demonstrative identification can be a thought, a feeling, or a sensation, as in the first example of (7), where "this" refers to a thought or a memory and in the second, where it refers to a sense-datum. Each of these Es represents, as in Hume, "some particular impression or other, of heat or cold, light or shade, love or hatred, pain or pleasure."

Thus, from the syntactic point of view, subjectivity in the E can be expressed elsewhere than in a third-person pronoun referring to the Self$_i$: in another shifter, such as the adverb "now," in an exclamation, or in a noun or adjective of the sort Milner calls "qualitative."[50] Such is the case with Geach's demonstrative "this"; it marks the sentence as subjective, refers to a particular, and hence is endowed with the certainty that we saw was missing from "cogitatur." These "represented thoughts," like Hume's particular impressions, need not be collected together into bundles—each may remain unintegrated with any other. The question is whether, unlike Hume's, each one must ultimately be attached to a referring expression representing the Self. Apparently unattached thoughts like those in (9) occur in the spoken language, of course, but these are interpretively assigned to the unique speaker, the "I." It is the absence of a speaker that problematizes the assignment of point of view. Es like those in (9) raise the question of who is thinking them because there is no speaking Self to attach them to. It is the detachment of the subject from the "I" that allows the question of the subject to arise. What are the conditions under which the Es in (9) can be interpreted? With their subjective grammatical element such as exclamations, "qualitative adjectives," and deictics, linguistically they ultimately demand to be attached to a noun phrase that refers to a thinker. But within the represented E, that thinker need not be referred to at all, as (9) demonstrates, since subjectivity resides in the subjective elements. Such unattached Es are typically assigned a thinker-subject by appearing in contexts—or rather, in our terminology, in

50. Milner, *De la syntaxe à l'interprétation* (Paris: Seuil), 1978.

Texts—where a parenthetical sentence or a contiguous E contains a noun phrase interpretable as the thinker, as in (10):

(10) He was really, Lily Briscoe thought, in spite of his eyes, but then look at this nose, look at this hands, the most uncharming human being she had ever met. [*TL*, 130]

Why could he never conceal his feelings? Mrs. Ramsay wondered, and she wondered if Augustus Carmichael had noticed. Perhaps he had; perhaps he had not. [*TL*, 145]

She could have wept. It was bad, it was bad, it was infinitely bad! [*TL*, 75]

The thought represented is not contained in the parenthetical or necessarily the contiguous E. Can either be considered to assign the E its point of view?

The assignment of point of view is accomplished by 1 E/1 Self. A sentence without a pronoun Self can represent a point of view. Linguistically speaking, the examples of (9) require the notion of the Self to account for their interpretation. But they do not require an explicit pronoun Self, even in a contiguous E. What they require is a noun phrase coreferential with Self, explicit or implicit, in the represented E.

Indeed, the grammatical status of the term coreferential with the Self permits certain important distinctions. A hierarchy distinguishes deictic pronoun, proper name, and Russellian description on the basis of the epistemological status of the sentences representing subjectivity. *Unspeakable Sentences* identified, on syntactic as well as semantic grounds, two levels at which subjectivity can be represented: reflective vs. nonreflective consciousness. The interpretation of reflective subjectivity is forced by the presence of exclamations, direct questions, or parentheticals. "Which was their house?" and "But how extraordinarily his note has changed!" both require reflective readings. On the other hand, Es containing only deictic and other "embeddable" subjective elements can be read as nonreflective, e.g., "But now his note had changed." (We can see that in none of the cases in (7) is the thought "(s)he was thinking" the object of reflection; it is nonreflective.) These distinctions correspond to the distinctions of referring expressions. Only a pronoun may *refer* to a reflective Self; the proper name as well as the pronoun may refer to a nonreflective Self and corefer with a reflective one; the description may only be coreferential with the Self, as a comparison of 11a, b, c demonstrates:

(11a) They had that—Paul Rayley and Minta Doyle—she, only this—an infinitely long table and plates and knives. [*TL*, 125]

(11b) they had that—Paul Rayley and Minta Doyle—Mrs. Ramsay, only this. [My example]

(11c) They had that—Paul Rayley and Minta Doyle—the children's mother only this. [My example]

The proper names or descriptions replacing the pronouns in the (b) and (c) sentences, respectively, no longer permit them to be read as representations of the point of view of the individuals so designated. In the contiguous E or parenthetical assigning point of view to an E of reflective consciousness, however, the constituent that refers to the Self may be either a pronoun or a proper noun. This "contiguous" E thereby becomes an E of nonreflective consciousness, by the simple presence of a proper noun or pronoun that refers to the Self, which subjectivizes the E, just as an exclamation subjectivizes an E of reflective consciousness. In no case can the Self be referred to by a definite description. The grammar of subjectivity in the novel thus distinguishes between three kinds of referring expressions, the relations among which have preoccupied all the major philosophical theories of reference.

The constraint restricting the noun phrases (NPs) referring to the Self does not rule out the possibility of other sentences in the narrative text containing definite (or indefinite) descriptions coreferential with the pronouns or noun phrases in the represented Es. The possibility of coreferentiality between NPs in different Es is one way that a sequence of Es is unified into a Text. The principle of the Text attaching Es of represented thought to a Self will make a distinction in the grammar between reference and coreference. Reference is determined on the basis of the material within a single E; coreference may also operate from E to E. That ontologically distinct NPs—personal pronouns, proper names (definite and indefinite), descriptions—can nonetheless corefer is perhaps more in need of explanation than is customarily thought. This may happen in a single E, as an identity statement: "I am AB" or "This is a chair" or in "Mrs. Dalloway said she would buy the flowers herself" (*MrsD*, 3) (and not "Clarissa Dalloway said that Clarissa Dalloway would buy the flowers"). We can speculate that the notion of character specific to the novel crucially involves the relation between the pronoun referring to the self, the proper name conceived of in the Kripkean fashion as a rigid designator, and the description. The different types of unspeakable sentences forming the style that I call "narrative fiction" translate one of these notions into another. For, since "[t]he chief importance of knowledge by description is that it enables us to pass beyond the limits of our private experience" (*PP*, 59), then that movement beyond privacy is marked in the language of narrative by replacing the disposible "this" and "(s)he" by an ordinary proper name or a description. This is the progression Virginia Woolf sees going from "his own past . . . a book known only to him" to "the title, James Spalding" to "a man with a red moustache":

> At Mudie's corner in Oxford Street . . . [t]he motor omnibuses were locked. Mr. Spalding going to the city looked at Mr. Charles Budgeon bound for Shepherd's Bush. The proximity of the omnibuses gave the outside passengers an opportunity to stare into each other's faces. Yet few took advantage of it. Each had his own business to think of. Each had his past shut in him like the leaves of a book known to him by heart; and his friends could only read the title, James Spalding, or Charles Budgeon, and the passengers going the opposite way could read nothing at all—save "a man with a red moustache," "a young man in grey smoking a pipe." [*JR*, 65][51]

We can conclude that the pruning of the "cogito" has been accomplished by the language of the novel, precisely that language Blanchot invokes in "The Narrative Voice" by a reference to "'the use of personal pronouns in the novel'" (*IC*, 380). Its "'he' marks the intrusion of the character: the novelist is a person who forgoes saying 'I', but delegates this power to others; the novel is peopled with little 'egos'" (*IC*, 381), where the little egos are not "I's" but "he's" or "she's."

CARTESIAN PRIVACY AS SHIFT OR DIFFERENCE IN POINT OF VIEW

> Where I am alone, I am not there; no one is there, but the impersonal is: the outside, as that which prevents, precedes, and dissolves the possibility of any personal relation. Someone is the faceless third person, the They of which everybody and anybody is part, but who is part of it? Never anyone in particular, never you and I. [*SL*, 31]

The category of referring expressions represented by the true, E-level shifters supplies, then, the grammatical means of formulating a

51. Ian Watt finds what is "[p]hilosophically" the novel's "particularizing approach to character" dependent on "defining the individual person" related "logically . . . to the epistemological status of proper names, whose function "was first fully established in the novel." (*The Rise of the Novel: Studies in Defoe, Richardson and Fielding* [Berkeley: University of California Press, 1965], 18).

"cogito" without the "I" that retains its linguistic subjectivity. The deictic term confers subjectivity on the statement it contains, marking its epistemological status as different from the corresponding statement without one. It is the language of narrative fiction that contributes to the deictics the name to designate the "short-term" Self of the reformulated "cogito." The principles of "1 E/1 Self-Now," independently required to account for the language of narrative fiction, have as their effect that the duration of the referentiality of the shifters "(s)he," where the pronoun refers to the Self, is the E: it is the linguistic domain of the "moment" of subjectivity. Since it is the only principle that mentions the notion of Self, the only domain in which all instances of a third-person pronoun referring to the Self must be coreferential is the E. The result is a kind of monadology of the E, what Blanchot has in mind when he says that the third person of the novel represents a "real . . . reduced to a constellation of individual lives, of *subjectivities,* a multiple and personalized 'he,' an 'ego' manifest under the cloak of a 'he' that is apparent" (*IC,* 381). The revised "cogito" thereby receives a deictic certainty. But it should also be apparent that it is no longer possible to conclude from it "ergo, sum," because there is no guarantee that both instances of the pronoun, even if coreferential, refer to the Self.

In principle, the third-person Self is free to shift from E to E, in striking contrast with the "I," which remains coreferential from E to E. In this sense, what literary criticism calls "shift in point of view" depends on the elimination of the "I." Outside the domain of E, nothing in the principles governing the E-level shifters prevents a new E from having a new referent for the pronoun interpreted as Self. Does this conform with the facts of the pronoun's behavior? At first glance, it is not at all apparent that the "(s)he" shifts with each use, as does "this" or "now." The normal interpretation of (6), with "he" substituted for "I," would treat the pronouns as coreferential, unless they are contrastively stressed. Although contrastive stress is arguably a feature of a shifter, our initial discussion of "I" in "I am thinking" noted the objections to its being stressed. The homonymy between "(s)he" as shifter and the same form as nondeictic pronoun suggests an alternative explanation: some instances of "(s)he" coreferential with the third-person Self are nondeictic pronoun homonyms that corefer to the deictic, treating the latter as their antecedent.

What is the crucial difference between the deictic and nondeictic pronoun? The ability of the third-person pronoun to shift its referent from E to E is, indeed, not restricted to the third-person Self; it is a general feature of the third-person pronoun. Benveniste states that "one characteristic of the person 'I' and 'you' is their specific 'oneness': the 'I' who states, the 'you' to whom 'I' addresses himself are unique each time. But 'he' can be an infinite number of subjects—or none."[52] This is one way of understanding what is meant by saying that the reference of the pronoun, as opposed to the anaphor, can be free, i.e., it does not require a linguistic antecedent. The difference lies with the manner in which the reference, when shifted, is fixed. As one of Milner's nonrigid designators, the reference of the nondeictic pronoun must be fixed by the grammar. Yet it does not have an independent reference, in that it nonetheless requires a lexically specified linguistic antecedent, either in the E or in the Text.[53] The momentary Self of the "cogito" is, by contrast, a nonrigid designator whose reference is fixed by being attached to the E's unique perspective; independent reference is thus defined as "E-independence" or the attachment to E, equivalent to the "subjectivity" of the shifters. It can thus occur in the first E of a sequence of related Es, i.e., a Text, without a lexical noun phrase antecedent, while pronouns cannot, as in these opening sentences of short stories by D. H. Lawrence:

(12) She was his second wife, and so there was between them that truce which is never held between a man and his first woman. ["Her Turn"[54]]

"After all," she said, with a little laugh, "I can't see it was so wonderful of you to hurry home to me, if you are so cross when you do come."

"You would rather I stayed way?" he asked. ["New Eve and Old Adam," *DHL,* 71]

She was too good for him, everybody said. Yet still she did not regret marrying him. ["A Sick Collier," *DHL,* 267]

52. Émile Benveniste, *Problems of General Linguistics,* trans. Mary Elizabeth Meek (Coral Gables, Fla.: University of Miami Press, 1971), 199.

53. The pronouns I mean are those traditionally termed "anaphors." I do not mean the term as in recent Government and Binding theory, to mean reciprocals and reflexives, but with the wider definition it is given in Stephen Neale's "Grammatical Form, Logical Form, and Incomplete Symbols," in *Russell and Analytic Philosophy,* ed. A. D. Irvine and G. A. Wedeking (Toronto: University of Toronto Press, 1993), 114.

54. D. H. Lawrence, *The Complete Stories of D. H. Lawrence,* volume 1 (Harmondsworth: Penguin), 39; hereafter *DHL.*

The requirement that the nondeictic pronoun have an antecedent, though not necessarily in the E, then sets a limit on its shifting. It is this pronoun, and not the deictic, that creates the impression that abrupt shifts from E to E are excluded.

This impression can be dispelled with some linguistic third-person experimentation. Not requiring a lexical noun phrase antecedent, a new third person shifter may in principle be introduced with each shift to a new E. Pragmatic considerations may make such abrupt shifts infrequent, but they are in no way impossible. The following passage from a story, again by Lawrence, illustrates such a shift:

> (13) He drank his tea in silence. They had been married a year. They had married quickly, for love. And during the last three months there had gone on almost continuously that battle between them which so many married people fight, without knowing why. Now it had begun again. He felt the physical sickness rising in him. Somewhere down in his belly the big, feverish pulse began to beat, where was the inflamed place caused by the conflict between them.
>
> She was a beautiful woman of about thirty, fair, luxuriant, with proud shoulders and a face borne up by a fierce, native vitality. Her green eyes had a curiously puzzled contraction just now. She sat leaning on the table against the tea-tray, absorbed. It was as if she battled with herself in him. ["New Eve and Old Adam," *DHL*, 71]

It is grammatically possible to read the first two sentences of the second paragraph, along with the entire first paragraph, from his point of view (note the deictic "just now," indicative of the subjectivity of the sentence) and to read the last two sentences from her point of view. One can construct examples where the shift is even more marked. The following two consecutive sentences represent his and her points of view, respectively:

> (14) Ah, he felt it was all over between her and himself. For her, it was as if she battled with herself in him. [My example]

The more familiar examples of shifts in point of view in narrative fiction "introduce" a new referent for the pronoun Self by means of a lexical noun phrase of some sort, either a proper noun or a Russellian description with which the pronoun may be coreferential. Such examples include those in (10) with a parenthetical whose subject is a proper noun. The NP "a beautiful woman of about thirty," arguably performs such a function in (13). But (14) demonstrates that a shift may occur where there is no such noun phrase.

Such cases, where no such lexical noun phrases intervene to fix the reference, introduce a new factor. Two pronouns differing in gender can only be interpreted as disjoint in reference—i.e., some Matching Condition must require coreferential NPs to agree in number, gender, and person. If all the pronouns in (14) are changed to the same gender, the result is a sequence like (15), which is well formed and even interpretable, perhaps not unambiguously, but which would no doubt be intuitively avoided by a writer wishing not to confuse:

(15) Ah, he felt it was all over between him and himself. For him, it was as if he battled with himself in him. [My example]

The contrast between (14) and (15) permits a surprising hypothesis. The tendency of the novel of point of view to represent otherness through sexual difference has its basis not simply in an extralinguistic reality, but in the fact that once the first person has been eliminated (and the second person along with it), the difference of "I" and "you" or "I" and "(s)he" must be replaced by some other of the remaining features. Number is ruled out, however, since the "privacy" of the Cartesian subject seems to exclude its being a plural pronoun. There remains the difference of gender. How the feature of gender comes to the pronoun from its role as Self is a question that awaits the crucial evidence.

THE NEUTER

> The discretion of the French language, which does not possess a neuter gender, is awkward but finally not without its virtue, for what belongs to the neuter is not a third gender opposed to the other two and constituting for reason a determined class of existents or beings. The neuter is that which cannot be assigned to any genre whatsoever: the non-general, the non-generic as well as the non-particular. . . . The unknown is neutral, a neuter. The unknown is neither object nor subject. [*IC*, 299–300]

> [T]he *il y a*, because neutral, mocks the questions which bear upon it. [*WD*, 65]

But Blanchot's pronoun of the "narrative voice" is not uniquely the third-person pronoun, unspecified as to the feature masculine or feminine. Rather, the "il" "has split in two: on the one hand, there is something to tell, and that is the *objective* reality as it is immediately present to the interested gaze; and on the other, this reality is reduced," as we saw, to "*subjectivities*" (*IC,* 136). This division of the pronoun, I have argued elsewhere, is masked by the English translations of "The Narrative Voice," whose subtitle, "(le 'il,' le neutre)" explicitly gives this pronoun its "neuter" or "impersonal" value.[55] French grammarians use the term "neutre" to refer to the expletive "il" in impersonal constructions such as "il pleut" and "il y a." To translate Blanchot's "il" as "he," as both Lydia Davis and Susan Hanson do, is to mistranslate its impersonal use; "it" is the proper translation of expletive "il."

Hence, the neutrality of "il" for Blanchot in the novel is a function of two possible readings it can have: it can be the subjective center of sentences (Es) representing point of view, a particular literary development of its role as personal pronoun, or it can be the semantically empty "dummy subject" of impersonal constructions, "neuter" in the sense that it neutralizes not so much the gender distinctions but the reference to persons that "il" otherwise has. In the first case, the traditional term "personal" for such pronouns will itself have to be neutralized: the Self is not a person, as we have seen, because it requires no linguistic antecedent; it is E-independent. French "il/elle" has the personal reading when it is coreferential with noun phrases that have a feature +person; English "(s)he" is normally only coreferential with noun phrases referring to persons. What is unique about the novelistic use of the third-person pronoun is that it may refer to Selfs without a lexically fixed noun phrase antecedent. In the second case, the neuter "il" for Blanchot is importantly not a neuter pronoun referring to things. Instead, having no sense or reference itself, it completes the syntax of a sentence whose reference is a proposition representing an event or state of affairs, the "il se passe quelque chose" of what is "uneventful everyday life, what happens when nothing happens, the course of the world as it is unnoticed, the passing of time, routine and monotonous life" (*IC,* 136). It occurs in statements of the kind proposed in various versions of the Lichtenbergian "cogitatur." But its "objective" neutrality, we concluded, is not sufficient for certainty. This was the point of the difference between "there is a triangle" and "here is a triangle!", our translation of Russell's distinction between "il y a" and "voilà." Blanchot makes one "il" stand for a "subjective"

55. See my "*Ecriture,* Narration and the Grammar of French," in *Narrative: From Malory to Motion Pictures*" ed. Jeremy Hawthorn, *Stratford-upon-Avon Studies* (London: Edward Arnold, 1985), 8–9.

reality and the other an "objective" one. Russell's neutrality, we recall, was likewise suspended between subject and object, neither one nor the other. Here lies the justification of our perhaps unexpected linking of these two quite distinct thinkers, "B. Russel," as Blanchot calls him in the one reference I have found that he makes to Russell (*L'entretien infini*,[56] corrected in *The Infinite Conversation*, 397), and Blanchot. In both cases, the project is the Cartesian one revised. It first finds an endpoint to scepticism in a neutral, impersonal subjectivity. But the goal for both remains what Blanchot calls "the outside"—a world in some sense external to the Self. In both cases, the neutral never completely abolishes dualism—it merely reduces the distance between the two. From an impersonal subjectivity an impersonal objectivity becomes a short step outside the confines of Cartesian privacy.

We recall that against our expectations Russell explicitly translated the "there is" of his final revision of "I see a triangle" not as "voilà" but as "il y a." Perhaps that can be explained by the aim to reach an objective knowledge. In Russell, that knowledge would be represented by a language that, paradoxically, translated deictic certainty into a statement that is by definition uncertain: a proposition with truth value, i.e., one that can be affirmed or denied. The translation operates via the analysis of what Russell called a "fact." A fact is different in form from a particular by virtue of its correspondence to the proposition, which does show the duality of true and false. The fact is "complex." For this reason, naming is not adequate to represent it. Wittgenstein's ontology of facts also rejects "the traditional conception of the universe as something that can be referred to by a name," as Max Black puts it.[57] The simplicity of the named object is reflected in the simple symbol that is the logically proper name. Simple naming, where the possibility of falsehood does not arise also, we saw, stands for a kind of knowledge. Its structure shows what Russell calls a "two-term relation," "a dual relation of the mind to a single objective" (*PE*, 157); this is the relation of acquaintance.

The statement that represents Descartes's first step outside absolute certainty is "ergo, sum." We have already seen that it requires a leap via coreference from the deictic reading of the pronoun subject of "cogito" to a pronoun which, if it is not the Text-level "I," requires a linguistic antecedent. Now we note that "sum" or "je suis" posits

56. Blanchot, *L'entretien infini*, (Paris: Gallimard, 1969), 495.
57. Max Black, *A Companion to Wittgenstein's "Tractatus"* (Ithaca, New York: Cornell University Press, 1964), 28.

existence of the referent of the pronoun. If that pronoun is a particular, i.e., an E-level shifter, the statement is nonsense; if it is not, then the statement is no longer certain. Perhaps this is why Thomas's meditations in *Thomas the Obscure* arrive at "'I think, therefore I am not'" (*TO*, 99), as the outside and negation of certainty.

LYNNE HUFFER

Blanchot's Mother[1]

The death of the other restores men to each other.
—Nancy K. Miller, "The Exquisite Cadavers: Women in Eighteenth-Century Fiction"

I have to admit, the first time I read Maurice Blanchot's *The Space of Literature*[2] over a decade ago, there was much that I just didn't get. Strangely, though, the book haunted me—not because I understood it, but because its pages were filled with the yearning of ghosts. Blanchot's story of literary space responded to my own romantic sensibilities; and despite—or perhaps because of—its mysterious, elliptical language, I felt a shudder when I read it. Now, rereading Blanchot for the umpteenth time, I still shudder, but for different reasons. I haven't completely escaped Blanchot's spell, but as my own libidinal yearnings have changed over the course of time, I have learned to demystify the mythical romance that frames his tale of poetic communication.

That demystification began, for me, with the realization that much of Blanchot's haunting power comes from his implicit appeal to nostalgia. Nostalgia, I thought, is inherently conservative: nostalgia wants us to retrieve the past, to return to the good old days when men were men and women knew their place. So if that's the case, I mused, perhaps there's a link between the romantic frame and the nostalgia that drives it. Blanchot's appeal to the myth of Orpheus is certainly romantic, but there's more to it than that. OK, I surmised, it all seems to come back to Blanchot's mother. She's the one he's really writing about.

This essay gives some analytical shape to those musings from my days in graduate school. My purpose here is to explore the nostalgic structure underlying Blanchot's concept of literary space. In so doing, I

1. Adapted in part from Chapter One in *Maternal Pasts, Feminist Futures: Nostalgia, Ethics, and the Question of Difference,* forthcoming from Stanford University Press. Used with the permission of the publishers. Rights in the Stanford version are held by the Board of Trustees of the Leland Stanford Junior University.

2. Maurice Blanchot, *The Space of Literature,* trans. Ann Smock (Lincoln: University of Nebraska Press, 1982).

YFS 93, *The Place of Maurice Blanchot,* ed. Thomas Pepper, © 1998 by Yale University.

ask the following questions: To what extent is Blanchot's nostalgic model necessarily founded in heterosexual desire? Is that model paradigmatic of literary communication, as Blanchot seems to claim? What is the role of the mother in that nostalgic structure? Finally, is Blanchot himself, like Orpheus, engaged in a heroic quest to bring his own work into being? Who, ultimately, is his Eurydice?

ORPHEUS

Indeed, the myth of Orpheus and Eurydice is a good place to start. In *The Space of Literature,* Blanchot retells the story of Orpheus, the tragic poet engaged in a heroic quest for his lost lover, Eurydice. Using the myth of Orpheus and Eurydice to describe the concept of literary space, Blanchot draws on the conventional frame of a heterosexual plot to give his theory of poetic communication the shape and movement of a romantic narrative. Here's a reminder of the story:

Orpheus, a brilliant musician who sings and plays the lyre, becomes listless and silent with inconsolable grief at the death of his wife, Eurydice. Eventually, wandering into the Underworld where Eurydice has come to dwell, Orpheus once again begins to play. Enchanted by his music, the guardians of the Underworld grant him the favor of retrieving Eurydice under one condition: that he lead the way up to the light of day without looking back at his beloved wife. But just as Orpheus approaches the end of his journey, he is overcome with desire for Eurydice and, turning to gaze at her face, loses her forever.

The Orpheus myth is central to Blanchot's concept of literary space. As he states in the epigraph to *The Space of Literature,* every book has a "center" that, like Eurydice, is harder to reach the more closely it is approached. In *The Space of Literature,* Blanchot explicitly tells us that the book's center—the point toward which "the book is headed"—is the section entitled "The Gaze of Orpheus." There Blanchot links the moment of Eurydice's disappearance to the movement of limitless desire that brings a literary work into being. This moment in the Orpheus myth thematizes Blanchot's project in *The Space of Literature:* to describe the operation through which the negativity of loss opens toward a promise of poetic communication. Eurydice's disappearance symbolizes a loss that is recuperated by the compensatory gift of Orpheus's song. "Orpheus's error," Blanchot writes, "seems to lie in the desire which moves him to see and to possess Eurydice, he whose destiny is only to sing of her. He is Orpheus only in the song" (172).

"He is Orpheus only in the song. . . . " Blanchot uses Orpheus to describe the coming into being of the literary work as an infinite movement between terms. Just as Orpheus approaches Eurydice only to lose her, so too artistic communication is the movement of one term in relation to another. Simultaneously, one term appears as the other disappears. The first, disappearing term is the object that inspires the artistic expression, while the second is the artistic representation of that object in the form of an image. Described in the vocabulary of the myth, Eurydice is the object or source of inspiration, and Orpheus's song is the image that represents her. Thus his song comes into being at her expense: the more he is heard, the more absolutely she is lost. In fact, in order for the image to appear, the real object that it names *must* disappear. To state the same process in semiotic terms, Eurydice is the referent that disappears behind the sign—Orpheus-as-song—which comes to name the referent, to give it "form, shape, and reality in the day" (171). Such is the price of representation, the abyssal loss at the heart of writing.

To speak of the abyss at the heart of writing is, admittedly, to engage in a discourse of which many of us have long grown weary. When Foucault wrote, in a 1966 essay on Blanchot, that "we are standing on the edge of an abyss that had long been invisible," he was, in fact, saying something new.[3] That "something new" was the decentering of the subject of thinking and writing, Barthes's "death of the author"[4] or, as Foucault put it in the Blanchot essay, the recognition that "the being of language only appears for itself with the disappearance of the subject" (15). We've heard about this, *ad nauseam*. We've also heard, since the early 1980s, about the feminist response to the celebration of the decentered subject.[5] As feminist critics have noted, theories that de-

3. Michel Foucault, "Maurice Blanchot: The Thought from Outside," trans. Brian Massumi, in *Foucault/Blanchot* (New York: Zone Books, 1987), 15.

4. See Roland Barthes, "The Death of the Author," in *Image/Music/Text*, trans. Stephen Heath (New York: Noonday Press, 1977), 142–48. Also see Foucault, "What Is An Author?" in *Textual Strategies*, ed. Josué Harari (Ithaca: Cornell University Press, 1979), 141–60.

5. For example, see the early debate (1982) between Peggy Kamuf and Nancy K. Miller, and its more recent epistolary sequel (1990) on the question of killing the female author, in Peggy Kamuf, "Replacing Feminist Criticism," *Diacritics* 12 (1982): 42–47; Nancy K. Miller, "The Text's Heroine: A Feminist Critic and Her Fictions," *Diacritics*

center the (masculine) subject paradoxically privilege the feminine by turning her into a seductive figure of absence. To put it simply, they celebrate woman by effectively making her disappear.[6]

Curiously, in that unfolding drama about the gendered articulation of a decentered subject, Blanchot's voice is scarcely heard. And yet, most critics agree that Blanchot's work is crucial to the theoretical developments that have come to be known as "French discourse," a rubric that generally describes thinkers as divergent as Barthes, Foucault, and Derrida. P. Adams Sitney points out that in the late forties, *Yale French Studies* described Blanchot as "the most important critic in France."[7] And Geoffrey Hartman asserts: "When we write the history of criticism for the 1940 to 1980 period, it will be found that Blanchot, together with Sartre, made French 'discourse' possible."[8] Similarly, Timothy Clark professes that Blanchot's 1949 essay on Mallarmé in *La part du feu* is "a kind of crude harbinger of deconstruction."[9] Indeed, Blanchot's influence on twentieth-century French thought can hardly be overstated, and yet, as Sitney makes clear, Blanchot has been relatively neglected by the American intellectual establishment when compared with Barthes, Foucault, or Derrida. It is not so surprising, then, that while certain feminist critiques of "French theory" are by now well known, very little critical work has engaged Blanchot from a feminist theoretical perspective.[10]

12 (1982): 48–53; and Kamuf and Miller, "Parisian Letters: Between Feminism and Deconstruction," in *Conflicts in Feminism,* ed. Marianne Hirsch and Evelyn Fox Keller (New York: Routledge, 1990), 121–33. See also Naomi Schor, "Dreaming Dissymmetry: Barthes, Foucault, and Sexual Difference," in *Men in Feminism,* ed. Alice Jardine and Paul Smith (New York: Methuen, 1987), 98–110.

6. The work of Luce Irigaray remains, in my opinion, the most clear and rigorous articulation of this phenomenon. See especially *Speculum of the Other Woman,* trans. Gillian C. Gill (Ithaca: Cornell University Press, 1985). For an early feminist overview of the celebration of the feminine in French modernity see Alice Jardine, *Gynesis: Configurations of Woman and Modernity* (Ithaca: Cornell University Press, 1985). Also see Linda Nicholson's introduction to *Feminism/Postmodernism* (New York: Routledge, 1990), 1–16.

7. P. Adams Sitney, "Afterword," in Blanchot, *The Gaze of Orpheus and Other Literary Essays,* trans. Lydia Davis, ed. P. Adams Sitney (Barrytown, NY: Station Hill Press, 1981), 166.

8. Geoffrey Hartman, "Preface," in Blanchot, *The Gaze of Orpheus and Other Literary Essays,* xi.

9. Timothy Clark, *Derrida, Heidegger, Blanchot: Sources of Derrida's Notion and Practice of Literature* (Cambridge: Cambridge University Press, 1992), 78.

10. This said, I am extremely indebted to the work that has been done on Blanchot from a feminist perspective. See Ann Smock, "Où est la loi?": Law and Sovereignty in *Aminadab* and *Le très-haut,*" *Sub-stance* 14 (1976): 99–116; Larysa Mykata, "Vanishing

So despite my reluctance to gaze yet again into Blanchot's abyss of writing, that is precisely what I'm doing here—not simply because few have done so through a feminist lens, but also because engaging Blanchot opens up new insights into the history of modern French thought. Indeed, the concepts developed in *The Space of Literature*—as well as in *Faux pas* (1943), *La part du feu* (1949), *Le livre à venir* (1959), and *L'entretien infini* (1969)—are fundamental to the destabilization of discourse and subjectivity that marks much late twentieth-century theoretical discourse. Most crucially, Blanchot links the production of a decentered subject to the production of a literary work. Unlike later theorists influenced by his ideas, and most notably Derrida, Blanchot theorizes the specificity of literary space by distinguishing between poetic and other forms of communication.[11] In so doing, he pushes to the extreme a form of thought that insists on the radical breach between the world of things and the world of representation. In Blanchot's work, this breach is epitomized by the coming to being of the literary work; according to him, in poetic communication the divorce between word and thing is absolute. And with the unmooring of the sign from its referent comes the epistemological crisis of what Lyotard calls our "postmodern condition": a loss of the belief in absolute truth.[12]

This loss of truth, then, is a corollary to the postulation of the decentered subject. Further, the radical skepticism underlying that

---

Point: The Question of the Woman in the Works of Maurice Blanchot," Ph.D. dissertation, State University of New York at Buffalo, 1980, and Jane Gallop, "Friends/Corpses/Turds/Whores: Blanchot on Sade," in *Intersections: A Reading of Sade with Bataille, Blanchot, and Klossowski* (Lincoln: University of Nebraska Press, 1981), 35–66. The work of Mykata, although it focuses on Blanchot's fiction, resonates with my work, as is evidenced by her incisive question, "Even if women cannot be treated as subjects or themes because they represent the void, if they are nonetheless pervasive in Blanchot's fiction and necessary for the elaboration of his theoretical positions, why has no effort been made to relate their negative identity to the fundamental questions?" (8).

11. Of course, Blanchot is not alone in theorizing the specificity of literary discourse. See the work of structuralists, especially Roman Jakobson, "Linguistics and Poetics," in *Style in Language*, ed. Thomas A. Sebeok (Cambridge: MIT Press, 1960), 350–58. See also Roman Ingarden, *The Literary Work of Art: An Investigation on the Borderlines of Ontology, Logic and Theory of Literature*, trans. George Grabowicz (Evanston: Northwestern University Press, 1973); Karl Bühler, *Theory of Language: The Representational Function of Language*, trans. Donald Fraser Goodwin (Philadelphia: J. Benjamins Pub. Co., 1990); and René Wellek and Austin Warren, *Theory of Literature* (New York: Harcourt Brace Jovanovich, 1977).

12. See Jean-François Lyotard, *The Postmodern Condition: A Report on Knowledge*, trans. Geoff Bennington and Brian Massumi (Minneapolis: University of Minnesota Press, 1984).

philosophical stance has also led to a collapsing of the boundaries that distinguish literary from nonliterary discourses, epitomized, again, by the work of Derrida.[13] Given this context, my interest in Blanchot lies in the connection between gender and a distinct literary space. The gendered structure of literary space is also, and at the same time, a nostalgic structure: nostalgia is characterized by the loss of a feminine object of desire. And it is precisely that gendered form of nostalgia that distinguishes literary from nonliterary communication in Blanchot. Blanchot's nostalgia, therefore, constitutes a conceptual map to be traced and eventually reconfigured with feminist theoretical tools. Thus, this essay challenges Blanchot by interrogating the boundaries of sexual difference within which he postulates the breach between sign and referent: the gap that separates Orpheus from Eurydice.

OEDIPUS

While the Orpheus story is indeed essential to Blanchot's description of poetic communication, there is another story at work in *The Space of Literature* as well. This second story both reinforces and complicates the first one, and its structure repeats the movement between appearance and disappearance sketched out in the story of Orpheus. The second myth is the psychoanalytic drama of the son and his mother. In Freud's Oedipal version of the story, the son must move beyond the incestuous desire he feels for his mother by leaving her behind in the world of childhood, thereby entering adulthood and the world of men. Like the Orpheus myth, this story is played out as a heroic quest involving love and irrecuperable loss. Also, like the Orpheus story, the Oedipal story is inscribed in the frame of a romantic plot driven by heterosexual desire. Just as Orpheus must lose Eurydice in order to appear as a tragically poetic hero, so too the son must lose his mother in order to attain a similarly heroic status.

In *The Space of Literature,* the psychoanalytic story of Oedipus appears only implicitly through its structural parallels to the Orpheus

13. See especially Jacques Derrida, "White Mythology," *New Literary History* 6 (1974): 5–74; and "The Law of Genre," *Glyph* 7 (1980): 202–32. Significantly, "The Law of Genre" is built around a reading of Blanchot's *La folie du jour* (Montpellier: Fata Morgana, 1973). For a critique of this slippage in Derrida, see especially Jürgen Habermas, "Excursus on Leveling the Genre Distinction between Philosophy and Literature," in *The Philosophical Discourse of Modernity,* trans. Frederick G. Lawrence (Cambridge: MIT Press, 1987), 185–210.

story.[14] Blanchot never names the Oedipal son, except as "the fascinated child" (33), consumed by his deadly attraction to the maternal face. Unlike the Orpheus story, which Blanchot explicitly locates at the book's center, at first glance the Oedipal story would seem to play a marginal role in Blanchot's theory of literary space. The mother and son appear only once in the main body of the text, in the section entitled "The Essential Solitude," and once again in an appendix entitled "The Two Versions of the Imaginary." Nonetheless, like the story of Orpheus and Eurydice, the romantic narrative of the son and his mother is crucial to Blanchot's concept of poetic communication.

Both the Orpheus and Oedipus myths describe a movement of separation and return that forms the skeletal structure of nostalgia. Moreover, in both myths the point of loss is a feminine object of masculine desire: in the Orpheus story, this object is Eurydice; in the story of the Oedipal son, it is the mother. This parallel points to the gendered articulation of the nostalgic structure underlying Blanchot's model of literary communication. Correspondingly, Blanchot's two stories of nostalgic longing not only explain the specificity of literary communication as a structure of loss; they also, significantly, reveal a collapse of the figure of feminine absence into Eurydice and the mother. This collapse, symbolized by the moment of Orpheus's gaze, forms the center of Blanchot's theory of poetic communication.

ORPHEUS: TAKE TWO

One of the difficulties of Blanchot's use of the Orpheus myth is its deceptively straightforward plot. Superficially, the movement of literary communication would appear, like the Orpheus myth, to follow a simple story line from separation to return, from loss to recuperation. However, a closer look both at the myth and at Blanchot's appropriation of it suggests that the story is more complex than this. Crucial here is the distinction Blanchot makes between everyday and poetic communication. While both everyday and poetic communication involve a moment of loss, only poetic communication becomes a self-perpetuating process where, like a whirling dog chasing its own tail, loss pursues itself. It is precisely this infinite structure of loss that links Blanchot's concept of poetic communication to the problem of

14. For a more explicit engagement with the Oedipus myth, see the third section of "The Most Profound Question" in Blanchot's *The Infinite Conversation* (*L'entretien infini* [1969]), trans. Susan Hanson (Minneapolis: University of Minnesota press, 1993), 17–24.

nostalgia with which I am concerned here. More specifically, the continual movement between infinite loss and the infinite promise of restitution defines both the subjective experience of nostalgia and the rhetorical structure of trope.

In the Orpheus story, as Blanchot retells it, everything begins with Eurydice. As the initial loss that Orpheus must grieve, Eurydice is the origin of Orpheus's song, his source of inspiration. In that sense, Eurydice's death marks both an absence and the birth of desire provoked by that absence. Orpheus is the poetic subject whose task it is to bring absence into light as representation. The figure *par excellence* of the poet's muse, Eurydice thus produces the movement of poetic expression: "For him [Orpheus] Eurydice is the furthest that art can reach. Under a name that hides her and a veil that covers her, she is the profoundly obscure point toward which art and desire, death and night, seem to tend" (171). As an abyssal absence, Eurydice thus simultaneously reveals and hides herself. Coming to the fore through the artifice of appearance ("sous un nom qui la dissimule"[15]), Eurydice shows herself in Orpheus's song. At the same time, retreating into her disappearance behind the curtain that screens her ("sous un voile qui la couvre" [225]), Eurydice vanishes behind the song. Thus Blanchot describes the lost object's self-disclosure in poetic communication: its appearance as disappearance is the paradoxical coming to being of the literary work.

The paradox of Blanchotian writing lies precisely in the imperative to transform absence into its substitute as figure; in order for Orpheus to find Eurydice again he must replace her absence with its figural representation: the sign replaces the referent it names. However, this process of figuration, through which Orpheus would find Eurydice, also guarantees that he will never find her again; he will only see her as she disappears behind the figure that will replace her. Following the constraints imposed by the guardians of the Underworld, Orpheus can only see Eurydice again by not seeing her, by turning away. He cannot face Eurydice in her absence, but rather must give that absence a false face through the gesture of turning away, or of troping her.

At this point in the process Blanchot has simply described the movement of figuration that defines any linguistic act: when we utter a word to describe a thing, we no longer see the thing. Like Orpheus, we turn away from the Eurydice-thing and, in so doing, replace her with a

15. Blanchot, *L'espace littéraire* (Paris: Gallimard, 1955), 225.

linguistic utterance. We know she is still there behind us, so to speak; but the rules of semiotics can't allow us to see her and speak her at the same time. To speak means necessarily to turn the thing into a trope or figure. Thus Eurydice, the referent, becomes an utterance with a meaning (signifier/signified): the sign that is her replacement.

While this gesture of replacement is fundamental to the linguistic act, it is *not* the nostalgic center toward which *The Space of Literature* is headed. Rather, the book's center—"The Gaze of Orpheus"—focuses on the moment of Orpheus's *transgression* of the rules of semiotics described above. Having turned *away* from, and thus troped Eurydice, Orpheus does the one thing he is forbidden to do: he turns *toward* her to face the loss itself ("looking this point in the face" [171]), and, in that *second* turning, loses her forever. So it is not in Eurydice's death, but in Orpheus's attempt both to retrieve *and* see her as figure—in her disappearance a *second time*—that Eurydice is lost forever.

For Blanchot, then, poetic communication is a transgressive linguistic act that involves an extra turn of the tropological screw. In describing Orpheus's extra turn, Blanchot points to what is commonly characterized as the heightened metaphoricity of poetic language, a language that removes itself from the world of things so as to create a suspended world of its own. Paradoxically, what is already a figure becomes even more of a figure; in turning *toward* Eurydice—the poetic thing—Orpheus forces her into a shape that is even further removed from the thing itself than before. Thus, with that moment of *secondary* loss, Blanchot marks the suspended time and space of poetic appearance: the "death sentence" that is also a "suspended sentence" condemning the literary work to the continual but impossible pursuit *of itself* through the figural replacement of absence.[16]

It is precisely this concept of secondary loss that constitutes literature's nostalgic structure. Most crucially, just as the heightened metaphoricity of poetic language requires an extra turn of the trope, so too

16. Derrida, for example, in *Parages* (Paris: Galilée, 1986), describes the Blanchotian "death sentence" as "death *and* survival" (208, translation mine). Similarly, Geoffrey Hartman describes Blanchot's characters as "despairing men [who] are sick unto death yet deprived of the ability to die" (107). See Hartman, "Maurice Blanchot: Philosopher-Novelist," in *Beyond Formalism: Literary Essays 1958–1970* (New Haven: Yale University Press, 1970), 93–110. Blanchot's *Death Sentence* (trans. Lydia Davis [Barrytown, NY: Station Hill Press, 1978]), exemplifies the contradictory imperative of figuration and disappearance that characterizes the literary work: "When someone who has disappeared completely is suddenly there, in front of you, behind a pane of glass, that person becomes the most powerful sort of figure [*une figure souveraine*] " (43).

the specifically *nostalgic* desire that produces literature requires an extra turn. In terms of nostalgia, this second turning produces memory. Without the detour of memory—Orpheus's second turn—a structure of loss cannot be nostalgic. Nostalgia requires memory, just as poetic language requires the troping of trope that is the extra turn.

Thus this secondary movement introduces memory into the nostalgic structure underlying literary communication in Blanchot. Orpheus's second look reveals that the work, chasing its own tail, can only ever retrieve *itself*. Eurydice—the beginning, or origin of the work—is only there as a distant memory, a linguistic construct, a figure. When Orpheus turns toward her, she is already dead, replaced as a trope: "for is there ever a work? Before the most convincing masterpiece, where the brilliance and resolution of the beginning shine, it can also happen that we confront something extinguished: a work suddenly become invisible again, which is no longer there, has never been there. This sudden eclipse is the distant memory of Orpheus's gaze; it is the *nostalgic* return to the uncertainty of the origin" (174, emphasis added).

Orpheus's second look is a nostalgic look toward the work's origin, precisely because that origin is long gone, or rather, was never really there. Paradoxically, in this nostalgic turn toward the origin, Orpheus guarantees that he will fail to see it. He can only ever see it as a memory, a fiction of his own making. Thus Orpheus's memory is an eclipse: a recalling that blinds itself in the very gesture of looking back, a nostalgic return to an inaccessible origin. Eurydice, whose replacement as memory stands in for the origin, was never really there to begin with. For Blanchot, her interest lies only in her death and disappearance. And it is precisely in that guise of absence—as death and disappearance—that Eurydice remains the imperious and forever unattainable source of the literary work.

Thus literature records the memory of Eurydice: in other words, literature remembers that which is merely a product of its own desire, which is to be itself, as literature. Again, Orpheus is Orpheus only in song (172). This point is crucial in Blanchot's construction of literature's self-removal from any contextual reality: according to him, the secondary communication of literary language makes none of the truth-telling claims of mimetic representation.[17] Literature does not

17. Here Blanchot follows the structuralists, and in particular Jakobson, who distinguished between the poetic function and the functions of everyday speech. As Habermas puts it in his critique of Derrida's denial of this distinction: "when language fulfills a poetic function, it does so in virtue of a reflexive relation of the linguistic expression to

contain images that reproduce reality as its figural copy, nor does it mimetically reflect empirical experience—giving life to that which is dead—by recalling it and filling it with poetic form. Blanchot's conception of poetic communication emphasizes the *gap* between the world and literary representation, where poetic language merely gives a false appearance to the disappearance of reality, or death of the object. Consequently, according to Blanchot, poetic language makes no claims to being an accurate or truthful imitation of the world. Rather, in poetic communication language reproduces itself in its own image, in a self-reflective system of mediation. As Blanchot puts it:

> Doesn't language itself become altogether image? We do not mean a language containing images or one that casts reality in figures, but one which is its own image, an image of language. [34, n. 3]

Literature is the space where language becomes an image of itself, where language speaks as an image of words.

Thus, unlike the objective, concept-building discourses of philosophy, history, or the sciences, the literary work constitutes itself in a negative relation to meaning, value, and truth. Its structure is circular: initiated by a loss requiring a replacement, literary fiction-making at the same time *creates* the absence requiring a replacement, that is, its own origin as loss. Orpheus loses Eurydice *because* he turns to face her; at the same time, he *must* turn to face her in order to lose her. Eurydice *is* that loss, and without the secondary turning that causes her to disappear forever, there would be no work to speak her *as* loss. Correspondingly, Orpheus exists only as the song that speaks this loss. As such, he is no more than the dispersed subject of a movement that both produces and requires its own inaccessible origin in loss. And this origin can only exist as the fictional construct, or memory, of an origin.[18] Thus the necessary but illusory source of the literary work was, from the start, a figural replacement: a woman who, in appearing, must disappear.

---

itself. Consequently, reference to an object, informational content, and truth-value—conditions of validity in general—are extrinsic to poetic speech" ("Excursus . . . ," 200).

18. Mary Jacobus's reading of Freud's "Childhood Memories and Screen Memories" in *The Psychopathology of Everyday Life* (1901) is pertinent here. Jacobus demonstrates that with Freud's concept of screen memories "the status of memory is put in question. Instead of being a recovery of the past in the present, it always involves a revision, reinscription, or representation of an ultimately irretrievable past" (118). See Mary Jacobus, "Freud's Mnemonic: Women, Screen Memories, and Feminist Nostalgia," in *Women and Memory*, ed. Margaret A. Lourie, Domna C. Stanton, and Martha Vicinus, special issue of *Michigan Quarterly Review* 26/1 (1987): 117–39.

So for Blanchot, the gaze of Orpheus lays bare the illusion of the origin of the literary work, highlighting literature's self-removal from truth in the very gesture of seeking it. In other words, in both producing and laying bare the illusion of the origin, literature brings itself forth as deception, as fiction, as "untruth." Correspondingly, the nostalgic longing for an origin that drives that process is itself both the product and cause of an illusion whose ground is nothing but itself. In the moment of the gaze back toward Eurydice, Orpheus perceives no real object or figure because all he sees is the reflection of his own looking as movement. What Orpheus perceives, then, is a reality that is rendered poetic because it is *twice* mediated, *twice* deferred, *twice* removed from itself as truth. Further, because it is illusory, this poetic space is also duplicitous: it is both the depth behind every poetic image, and thus a limitless source from which to draw inspiration and, at the same time, nothing but the image itself, a reflection of itself as mere words. The look thus creates its own origin, the fascinating depth of memory. Like an image ricocheting in a hall of mirrors, literature remembers and longs for itself.

Blanchot's concept of literary space could thus be described, in philosophical terms, as the appearance of truth in its veiling; to look at truth in order to face it means, at the same time, to lose the possibility of seeing it. Philosophically, at least since Plato, truth is linked with seeing: the more we see, the closer we get to truth. For Blanchot, however, truth is always the reserve of the visible, the dark edge of the knowable, the thing we can't see. Thus the conditions of possibility of poetic communication and the conditions of possibility of seeing the truth are linked—through the structure of Orpheus's gaze—by the conditions of possibility of vision. To look at the visible—Eurydice-as-figure—means, at the same time, to look at the possibility of visibility itself. And to look at that possibility means to be blinded, for one cannot see oneself looking, except in a mirror, and then one is no longer seeing the looking itself.[19] To look at visibility—the possibility of vision—means, paradoxically, to look at the impossibility of seeing.

19. See Jacques Lacan on the structure of the look and the deception of philosophical contemplation: "That in which the consciousness may turn back upon itself—grasp itself, like Valéry's Young Parque, *as seeing oneself seeing oneself*—represents mere sleight of hand. An avoidance of the function of the gaze is at work here" (Lacan, *The Four Fundamental Concepts of Psychoanalysis*, ed. Jacques-Alain Miller, trans. Alan Sheridan [New York: W. W. Norton and Company, 1981]). Also see Jacqueline Rose, *Sexuality in the Field of Vision* (London: Verso, 1986).

Literature thus exposes the trap of truth: the closer we get to it, the more we lose it, because the only way we can say it is by holding up the reflective screen of language, the mirror in which all we see is ourselves.

Thus literature is the space where speaking is only the image of speaking and where seeing is only the look in the mirror. So when Orpheus tries to bring Eurydice into the light of day, he must do so, in turning away, through the metaphorical operation of not-seeing, that is, through the detour of figuration. And when he transgresses the law in order to turn to face her, he can only see through memory, which is necessarily self-reflective, a mirroring of his own gesture of looking. His song, then, is the look in the mirror, language reflecting itself as image. Thus in the very gesture of looking at Eurydice-as-truth, at the very possibility of his own seeing, Orpheus loses her (that truth, that possibility of seeing) forever. This explains even further why Blanchot emphasizes the gap between literature and truth, the necessity in literature to "belong to the shadow of events, not their reality, to the image, not the object, to what allows words themselves to become images, appearances—not signs, values, the power of truth" (24). For Blanchot, literary language does not signify or carry meaning, does not refer, and does not function within a system of values where it would make claims as truth. In other words, the loss that constitutes literature's nostalgic structure—the loss of Eurydice, the loss of the origin—means not only that literature cannot tell the truth (i.e., fiction as the opposite of veracity), but, most crucially, that literature is literature *because* it lays bare its self-recognition as untruth.

OEDIPUS: TAKE TWO

Literature's self-recognition as untruth brings us back to the realm of self-reflective illusion dramatized by the Orpheus myth. This realm of illusion is also the space where the drama of the mother and son unfolds. Just as the Orpheus story occurs in a shadow-world, so too the equally romantic story of the Oedipal son takes place in a space of self-mirroring images. This space—the space of literature—is what Blanchot calls the milieu of fascination: "where what one sees seizes sight and renders it interminable, where the gaze coagulates into light, where light is the absolute gleam of an eye one doesn't see but which one doesn't cease to see since it is the mirror image of one's own look" (32–33). Fascination names the in-between space of the second look, a self-blinding, self-mirroring turning to see: "the gaze turned back upon itself and closed in a circle" (32).

Most crucially for Blanchot's Oedipus, this fascinating "limitless depth behind the image" (32) is described as the realm of childhood, the maternal place to which the son—like Orpheus to Eurydice—nostalgically returns:

> If our childhood fascinates us, this happens because childhood is the moment of fascination, is itself fascinated. And this golden age seems bathed in a light which is splendid because unrevealed. But it is only that this light is foreign to revelation, has nothing to reveal, is pure reflection, a ray which is still only the gleam of an image. Perhaps the force of the maternal figure receives its intensity from the very force of fascination, and one might say then, that if the mother exerts this fascinating attraction it is because, appearing when the child lives altogether in fascination's gaze, she concentrates in herself all the powers of enchantment. It is because the child is fascinated that the mother is fascinating, and that is also why all the impressions of early childhood have a kind of fixity which comes from fascination. [33]

Here again, as in the Orpheus myth, Blanchot's theory of literary space turns on the fulcrum of the disappearing appearance of a feminine figure, this time in the guise of the mother. In this way Blanchot sets up a parallel between Eurydice and the mother as the figures of loss and illumination that constitute the "elemental deep" (34, n. 3) through which the literary work comes into being. In this context, both Eurydice and the mother are examples of the feminine figuration of the fiction of truth:[20] the far edge of the sayable, "the furthest that art can reach" (171). Like Eurydice, or like truth, the mother appears, but only as dissimulation: "under a name that hides her and a veil that covers her" (171). Once again, literature is literature because it lays bare its "feminine" other, its self-recognition as untruth.

Why should we care about Blanchot's mother in her role as feminine other? Indeed, most readers of Blanchot have focused on Eurydice's role in Blanchot's theory of literary communication. But the link between Eurydice and the mother is crucial; by focusing not only on Eurydice, but also on the mother, we can unmask the *collapse* of the feminine at the heart of nostalgia. It is precisely this collapse that allows us to interrogate the theoretical and political implications of Blanchot's aesthetic theory. In other words, Blanchot's collapse of

20. For a similar formulation, see Derrida, *Spurs: Nietzsche's Styles/Eperons: Les styles de Nietzsche,* trans. Barbara Harlow (Chicago: University of Chicago Press, 1987).

woman into mother allows for an interrogation of the ways in which gender and nostalgia are linked in literary communication.

The unmasking of the link between gender and nostalgia puts into question Blanchot's well-known concept of neutrality. Blanchot uses the term "neutrality" to describe the self-reflective realm of poetic communication that displays its own removal from a world of meanings and relative values. Further, he specifically uses the figure of the mother to mark the "neutral" (33) space of pure reflection in which that poetic communication occurs. However, the mother reveals that there is more to Blanchot's neutrality than meets the eye.

On the one hand, the mother is the "neutral" marker of a space of pure reflection in which poetic production occurs, the absence that constitutes the irreducible ground of figuration as movement. As such, she marks meaninglessness itself, "a bit of non-sense, an X,"[21] the interruption or suspension of signification that constitutes the Blanchotian literary space. To put it in terms used earlier to describe Orpheus and Eurydice: the mother marks literature as the tropological movement that recognizes itself as mere self-reflection and, therefore, is itself pure mediation, or language as a mere mirroring of itself. A deceptive place-holder[22] that signifies nothing but the illusion of mediation as a referential mirror, the mother is the self-reflective realm of fascination that displays its own removal from a semiotic grid of relational values. Thus Blanchot describes the mother in terms of neutrality: "neutral, impersonal presence . . . the immense, faceless Someone" (33) of fascination.

However, that apparently neutral, nonfigural maternal absence is at the same time described by Blanchot as a figure: "Perhaps the force of the *maternal figure* (*la figure maternelle*) receives its intensity from the very force of fascination. . . . [S]he [the mother] concentrates in herself all the powers of enchantment" (33, emphasis added). Thus the mother is both a figure and a nonfigure. On the one hand, she carries the force of meaning within a semiotic system of values constituted, at least in part, through a family structure in which gender functions as the binary opposition between paternal and maternal poles. At the

21. See Andrzej Warminski, *Readings in Interpretation: Hölderlin, Hegel, Heidegger* (Minneapolis: University of Minnesota Press, 1987), xlix.

22. This idea of the "mother" as a "place-holder" assumes a context in which language is understood as pure iterability, and where the word "mother" is the "differential, nonsignifying, syntactical marker put in the place of that which was *not there* in the first place" (Warminski, xxxiv).

same time, she is removed into a ghost-world of nonsignifying relationality. She is both the lost object with a face toward which the child nostalgically longs to return, and the nonhuman loss itself, the irreducible blank that, like Eurydice, was already lost from the start.

In this way, the woman-as-mother of Blanchot's literary space remains, simultaneously, superficial and deep, the disappearing point that is both the acme of light and the vortex of darkness: "light which is also the abyss, a light one sinks into, both terrifying and tantalizing" (33). She is both the marked "thing" that must be there for anything to happen at all, and the neutral "nothing" whose existence is an illusion. As Derrida puts it in a different context: "The mother is the faceless figure of a *figurant*, an extra. She gives rise to all the figures by losing herself in the background of the scene like an anonymous persona. Everything comes back to her, beginning with life; everything addresses and destines itself to her. She survives on the condition of remaining at bottom [*au fond*]."[23] That foundational but empty condition of language as mediation, its inaccessible but necessary ground, is the "anonymous, impersonal being" (Blanchot, 31) who can only appear in her feminine transformation as Eurydice or the mother. She is the paradoxical reminder of both survival and death, the *sur-vie* of surfaces that allows existence and creativity to continue, and the infinite depth of disappearance that swallows life and force behind an inescapable deception of appearances.

The key to understanding this maternal contradiction between figure and nonfigure, signification and non-sense, lies in its implications for Blanchot's central concept of the operation of writing itself. As the space of pure relationality, the mother is the condition of possibility of language, the structure of the between that both allows a tropological system to keep turning and, at the same time, reveals the illusory apparatus undergirding that system. As "the relation the gaze entertains" (33), the maternal image is that formless, indifferent space of suspension, the gap of the interval that underlies the very possibility of figuration. Blanchot's mother—"the fascinating . . . mother . . . of early childhood (*du premier âge*)" (33)—is neither an original space nor an originary time, but rather the continual movement of a relation between terms: the gap of the hyphen, of the *inter-dit*. However, in

23. Derrida, "Otobiographies: The Teaching of Nietzsche and the Politics of the Proper Name," trans. Avital Ronell, in *The Ear of the Other: Otobiography, Transference, Translation*, ed. Christie McDonald (Lincoln: University of Nebraska Press, 1985), 38.

Blanchot, her appearance as a figure vested with meaning marks the inevitable humanization of the movement of loss that is itself the condition of the possibility of writing. As Blanchot puts it: "In this way the image fulfills one of its functions, which is to quiet, *to humanize* the formless nothingness pressed upon us by the indelible residue of being" (255).

Like Eurydice, the mother is the appearance of disappearance itself; as such, she constitutes the fulcrum around which the structures of nostalgia and trope are linked in Blanchot's delimitation of literary space. It is important to remember here that the coupled figures of Eurydice and Orpheus, the mother and the son, are ways of naming the process through which literary communication happens. More precisely, that mythic structure of loss and figuration could most accurately be described as the movement of a relation. In that movement, something withdraws and, in that withdrawal, allows something else to come to the fore. Eurydice withdraws and, in that withdrawal, allows Orpheus to come to the fore. Similarly, the mother withdraws and, in that withdrawal, allows the son to come to the fore. That relation of disappearance and appearance constitutes the movement of figuration. In *The Space of Literature,* the heterosexual couplings of Eurydice-Orpheus and mother-son thus function—in the terms of a binary logic of complementary halves—as the internally divisible but inseparable markers of a nonhuman relational movement. The feminine half of these couplings—Eurydice or the mother—names the void or lack—the loss—at the center of the relation through which these apparently symmetrical opposites are produced.

The workings of the relational structure described above govern the mutually reinforcing structures of trope and nostalgia. In both the workings of trope and the thematics of nostalgia, the unattainable center of those movements of turning and return remains an irrecuperable void or point of loss. The result is a "poetics of pure figure"[24] where language is completely self-reflective and removed from meaning or truth.

However, even Paul de Man would admit that this notion of a purely poetic language completely severed from its referential ground is "properly inconceivable" (de Man, 49). Yet it is precisely such a reference-free notion of language that emerges in Blanchot's theory of liter-

24. See Paul de Man's reading of Rilke's *Sonnets to Orpheus* in "Tropes (Rilke)," *Allegories of Reading: Figural Language in Rousseau, Nietzsche, Rilke, and Proust* (New Haven: Yale University Press, 1979), 48.

ary communication. Blanchot explicitly links the paired stories of Eurydice and the mother to an "elemental deep" (34) that has nothing to do with signs that signify in the world. However, in order to appear, this limitless, formless, feminine, and maternal ground of babble—"the giant murmuring" (27)—must construct its own limits by opening into the form of an image—"language opens and thus becomes image" (27). That image both speaks and makes meaning. The illusion of a poetics of pure figure reveals itself as a rhetoric of value and meaning. Blanchot's space of literature is not in the uncharted void of outer space; it is always and necessarily tied to its referent: a space on a map of the world.

THE POLITICS OF SEXUAL DIFFERENCE

If it is true, then, that a reference-free language is "properly inconceivable" (de Man, 49), there is much that could be said about the politics of Blanchot's aesthetic theory. Despite Blanchot's repeated insistence on the specificity of literary space as removed from a referential system of truthful correspondence between word and thing, meaning must and does occur. One such meaning is the transformation of the void at the center of figuration into the voice of a speaking subject. As we have seen, that void is feminine—Eurydice, the mother—and that voice is masculine—Orpheus, the son. The purportedly neutral workings of figural language rely on an ideologically-charged, value-laden structure of meaning embedded in the politics of sexual difference. These politics, to put it simply, erase the feminine so that the masculine may speak.

So, despite Blanchot's removal of literature from the realm of truth, the workings of language have everything to do with truth and meaning. Moreover, because this meaning occurs in a context of relative value, the truth it tells is never ideologically neutral. Blanchot exposes this valuation in the stories he chooses to tell: the story of Eurydice and the story of the mother. Both of these stories thematize the movements of nostalgia, a nostalgia whose heterosexual, binary structure functions as a model for understanding Blanchot's central concept of figuration. The disappearing appearance of object-into-image that, for Blanchot, characterizes poetic communication *requires* the collapse of woman-into-mother as blank or void at the point of that disappearance. Correspondingly, the speaking that remains takes the form of a presence and a voice that articulates a meaning. That voice describes the contours of literary space. It may speak in the *name* of silence, but it is not silent.[25] The ones in whose name the voice speaks are the ones who are silent: Eurydice, the mother.

In thinking about Blanchot's text as itself a gendered fiction of literary communication, it is imperative, then, to interrogate his concept of neutrality as it relates to the nostalgic structure of trope. Further, such an interrogation not only opens up the question of value and meaning from which Blanchot attempts to remove the concept of literary space, it also points to the necessary but unacknowledged masculinization of the Blanchotian poetic subject. The valorization of that masculine subject has implications for the purportedly decentered subject of a theoretical text—the one by Blanchot—that is generally regarded as a paradigmatic twentieth-century model of literary authority. However decentered, disappearing, and dispersed he might be, Blanchot's "celui qui écrit"—"he who writes" (21)—nonetheless *requires* a structure of sexual difference anchored in meaning, value, and truth in order to exist at all. Thus Eurydice and the mother reveal, through the necessity of their own disappearance, the invisible logic of the subjective masculinization of Orpheus or the son, the "silent" discursive subject who, despite that silence, ends up speaking, signing his name, and thus authorizing a text with the power to communicate in a world of signs.

It is true that Blanchot himself accounts for the way literature ultimately comes to communicate in the world. But for Blanchot, it is precisely the purported neutrality of the structure of the "neutral, directionless gleam (*lueur neutre égarée*)" (32) that makes possible the transformation of hovering suspension into the promise of the com-

25. Characteristically, the biographical blurb for *L'espace littéraire* describes Blanchot as "silent": "Maurice Blanchot, novelist and critic, was born in 1907. His life is entirely devoted to literature and to the silence that is particular to him/it [qui lui est propre]" (translation mine). Along the same lines, French journalist Jean-Marc Parisis gives Blanchot "a perfect score [*noté vingt sur vingt*] for the effectiveness of his self-effacement" (cited in Steven Ungar, *Scandal and Aftereffect: Blanchot and France since 1930* [Minneapolis: University of Minnesota Press, 1995], 5). Of course, many have wondered about specific silences during Blanchot's career as a writer and, in particular, *his* silence regarding the articles he published during the thirties for the collaborationist newspapers *Combat* and *L'insurgé*. As Blanchot himself puts it in regard to Heidegger's notorious refusal to address his ties to the Nazi party during the war: "Allow me after what I have to say next to leave you, as a means to emphasize that Heidegger's irreparable fault lies in his *silence* concerning the Final Solution" (Ungar, 63, my emphasis). See also Mehlman, "Blanchot at *Combat:* Of Literature and Terror," in *Legacies of Anti-Semitism in France* (Minneapolis: University of Minnesota Press, 1983), 6–22.

munication of meaning. Blanchot describes that transformation as the filling up, through reading, of the radical opening of the origin with the life of the world and history: "filled with the world's life and with history's" (205). Thus the in-between space of pure reflection—"that which, in the work, was communication of the work to itself, *the origin blossoming into a beginning*" (205)—becomes anchored in the world of mimetic representation: "in the image of this world of stable things and in imitation of this subsisting reality" (205). In this way the in-between of pure relation is stabilized into the containment of meaning—"the 'empty' movement takes on content" (205)—and, as a result, "becomes the communication of a something [*de quelque chose*]" (205, translation modified).

This is how Blanchot accounts for the fact of reading and interpretation. It is through reading that the literary space disconnected from meaning becomes a movement toward signification, value, and truth. Most important, in that process the poetic subject disappears, swallowed, like Eurydice, into the violent opening of neutrality. And in that neutrality, according to Blanchot, the world settles into its place of endless interpretation, like a package wrapped in an anonymous reading. No longer a subject, the Orphic voice becomes the pure opening of song: "he is Orpheus only in the song" (172).

However, Blanchot's description of a fragmented and dispersed Orphic voice in fact hides its own foundation in the binary and gendered structure of the origin and its loss. That structure is the structure of nostalgia. The lost origin—Eurydice, the mother—is recuperated, as loss, into a form that is not only thoroughly human but, like humanism itself, decidedly masculine as well. Moreover, that trembling neutrality describes a logic that attempts to go beyond dialectical thinking toward the pure neutrality of a poetic economy. Still, the seeming invincibility of the system's purportedly neutral logic is also the mask marking the system's failure. Blanchot's neutral system of literary communication uses a structure of sexual difference in order to describe itself as neutral. In other words, it uses a value-laden discourse to describe the absence of value or truth. The neutral poetics of figure that, for Blanchot, is the outcome of loss, nostalgic longing, and the impossible return is not at all neutral. Released from the irrecuperable void of Eurydice's fall, this Orphic neutrality comes to speak as a voice in which "we," the reader, see "ourselves" reflected.

That "we," to be sure, is a masculine one. Correspondingly, the fall of Eurydice is a feminine condition from which "we," after all, must be delivered. It is precisely the production of the "we"—the "celui qui écrit"—that reveals the binary, gendered logic underlying what appears to be a space of neutrality.

So again, why should we care about Blanchot's mother? Despite the radical opening that, through reading, releases literature from the self-reflective circle in which it is trapped, the gendered structure Blanchot's theory requires produces an equally radical *containment* of meaning. That containment is the homogenization of the feminine as origin, disappearance, and elusive silence. From a feminist perspective, then, the opening of reading is already constrained by an always prior closing of the feminine at the moment of enunciation. The world that fills Blanchot's "neutral" literary space is already dualized, binaristic, gendered. And in that gendered constraint, interpretive possibilities—other possibilities of speaking—are lost, so to speak, from the start.

I'm not sure what it would look like to do things differently, but surely we can start thinking in other, nonnostalgic directions. Let's begin with the assumption that Eurydice and the mother aren't lost at all; they've just been lost to "us" because "we" can't hear them. Let's assume they're present. I imagine they're pissed off. I imagine them resisting, refusing their collapse as well as their effacement. So what would happen if we took them seriously? What would happen—to Blanchot, to literature, to theory—if the feminine opened up, if the feminine became feminist, if Eurydice and the mother began speaking to each other?

DAVID R. ELLISON

Narrative and Music in Kafka and Blanchot: The "Singing" of Josefine

In his review of Blanchot's early "fantastic" narrative entitled *Aminadab,* Sartre found a resemblance between this strange tale and the uncanny fictions of Franz Kafka, but noted in passing that Blanchot himself denied, at that point, having read Kafka.[1] Whether Blanchot was being entirely forthcoming in his denial or merely coy, the resemblances between the mysterious tone of *Aminadab* and a certain Kafkaesque atmosphere are unmistakable. However, it is later in his career, when he had moved away from fantastic or allegorical narratives and begun to write his concentrated, elliptical *récits* that Blanchot, in my view, came much closer to Kafka's essential concerns as writer.[2] As the theoretician of *Le livre à venir, L'espace littéraire,* and *L'entretien infini,* as the scriptor of *Celui qui ne m'accompagnait pas, Au moment voulu,* and *L'attente l'oubli,* Blanchot distanced himself from the imitative atmospherics of the "Kafkaesque" and began to participate in the fundamental *Unheimlichkeit* of the narrative universe created by Kafka.

There is uncanniness in the *récits* of Blanchot, but there are also points of narrative convergence between Blanchot and Kafka that can only be called, themselves, uncanny: it is as if Blanchot, the surveyor of literary forms, had "returned home" in reading Kafka, but this home presents the strangest form of defamiliarizing familiarity, so that the

1. Jean-Paul Sartre, "*Aminadab,* ou du fantastique considéré comme un langage," in *Situations I* (Paris: Gallimard, 1947), 122–42.

2. For an excellent recent analysis of the five texts Blanchot explicitly designated as *récits,* see Brian T. Fitch, *Lire les récits de Maurice Blanchot* (Amsterdam: Rodopi, 1992). In the second chapter of this book, Fitch discusses the distinction Blanchot makes between *roman* and *récit*—a distinction I shall be concerned with later in my essay.

YFS 93, *The Place of Maurice Blanchot,* ed. Thomas Pepper, © 1998 by Yale University.

encounter (*rencontre,* a crucial notion for Blanchot) of the latter-day writer and theoretician with his predecessor has none of the coziness of tranquil domesticity, but rather the expropriating dizziness of a confrontation with what Blanchot, in his "Kafka et l'exigence de l'oeuvre," will call "The Streaming of the Eternal Outside [*le ruissellement du dehors éternel*]."[3]

In the pages that follow, I shall concentrate on the relation between the act of narration and a certain kind of music (or "song") in both Kafka and Blanchot. I shall analyze in some detail the last short story Kafka wrote, "Josefine, die Sängerin oder das Volk der Mäuse" ["Josephine the Singer, or the Mouse Folk"], completed in 1924, the year of the writer's death.[4] It is my contention that this convoluted and, in some ways, self-destructive tale marks the culmination of an idiosyncratic narrative form that Kafka had been developing in the later years of his life, and that Blanchot was able to mine the considerable theoretical possibilities thereof better than any other contemporary writer. My analysis will unfold in three distinct stages. First, I shall concentrate on the initial paragraph of "Josefine" in a *micro-lecture,* then move on to examine several of the interpretive problems raised in later sections of the text; second, I shall turn to some of the crucial theoretical distinctions made by Blanchot in his discussions of narrative fiction as they relate to Kafka (it is here that the points of encounter between the two writers reach the level of properly uncanny similarity); and finally, I shall discuss quite briefly the enigmatic conclusion of "Josefine," in which the constitution of community is linked in a fundamental way to the effacement of the protagonist, to her disappearance in death. In the end, I shall suggest that Kafka's late

3. Maurice Blanchot, "Kafka et l'exigence de l'oeuvre," originally published in 1958 and included in *De Kafka à Kafka* (Paris: Gallimard "Idées," 1981), 94–131. Michel Foucault makes reference to the "ruissellement du dehors éternel" in his important essay "La penseé du dehors," *Critique* 229 (1966): 514–42. For an English translation of this essay in conjunction with a translation of Blanchot's *Michel Foucault tel que je l'imagine,* see *Foucault/Blanchot,* trans. Jeffrey Mehlman and Brian Massumi (New York: Zone Books, 1990).

4. Franz Kafka, "Josefine, die Sängerin oder das Volk der Mäuse," in *Gesammelte Werke,* ed. Max Brod (Frankfurt am Main: Fischer Taschenbuch Verlag, 1976), vol. 4, 200–16. All quotations from the original German text of "Josefine" are from this edition. For translations of the text into English, I refer to the version of Willa and Edwin Muir as published in: *Franz Kafka: The Complete Stories,* ed. Nahum N. Glatzer (New York: Schocken Books, 1971), 360–76. When page numbers stand alone, they refer to the German edition.

story is founded on the notion of forgetfulness (*oubli*) as theorized and fictionalized by Blanchot.

I. "JOSEFINE, DIE SÄNGERIN ODER DAS VOLK DER MÄUSE": THE TEXT AS NARRATIVE UNWEAVING

Perhaps the best way to encounter a text as rich and as narratively unusual as "Josefine" is to plunge *in medias res.* Following is the story's first paragraph, which contains, in a highly concentrated declarative (assertive) exposition, the essential elements of the narrative's eventual undoing:

> Unsere Sängerin heißt Josefine. Wer sie nicht gehört hat, kennt nicht die Macht des Gesanges. Es gibt niemanden, den ihr Gesang nicht fortreißt, was um so höher zu bewerten ist, als unser Geschlecht im ganzen Musik nicht liebt. Stiller Frieden ist uns die liebste Musik; unser Leben ist schwer, wir können uns, auch wenn wir einmal alle Tagessorgen abzuschütteln versucht haben, nicht mehr zu solchen, unserem sonstigen Leben so fernen Dingen erheben, wie es die Musik ist. Doch beklagen wir es nicht sehr; nicht einmal so weit kommen wir; eine gewisse praktische Schlauheit, die wir freilich auch äußerst dringend brauchen, halten wir für unsern größten Vorzug, und mit dem Lächeln dieser Schlauheit pflegen wir uns über alles hinwegzutrösten, auch wenn wir einmal—was aber nicht geschieht—das Verlangen nach dem Glück haben sollten, das von der Musik vielleicht ausgeht. Nur Josefine macht eine Ausnahme; sie liebt die Musik und weiß sie auch zu vermitteln; sie ist die einzige, mit ihrem Hingang wird die Musik—wer weiß wie lange—aus unserem Leben verschwinden. [200–201]

> Our singer is called Josephine. Anyone who has not heard her does not know the power of song. There is no one but is carried away by her singing, a tribute all the greater as we are not in general a music-loving race. Tranquil peace is the music we love best; our life is hard, we are no longer able, even on occasions when we have tried to shake off the cares of daily life, to rise to anything so high and remote from our usual routine as music. But we do not much lament that; we do not get even so far; a certain practical cunning, which admittedly we stand greatly in need of, we hold to be our greatest distinction, and with a smile born of such cunning we are wont to console ourselves for all shortcomings, even supposing—only it does not happen—that we were to yearn once in a way for the kind of bliss which music may provide. Josephine is the sole exception; she has a love for music and knows too how to transmit

it; she is the only one; when she dies, music—who knows for how long—will vanish from our lives. [360]

The first paragraph of the story establishes the *dramatis personae:* there is one character called Josefine who stands out from the rest of her "race" ("Geschlect") as being talented in music, as being a singer, whereas the remainder of the group (we later learn they are "mouse folk"), being possessed only of a "practical cunning," seem unable to "raise themselves" ("sich erheben") to the lofty heights of the musical as such. Kafka begins his narrative in the most classical way, with a dramatic opposition between the mass of the people, devoted to the practical concerns of everyday life, and Josefine, servant of the sublime (the substantive *das Erhabene,* the sublime, being derived from the verb Kafka uses here, *sich erheben*). The paragraph points to the eventuality of a tension between Josefine and the mouse folk: they are so different in their fundamental *Auffassungen* or *Weltanschauungen* that the reader might easily imagine a conflict arising as the narrative develops, the kind of conflict that nourishes, or even makes possible the differential movement of narrative itself. When we find out, in the latter stages of the tale, that Josefine is somewhat of a prima donna, critical of her audience's ignorance and capricious in the demands she places on the material conditions of her performances, it would seem that the dramatic potential of the first paragraph has been realized.

At the same time, however, in order for there to be the highest level of conflict, drama, pathos, there must be oppositional pressure exerted from both sides. Now it may be true that, late in the story, Josefine and her retinue attempt to gain special favors from the mouse folk as a whole (thereby proclaiming Josefine's difference from the multitude); but their efforts are met, not by polemic or contention, but by calm indifference—an indifference that emerges subtly in the first paragraph, where the narrator makes clear that the mouse folk's inability to "raise itself" to the level of music is no matter of great concern. The narrator, who speaks *for* the mouse folk (and this speaking-for is no innocent rhetorical gesture),[5] asserts not only that "stiller Frieden ist

5. Most early critical readings of "Josefine" tended to emphasize the oppositional relationship between the heroine of the story and the mouse folk, while leaving in the dark the complex rhetorical position of the narrator. In recent years, this has changed. Thomas Vitzthum finds that "the narrator consciously and skillfully [uses] language to establish his art, or his artful irony, in opposition to Josefine's naïve singing" ("A Revolution in Writing: The Overthrow of Epic Storytelling by Written Narrative in Kafka's *Josefine, die Sängerin,*" *Symposium* 47/4 [Winter 1993]: 275).

uns die liebste Musik"—i.e., that silence, rather than music in the usual sense, is most appealing to the mouse folk, but that, after all, it is not certain, not proved, that music leads to happiness. The conditional mode of the narrator's statement is worth noting, and is typical of the modality of the story as a whole: "auch wenn wir einmal—was aber *nicht geschieht*—das Verlangen nach dem Glück *haben sollten*, das von der Musik *vielleicht* ausgeht" ("even supposing—only *it does not happen*—that we *were* to yearn once in a way for the kind of bliss which music *may* provide"—my emphasis).

From the very beginning of the story there is a fundamental narrative skepticism about music—about its "essence"—as well as an interesting indifference to the efforts of Josefine, which tends to complicate the assertive tone of the remainder of the paragraph. On the one hand, Josefine is presented as an exception, as a singer among non-singers, as someone who not only communicates with a beyond, a transcendental *jenseits* or *au-delà*, but who is also capable of communicating it (in the transitive sense) to the mouse folk: "Nur Josefine macht eine Ausnahme; sie liebt die Musik und weiß sie auch zu vermitteln; sie ist die einzige" ("Josephine is the sole exception; she has a love for music and knows too how to transmit it; she is the only one"). Thus it would appear that Josefine might mediate between the un-

---

Both Deborah Harter and Christine Lubkoll emphasize the crucial creative role of the narrator as "historian" of his people. Harter asserts that the narrator is self-consciously concerned with his own craft as storyteller and that it is he who controls the destiny of the protagonist: "Josefine may represent for him [the narrator] that part of his imaginative act which seeks to objectify its own meaning, to explore its own relationship (or non-relationship) to art. In a movement which makes her the very embodiment of his writerly act, the narrator brings her forth, examines her character, prepares her disappearance" ("The Artist on Trial: Kafka and Josefine, 'die Sängerin'," *Deutsche Vierteljahrsschrift für Literaturwissenschaft und Geistesgeschichte* 61/1 [March 1987]: 156). According to Lubkoll, the male narrator attempts to "domesticate" the musicality of Josefine and to discredit her talents through descriptions of her "hysterical" mannerisms ("'Dies ist kein Pfeifen': Musik und Negation in Franz Kafkas Erzählung *Josefine, die Sängerin oder Das Volk der Mäuse*," *Deutsche Vierteljahrsschrift für Literaturwissenschaft und Geistesgeschichte* 66/4 [December 1992]: 754).

Lubkoll begins the first section of her argument with an interesting comment on the relation of femininity to musicality—a comment that will have some bearing on the Blanchot essay entitled "Le chant des sirènes" that I analyze later in this essay: "That the musical passes for the domain of the feminine is, of course, no discovery of Kafka's. Already Homer makes clear that the Sirens sing in order to lure male protagonists away from their set course—or dis-course. The fact that Odysseus resists allows, so to speak, for the founding of Western history: he translates the female song into a male text" (751; my translation).

musical folk and "the power of song," that she might play a properly pedagogical role in her society. On the other hand, however, it is not clear from the first paragraph whether the mouse folk has enough interest in music or in the performance activities of Josefine to accept or receive this potentially mediated song. "Josefine" seems, at first glance, to be a fine parable of *Rezeptionsästhetik;* but the question is whether the artistic performance has any effect on its audience whatsoever.

The two key words of the paragraph may well be the first and the last: "*unsere*" ("our" as in "our singer, Josefine"), and "*verschwinden*" ("to disappear"—a verb that seems, in the first paragraph, to be a euphemistic replacement for the starker "to die" or "*sterben*," but that has a prophetic ring to it, in that Josefine, at the end of the tale, does indeed disappear, mysteriously and without a trace). Both words—"our" and "disappear"—help to define the ultimate effect Josefine has on her community in the narrator's telling of the tale. The use of the first-person plural possessive adjective is unusual for Kafka: of the other longer stories, only the second version of "Die Abweisung" ("The Refusal") begins with the word "unser" or "our," with all other stories being fairly evenly divided between a first- or third-person singular narrating voice. Although the use of the possessive form can allow for intimacy and complicity in narratives that emphasize the emblematic heroism of one member of a group, in the case of "Josefine" the possessive emerges progressively as a form of envelopment or containment whereby the protagonist's difference is gradually effaced and eradicated.[6] In the end, although Josefine has manifested her desire to be appreciated in her uniqueness, in the quality of her musicality, she is fated (by the leveling-effect, the driving *in*-difference of the narrative movement) to disappear, to vanish, along with her music—i.e., not to die a tragic or pathetic or perhaps "operatic" death.

6. Although "Josefine" is not as much commented upon as many of Kafka's earlier works, this story has been the object of considerable critical interest in recent years. In my view the best close reading of the text is that of Margot Norris, "Kafka's 'Josefine': The Animal as the Negative Site of Narration," in *Beasts of the Modern Imagination: Darwin, Nietzsche, Kafka, Ernst, and Lawrence* (Baltimore: The Johns Hopkins University Press, 1990), 118–33. Norris's analysis is an excellent demonstration of the way in which the narrative movement of "Josefine" cancels itself out through the kind of erasing of differences to which I am now alluding in my own argument. Put succinctly: "Narrative depends on the ability to sustain differences, and as Josefine's experience illustrates, it is impossible to maintain difference among the mice folk. The narrator, like Josefine, fails, and instead of being told, Josefine's story becomes negatively inscribed in this failure of the narration" (120).

She becomes subsumed within the streaming multitudes of her ceaselessly proliferating people (with apologies to Blanchot: *le ruissellement du peuple éternel*), enveloped in a general forgetfulness.

At the conclusion of the first paragraph, the reader is left with two related questions: 1. What *is* music according to this story? What is its significance, its content, its "inner essence?" 2. How will the narrator develop Josefine's relation to the mouse folk in the remainder of the story? What kind of narrative progression will characterize this tale? The first paragraph only alludes to "die Macht des Gesanges"—that is, the powerful effect of song rather than the essence of song; and the question of Josefine's mediating influence on the mouse folk is merely raised without being answered. At the very least, the text must stage some of Josefine's performances (it does, it will), and it is in the encounter (*Begegnung, rencontre*) of these performances, where protagonist and folk are united in a community, that the nodal-points of the narrative are to be found.

The section of the story immediately following the first paragraph is devoted to the narrator's musings on the significance of music. But these reflections never focus on the musical as exterior object of disinterested contemplation: rather, from the very beginning of the narrative, it is clear that the phenomenon of music or musicality can only be understood in relation to the mouse folk and its interactions with Josefine. The first sentence of the second paragraph is crucial in this regard, as is its problematic translation by Willa and Edwin Muir (the reader will note in passing that, as of the second paragraph, the narrator begins to alternate between the first-person singular and first-person plural forms, the former being used to express private thoughts which may or may not correspond with the received opinions of the mouse folk as a community):[7] "Ich habe oft darüber nachgedacht, wie es sich mit dieser Musik eigentlich verhält" (201). The Muir translation reads: "I have often thought about what this music of hers really means" (360). The translators not only have added the phrase "of hers" to the original text, but they have made the Kafkan idiom more precise than

7. On the alternation of pronoun forms, see Thomas Vitzthum: "Though the narrator identifies himself as one of the mouse-folk, he often seems much too outspoken, knowledgeable, and curious to be counted among their ranks. In fact, his confusing use of pronouns shows him to be sometimes one of them, sometimes not. . . . Whereas in most cases the narrator does use 'wir' or 'unser' to describe his relation to the mouse-folk, he often seems to stand outside of or above the mouse-folk's tradition. He is the subverter of both the tradition and Josefine in that the very act of his writing undermines Josefine's position as Singer" ("A Revolution in Writing," 271–72).

the author intended it to be in this context. They have rendered the narrator's cautious and, it must be said, rather vague and inelegant phrase "wie *es sich* mit dieser Musik *verhält*" (which means something like "how things stand with this music," or "what is the case with this music") by "what this music of hers *really means*." What the Muirs have done is a very interesting exercise in what might be called translator's (or reader's) wish-fulfillment: they, like all readers of "Josefine," would like to know what the text is going to propose as the meaning of music; they wish to penetrate the essence of music, its interiority, and their wish is so strong that they mistranslate the Kafkan story, inserting the verb "to mean" where it does not exist, where it is notably absent. The narrator's verb phrase "wie es sich . . . verhält" is, of course, connected to the word for relationship: "das Verhältnis"—and the issue of the story (issue in the sense of topic as well as the sense of ending or final point), from beginning to end, is the relation of the mouse folk to Josefine, who, in some sense, represents or incorporates the mysterious phenomenon of music.

As the story progresses, not only is the interiority of music increasingly inaccessible to what one might call "mouse consciousness," but the question arises whether Josefine is actually singing, or whether she is merely piping—piping ("das Pfeifen") being, in the narrator's pseudophilosophical vocabulary, "die eigentliche Kunstfertigkeit unseres Volkes, oder vielmehr gar keine Fertigkeit, sondern eine charakteristische Lebensäußerung" (201) ("the real artistic accomplishment of our people, or rather no mere accomplishment but a characteristic expression of our life" [361]). The narrative proceeds in a cascade of descending logical hesitations that can be resumed as follows: Josefine is the singer of the unmusical mouse folk (200); but does she sing or does she pipe? (201–202); does her song enrapture her audience, or is it the silence that surrounds that song? (203); why does the mouse folk attend her performances in the first place when it is clear that this community is not only unmusical, but, in fact, incapable of unconditional devotion ("bedingungslose Ergebenheit kennt unser Volk kaum" [205])?

The first section of the text leads from a highly skeptical discussion of Josefine's supposed musicality (in German this would be "*angebliche* Musikalität") to an interesting development on the (quasi-Heideggerian) theme of *care* ("die Sorge"). As the text moves forward, it becomes evident that the nature of Josefine's vocal production (whether it be artistic singing or everyday piping) will not be solved, which leaves the philosophical question of the relation of art to life open, undecidable. At the same time, however, the very fact of Josefine's performances (i.e., the fact that they take place at all) gains increasing weight in the story. At the midpoint of the tale, the narrator reaches what might be considered an extreme point of skepticism when he asserts: "Es ist nicht so sehr eine Gesangsvorführung als vielmehr eine Volksversammlung" (207) ("It is not so much a performance of songs as an assembly of the people" [367]). But this is perhaps the essential turn or defining twist of the narrative line, in which the text reveals to the reader what had been present, *sotto voce,* from the beginning: namely, that the content of the performance (and the meaning of the song) are unimportant in their potential emptiness, but that the existence of the performance, its social reality, is the one fact that counts. It is at this point of the narrative that the title of the story—"Josefine, die Sängerin oder das Volk der Mäuse"[8]—becomes fully understandable. The story is about the mouse-people as much as it is about Josefine; it is constructed on their mutual devotion (at the exact middle of the tale there is a comical sequence of paragraphs in which the narrator describes how the folk is convinced that it must care for its beloved but demanding and not always pleasant Josefine, whereas she is just as certain that her job is to protect her people from the dangers of the outside world through the uplifting power of her song [205–207]).

The second half of the text can be characterized as Josefine's gradual disappearing act. In a first section, the protagonist vanishes from the scene as the narrator describes in some detail the difficult existence of the prolific mouse folk and its curious "prematurely old" but also "ineradicably young" outlook (209).[9] In a second part, we learn of the

8. It is only shortly before his death that Kafka added the second half of the title to his story. In his *Franz Kafka: Eine Biographie* (New York: Schocken Books, 1946), Max Brod reports Kafka's explanation of this addition in the following terms: "Solche Oder-Titel sind zwar nicht sehr hübsch, aber hier hat es vielleicht besonderen Sinn. Es hat etwas von einer Waage." ("Such 'or-titles' are certainly not very pretty, but in this case there may be a special meaning. There is something of a balance [or scales, as in scales of justice] here" [quoted in Christine Lubkoll, " 'Dies ist kein Pfeifen,' " 756]). There is an interesting development on the juridical connotations of the image of the scales in Christine Lubkoll's article.

9. Until now I have concentrated on narrative issues raised by "Josefine," and have (purposefully) not suggested who the protagonist and the mouse folk might "symbolize." As is easily imaginable in the case of the vast corpus of Kafka criticism, a number of critics have proposed that the relation between Josefine and the mouse folk "in fact" stands for something else. The search for this something else is no doubt inevitable in all literature, but especially inevitable in the texts of Kafka, who is more adept than most

various excuses for not performing and demands for special treatment Josefine makes on the mouse folk (including her proposal not to work, in order to devote herself entirely to her art), all of which are qualified as illogical or dismissed out of hand since Josefine, after all, is no different from other mice in her questionable "singing," which may be nothing more than everyday piping (211–15). And finally, in four short paragraphs the narrator discusses her disappearance (215–16)—a section to which I shall return.

Viewed as a structural whole, "Josefine" is the story of the disappearance of music and the unweaving of narrative. Put more precisely, one should say that the primary narrative, at its most literal thematic level, dismantles the protagonist's pretentions to musicality as sublime artistic activity, and in this gradual dismantling, focuses increasingly on the power of the mouse folk to contain or even eradicate Josefine's defiant individuality. The envelopment or swallowing-up of music in the primary narrative produces a secondary, metanarrative that is about the unweaving of narrative as such. The text becomes self-reflexive in that it tells the story of its own undoing, of its own impossible construction. In "Josefine" Kafka has gone far beyond the pathos and high melodrama of earlier stories such as "Das Urteil" ("The Judgment," written in 1912) and "Die Verwandlung" ("The Metamorphosis," 1913), both of which develop along a steady narrative line from an initial, clearly-defined existential situation to a tragic conclusion. In negating pathos and *peripeteia* as such in his later fiction, in replacing the bourgeois family milieu with the strangeness of an animal kingdom, Kafka seems to be espousing what might be called a pure hypothetical narration, which is, in a sense, an antinarration, or

---

writers at creating an open, indeterminate symbolism—a textuality that allows for many, if not innumerable, interpretive grids.

Given Kafka's well-documented interest in Judaism, Zionism, and the Hebrew language during the last six years or so of his life, Robert Alter's proposal to equate the mouse folk with the Jewish people in its historical reality is no doubt one of the more convincing symbolic options: "The mouse folk, leading as it does a constantly precarious existence, often in need of consolation, collectively childish yet prematurely old, haunted by a tradition of singing ("in the old days our people did sing") though fallen into an era of unmusicality, presents a whole series of correspondences to the Jewish people in its Diaspora history. Because of the analogy intimated between the real singing of the old days and the grandeur of biblical Israel, the narrator's exposure of the true nature of Josephine's singing is not just a questioning of the possibility of sublime art but also a critique of the idea of transcendent language (Benjamin's or the Kabbalah's notion of Hebrew)" (Robert Alter, *Necessary Angels: Tradition and Modernity in Kafka, Benjamin, and Scholem* [Cambridge: Harvard University Press, 1991], 54).

nonnarration. And while there is a stylistic evolution away from narrative progression in the classical sense (a progression dependent upon the differentiation of the protagonist from his/her milieu), there is also a shift from the emphasis on an individual's struggles with a family group toward a delineation of the relations that compose a community.

At this juncture, I would like to leave the fictional universe of "Josefine" for a while and turn to some of Blanchot's theoretical writings on narrative—which deal in various ways both with the possibility of a pure narrative and with the relation of the aesthetics of storytelling to the ethical issues involved in the inclusiveness of community. The use of the possessive adjective "our" is not innocent; it may be violent; it is a speaking-*for* on the part of a narrator representing his folk that is also a robbery of the individual's voice, and one wonders if it is on the basis of that silencing of musicality that the community erects itself, or whether the voiding of "music" and the vanishing of the individual into the indifferentiation of the mass (the folk, the "race") is merely, allegorically stated, the quite natural and ultimately peaceful fate of the artist (who, of course, may be no artist at all) as she returns "home."

II. MUSIC AND NARRATIVE IN BLANCHOT

I have suggested, in the first part of this essay, that the meaning of music or musicality remains a difficult-to-encounter blind spot in "Josefine," and that the question of music as such emerges only in conjunction with, only in relation to, the narrator and the mouse folk who act as the protagonist's audience. In Kafka's story, the content of music is beyond the reader's apprehension, while the enactment of music is a constant *factum* in the lives of the mouse community. The various musical performances of Josefine punctuate the narrative rhythm of the story; the bringing-together of the mouse folk around the heroine's singing constitutes the narrative *as* movement. Thus, any interpretations of "Josefine" must take into account the interactions and intersections of musicality with narrativity as fundamental, foundational themes.

Maurice Blanchot, whose interest in Kafka's storytelling has been constant throughout his long career,[10] has written two essays that have a direct bearing on the constellation of interpretive problems I have

10. Proof of this abiding interest can be found in the volume *De Kafka à Kafka* (Paris: Gallimard, 1981), which contains eleven essays by Blanchot on Kafka spanning a period of twenty-five years.

raised up to this point. The first of these, "Le chant des sirènes,"[11] is uncannily close to the universe of "Josefine" in that it stages the act of singing as performance within an exposition on the problematic of narrativity per se. The second, entitled "La voix narrative, le 'il,' le neutre,"[12] treats the question of narrative voice in a way that prolongs the insights of "Le chant des sirènes" and leads to the explicit thematization of the possibility of a "pure" narrative—a notion that Blanchot develops theoretically through a discussion of Flaubert and Kafka and that subtends his own experimental *récits* in their spectral abstraction. I shall discuss both of these short essays in themselves before determining the ways in which they apply to Kafka's aesthetics in general and to "Josefine" in particular.

a. "Le chant des sirènes"

Thc point of dcparturc for Blanchot's theoretical meditation is the episode in *The Odyssey* in which Ulysses encounters the song of the Sirens, or rather, does not encounter it, since, making use of his habitual wiles, he stops his ears with wax and, by not hearing the enchanting singing, manages to survive the episode and move onward in his navigation. Blanchot is interested in the double-edged quality of this event/nonevent, this moment of high dramatic intensity in which a difficult encounter both does and does not take place. He sees in Ulysses's victory over the Sirens the inevitable result of the hero's obstinence and prudence, qualities that allowed him to "take pleasure in the spectacle of the Sirens, without risk and without accepting the consequences, this cowardly, mediocre and calm pleasure, measured, as it befits a Greek of the decadent period who never deserved to be the hero of *The Iliad*"—(11).[13] But this "victory" is only apparent, according to Blanchot, in that the encounter with the Sirens is an *attirance,* a magnetic attraction, that causes Ulysses to fall into narrative:

> Although the Sirens were defeated by the power of technique, which will always try to play without danger with unreal (inspired) forces, Ulysses did not escape so easily. They [the Sirens] lured him to a place into which he did not want to fall and, hidden at the center of *The Odyssey* now become their tomb, they enlisted him and many others in

11. Maurice Blanchot, "Le chant des sirènes," in *Le Livre à venir* (Paris: Folio "Essais," 1959), 9–18.
12. Blanchot, "La voix narrative, le 'il,' le neutre," in *De Kafka à Kafka,* 171–84.
13. This and all further translations into English of Blanchot's texts are my own.

> this happy and unhappy navigation, which is that of narrative [*le récit*], a song no longer immediate, but told, and rendered in the telling only apparently harmless, ode become episode. [11–12]

Thus Blanchot interprets the moment of the encounter between Ulysses and the Sirens as an allegory of narrative in which the protagonist's adventurous triumph (he manages to move beyond the Sirens, and this moving-beyond is the very forward rhythm that defines this epic in its essence as a successful return, through and beyond all perils, to the comforts of domesticity) is overturned in the very instant of the encounter: without knowing it, Ulysses, like so many others, has fallen into the narrative maelstrom. The song of the Sirens may not have been heard, but it becomes told ("ode" becomes "episode"), and the loss of immediacy that accompanies the transformation or translation of song into narrative in no way destroys the power or authority of the *récit* as it develops from within this central *point de rencontre.*

At the heart of Blanchot's essay is one crucial theoretical distinction—between *roman* (novel) and *récit* (narrative)—a clear polar opposition that organizes his argument and that helps the reader to understand what is at stake in Blanchot's own narrative fictions. Blanchot does not deny the importance of Ulysses's ongoing adventures, nor does his emphasis on the absolute quality of the moment of encounter with the Sirens negate the power of the events that lead up to and beyond that moment: rather, he chooses to distinguish between the flow of narrative events as a whole, which he calls *roman,* and the instantaneous explosive episode, which he designates as *récit.* Following are the definitions in Blanchot's words:

> With the novel [*roman*], it is the preliminary navigation that appears on center stage, that brings Ulysses up to the point of the encounter. This navigation is an entirely human story, it concerns human time, is linked to human passions, really takes place and is rich and varied enough to absorb all the power and all the attention of the narrator. [12]
>
> Narrative [*le récit*] begins where the novel does not go and yet leads through its refusals and rich negligence. Narrative is, heroically and pretentiously, the telling of only one episode, that of the encounter of Ulysses and of the insufficient and enticing song of the Sirens. [13]

A work as vast as *The Odyssey* is thus an amalgam of the *roman* and the *récit,* a text in which the "human time" of the novelistic flow of events is occasionally interrupted by the episodic immediacy of a decisive encounter such as the Song of the Sirens. And when this interruption occurs, the story turns, or metamorphoses, from its everyday human appearance into a pure fictive construct. According to Blanchot, whereas the *roman* advances through what he calls "the desire to allow time to speak" (time understood here in its usual human dimension), the *récit,* on the other hand, "progresses thanks to this *other* time [cet *autre* temps], this other navigation which is the passage from real song to imaginary song" (16). In the system of polarities that structures Blanchot's theoretical argument, all those qualities associated with the *roman* (human time, everydayness, the song in its reality) are both more understandable to the reader and also, quite evidently, less interesting to the critic than the more complex, nearly ineffable attributes connected to the *récit* (an *other* time, the fall into fiction, the song in its textual/imaginary recreation). What Blanchot has done is to organize an expository theoretical discourse in a classical way—by setting up contraries, dichotomies—in which each term appears to have a clear opposite. The problem, however, is that whereas an interpretive community might have a shared understanding of the meaning of "human time," the notion of an *other* time remains enigmatic; and it does not help to say that this *other* time is "the opposite of" human time, whatever that might mean. In the same way, the fall into fiction and the idea of an imaginary song are difficult to imagine: these notions hover, metaphorically (or turn, tropically), around a central inexpressible void that is the point of fascination of Blanchot the critic and writer of fictions. There is, within the experience of the Song of the Sirens (which, we have seen, is also a nonexperience, a nonevent), an abyss, a *béance,* and it is the magnetic attraction of this nothingness that causes the *récit* to coalesce, to take form. It is no surprise, given this scheme, that for Blanchot, like Kafka, the center of the song is not a plenitude, but a lack. Music seems to promise a transcendental beyond, an *au-delà,* but this beyond, in Blanchot's words, is a desert, and the ground of music is nonmusic: "The enchantment [of the Sirens] awakened the hope and the desire of a marvelous beyond, and this beyond only represented a desert, as if the home region of music were the only place completely devoid of music" (10). Narrative constructs itself around the nothingness of music, a nothingness that it attempts to metamorphose into an imaginary textual equivalent, or, in other words, a pure fiction.

b. "La voix narrative, le 'il,' le neutre"

Originally written in 1964, Blanchot's essay on narrative voice is perhaps his most explicit and (if such a term is ever appropriate for this writer) most systematic theoretical statement on narrative as such. It is in this text that the notion of a pure narrative emerges with greatest clarity, and it is no coincidence that this takes place within a discussion of Kafka's fictional works. Blanchot establishes, from the beginning of his argument, that the matter of narrative voice should not be confused with the naïve conception of writing as a transparent representation of an individual consciousness. Narrative always implies distance, and this distance entails the impersonality of what Blanchot, in this essay as well as elsewhere, calls *le neutre,* the neuter.

Crucial to Blanchot's conception of narrative is the subtle passage or, to use Michel Butor's term, "modification" that takes place in the literary-historical transition from Flaubertian aesthetics to the fictional praxis of Kafka. Although Kafka did admire Flaubert (who, along with Goethe, remained one of the Czech writer's constant references in his letters and *Diaries*), Blanchot cautions against the temptation of enlisting Kafka as a mere follower of Flaubert. Whereas aesthetic distance or "creative disinterest" defines the position of the writer and reader vis-à-vis the work of art for Flaubert, this same distance "enters into" the texts of Kafka:

> The distance—the creative disinterest (so visible in the case of Flaubert since he must fight to maintain it)—this distance, which was that of the writer and the reader facing the work, allowing for contemplative pleasure, now enters, in the form of an irreducible strangeness, into the very sphere of the work. [178]

It is within the "irreducible strangeness" of this interior narrative distance that the neuter, *le neutre,* constitutes itself and acts to overturn the centrality of subjective consciousness. Blanchot makes it clear that the neuter "il" does not simply replace the classical third-person singular pronoun, but calls it into question *as subject.* It is through the neuter "il" that the "other" (*l'autre*) speaks, but this "other" cannot be reduced to the mere opposite of the self. The neuter "il" can never be subsumed within a personalized narrative, a narrative tethered to the foundation of human time and events: it will always be outside the act or the subject in which it seems to manifest itself.

Hence the narrative voice as such has no place in the work, but is the void around which the work constructs itself:

> The narrative voice [*voix narrative*] (I do not say narrating voice [*voix narratrice*]) owes its voicelessness to this exteriority. A voice that has no place in the work, but that also does not dominate it from above . . . the "il" is not the notion of comprehensiveness according to Jaspers, but rather like a void in the work. [181]

As was the case in "Le chant des sirènes," in which the distinction between *récit* and *roman* structured the theoretical argument, the essay on narrative voice is organized around the foundational opposition between *voix narrative* and *voix narratrice.* And since the *voix narrative* is the voicelessness of exteriority emanating from a central neutral void, since it has no definable place in human time and reality, it is the voice of the *récit.* Although Blanchot never explicitly defines the *voix narratrice,* it seems clear that this narrating instance is the "opposite" of the *voix narrative,* and that it is the voice of the *roman* in the fullness of subjective consciousness. Jacques Derrida confirms this hypothesis when he states that, unlike the *voix narrative,* which has "no place" in its radical exteriority, the *voix narratrice* can be situated within the theoretical discourse of poetics precisely because it "derives from a subject who tells something, remembering an event or a historical sequence, knowing who he is, where he is, and of what he speaks."[14]

In philosophical terms, one would have to say that the notion of the *neutre* is an a-conceptual concept: it slips between the logical oppositions that organize rational or theoretical discourse. Thus, although once again Blanchot's argument is apparently based upon solidly-established polar oppositions, the *voix narrative,* being without location, *insituable,* cannot simply be called the contrary of the *voix narratrice,* the narrating voice of individual human subjectivity. That which is without location is without a ground, and in the void of its voicelessness, cannot merely be "opposed" to the centrality of a voice present-to-itself. This is why any definition of the *neutre* must necessarily take the apparent form of a logical paradox: since the neuter is neither this nor that, but somewhere (where?) in-between, it cannot be approached by a logic of simple assertive distinction or differentiation.

14. Jacques Derrida, *Parages* (Paris: Galilée, 1986), 150; my translation.

In this sense, the *neutre* is itself radically exterior to the reference points upon which discourse as logical continuity is constructed:

> The neutral word [*la parole neutre*] neither reveals nor hides anything. That does not mean that it signifies nothing (by pretending to abdicate meaningfulness in the form of nonsense), that means that it does not signify according to the manner in which the visible-invisible signifies, but that it opens within language an other power [*un pouvoir autre*], foreign to the power of enlightenment (or obfuscation), of comprehension or of misunderstanding. It does not signifiy according to the optic mode. [183]

Just as in "Le chant des sirènes" Blanchot had spoken of an "other time" (*autre temps*) outside of human everydayness, here he alludes to the "other power" (*pouvoir autre*) opened up within language by the neuter word—a word that is foreign to the founding metaphorical principle of cognition: the "light-darkness" imagery by which Western thought expresses the frustrations and accomplishments of human understanding. What Blanchot calls, with admirable economy, the "optic mode," is the very horizon of our logical discourse, the ultimate limitation within which discourse as understandable human communication is inscribed. To write (or to read), according to the *voix narrative* as it opens up the strange space of the *récit,* is to find oneself beyond that horizon, in a no-man's land, in the aridity of a desert which no land-surveyor can encompass. And it is in this unlocatable "place," I would contend, that Blanchot's own *récits,* like Kafka's "Josefine," "take place."[15]

15. Given the thematic limitations of this essay, and for reasons of discursive clarity, I have decided to focus on a couple of Blanchot's theoretical writings as they relate to Kafka's "Josefine," without reference to Blanchot's own fictional texts, those constructs of the *voix narrative* that defy the "optic mode" of critical analysis. Although Blanchot's fictions are by no means merely practical applications of his theory, there are certainly constitutive similarities between the two types of writing.

The reader who would like to "see" the narrativizing of *le neutre* as radical exteriority might wish to read the passage in *Au moment voulu* (Paris: Gallimard, 1951), in which the narrating voice finds himself/itself projected to the "outside of things." This section begins on page 92 with the observation "I understood that I found myself over there, in the light, calm, and in no way unpleasant cold of the outside," and concludes on page 94 with the interrogative gesture: "And so who was I if I was not this reflection of a figure that did not speak and to whom no one spoke, only capable, resting upon the infinite tranquility of the outside, of questioning the world in silence from the other side of a window?"

c. *Kafka in the Light of Blanchot*

If Blanchot's theoretical meditations exhibit a certain relevance to the fictional praxis of Kafka, it is in their insistence upon two essential points: 1. that at the center of narrative (understood rigorously as *récit*) lies a void, a nothingness, which is untranslatable in the terms of rational discourse but which generates the story in its radical exteriority; 2. that the *récit* as expression of *le neutre* is "voiceless," not attributable to a consciousness as human individuality and not subject to the laws of human time. The question that arises at this juncture is whether the writings of Kafka in some way correspond to these points, and if so, to what degree, in what manner? And, perhaps most crucially: *which* writings of Kafka are in proximity to Blanchot's theoretical concerns?

Because my space is limited, I will pass quickly over a subject that merits more detailed consideration, namely, the evolution of Kafka's prose style and narrative structures from the time of his first successful short story ("The Judgment," 1912).[16] As I have suggested in passing, I think it could be demonstrated that the early stories, such as "The Judgment" and "The Metamorphosis," are constructed in a classical progression, a movement-toward-the-end that allows for melodrama and an ultimate tragic resolution. In Blanchot's terms, these stories would be the product of the *voix narratrice* and would differ from the aesthetics of the *roman* only in their concentrated length, only in the rapidity with which they move toward their respective resting places. "The Metamorphosis" is really a short novel, quite untypical of the rest of Kafka's literary production in its clear tripartite structure, in its traditional theatricality. Most importantly, although Gregor Samsa is becoming an insect, he retains his very human consciousness, and the distance between his exterior appearance and his interiority produces a kind of irony that still derives from the aesthetic distance of Flaubert. In the case of "Josefine" (or "Forschungen eines Hundes" ["Investigations of a Dog," 1922] or "Der Bau" ["The Burrow," 1923]), however, the reader finds himself/herself immediately thrust into an animal world from which all human points of reference

16. "Das Urteil" ("The Judgment") is not Kafka's first story, but it is the first narrative that pleased him, the first literary attempt that seemed to promise further aesthetic accomplishment. On the importance of "The Judgment" as initiatory narrative, see my essay "Proust and Kafka: On the Opening of Narrative Space," *MLN* 101/5 (December 1986): 1135–67.

are absent.[17] The *voix narratrice* cannot function because the human subjectivity of which it is the reflection, the full expression, is no longer on the narrative stage. My contention is that the literary evolution of Kafka can be formulated, in Blanchot's terms, as a gradual effacement of the *voix narratrice* in favor of the *voix narrative,* as a final victory for the *récit* over the *roman.* "Josefine" can be read as a textualization of Blanchot's theoretical points in that the protagonist's song is, in fact, a void, an emptiness, a problematic sound that may or may not "be" song; but this emptiness generates the entirety of the narrative movement, which can be defined as the impossible effort of the animal narrator to rationalize through logical discourse that which is already situated in the realm of *le neutre.* The point of the narrative is that what Josefine is producing is neither song nor piping, but something else—in Blanchot's terms, *un autre chant.*

The passage from the *roman* to the *récit,* from the human fullness of the *voix narratrice* to the animal squeaking of the *voix narrative,* could not have been an easy one for Kafka, who wrote with more anguish and less serenity than Blanchot. The final ruminations of the philosophical dog, the paranoia of the burrowing rodent, and the nervous exertions of the singing mouse are the end-result not of a theoretical meditation, but of a lived drama—Kafka's own. Blanchot senses this when, in his probing essay entitled "Kafka et l'exigence de l'oeuvre," he shows from a close reading of the *Tagebücher* (*Diaries*) that Kafka's intense involvement in Judaism (his learning of Hebrew and what may have been a more than passing interest in the Zionist question) brought religion into conflict with the exacting demands (*l'exigence*) of writing. For Blanchot, whose unique allegiance is to writing, Kafka's turn toward religion in his final days created an existential conflict from which the creator of the animal stories had diffi-

17. For an excellent deconstructive reading of "Der Bau" which emphasizes the far from transparent reduction to "sense-certainty" of the final animal stories, see Henry Sussman, "The All-Embracing Metaphor: Reflections on 'The Burrow'," chapter five of *Franz Kafka: Geometrician of Metaphor* (Madison: Coda Press, 1979). In the introductory remarks of this chapter, Sussman writes: "Absurd as it may seem, given the complexity of the novels, to insist upon an evolution in Kafka's writing toward the circumscription in a here and now characteristic of the sense-certainty where the Hegelian *Phenomenology* takes off, not ends, the containment of 'The Burrow' serves indeed as an end to Kafka's writing, an ending worthy of the body, a culmination of its exploration into the limit disclosed in the process of metaphor. . . . Although the transposition of the limit to the stark setting of a hole may entail a certain simplification, this does not imply simple reduction. Kafka's fortitude, in this case, consists in the intricacy and ambiguity that he is willing to implant in a hole" (150).

culty disengaging himself. Proof of Kafka's ambivalence can be found in a haunting and much-cited *Diary* entry from 28 January 1922, in which the real world (the domain of families, of biological fulfillment, and of achieved religious community) is contrasted with the "desert" in which the writer wanders endlessly:

> Why did I want to quit the world? Because "he" [my father] would not let me live in it, in his world. *Though indeed I should not judge the matter so precisely,* for I am now a citizen of this other world, whose relationship to the ordinary one is the relationship of the wilderness to cultivated land (I have been forty years wandering from Canaan). . . . It is indeed a kind of Wandering in the Wilderness in reverse that I am undergoing: I think that I am continually skirting the wilderness and am full of childish hopes (particularly as regards women) that "perhaps I shall keep in Canaan after all"—when all the while I have been decades in the wilderness and these hopes are merely mirages born of despair, especially at those times when I am the wretchedest of creatures in the desert too, and Canaan is perforce my own Promised Land, *for no third place exists for mankind* (my emphasis).[18]

There is a striking dissimilarity between the nostalgic and despairing rhetorical tone of this entry and the tranquil indifference of the mouse-narrator in "Josefine"—a dissimilarity that marks the separation between Kafka's unmediated thoughts as expressed in his *Diaries* and the unearthly exteriority of his animal tales. In the passage quoted above, Kafka has set up an either/or alternative from which there is no escape,a polar opposition that exhausts all the possibilities, since we are told that, beyond Canaan on the one hand and the wilderness on the other, "no third place exists for mankind." Having been expelled from the world as "Promised Land" by his father, Kafka has been wandering in his own arid territories, unhappily and with sidelong wistful glances toward Canaan. Now this expulsion into the outside, the beyond, reminds one of what happens to the dispossessed human subject when precipitated from the *roman* into the *récit,* from the domain of the *voix narratrice* into the voicelessness of the *voix narrative.* Yet what separates Kafka the human subject, author of the *Diaries,* from Kafka the writer, author of "Josefine," is that in the *Diaries* he has not found his way out of discursive logic, beyond pathos, beyond immediate existential despair.

18. Franz Kafka, *Diaries 1914–1923,* ed. Max Brod, trans. Martin Greenberg with the cooperation of Hannah Arendt (New York: Schocken Books, 1965), 213–14.

As presented in the entry of 28 January 1922, the situation of the writer emerges as the mere logical opposite of the supposed happiness and fulfillment of ordinary humans, in which a note of self-pity is not absent. What Kafka achieves in "Josefine" is to move beyond an indulgence in differentiation (the representation of the artist as other, as sad foreigner, as outcast from society) toward a rhetoric of in-differentiation (Josefine may be singing, may be piping, is both same and different from all other members of the mouse folk). Yet it is just possible that the Kafka of the *Diaries* recognized the melodramatic tone of his rhetoric, that, to borrow from Proust's terminology, his *moi social* intuited what his *moi profond* was capable of achieving through writing.[19] This can be seen, I think, in a curious phrase that does not at first call attention to itself, a phrase like many others one finds in Kafka's writings that seems to express the writer's prudence in reaching a definite formulation, but which, in this case, may be more than a topos of modesty: "Though indeed I should not judge the matter so precisely" (in the German: "So klar darf ich es jetzt allerdings nicht beurteilen").[20] What is interesting here is the presence of a phrase that calls attention to the absolute quality of the polar oppositions structuring the remainder of the passage, and that calls into question the appropriateness of this very absoluteness. In other words: it may be that the Kafka of the *Diaries* recognized that the stark contrast of Canaan to the Wandering in the Wilderness is a theatrical simplification, the kind of trenchant distinction that makes possible structures like the Oedipal triangle and narrative order as such. Perhaps this kind of clarity is too clear; perhaps the act of judgment ("Das Urteil," "beurteilen") necessarily contains within itself a categorical separation in the form of a cut ("Teil," "teilen") that is too neat. The evolution in Kafka the storyteller is from a transparent Oedipal allegory of banishment by the father in "Das Urteil" to the impossibility of sustaining a differential narrative and of making aesthetic judgments (the undecidability of Josefine's "song") in his final fictional work. There is a "third place," which is beyond the horizon of Canaan *and* the Wilderness, but it is not for mankind; it is rather for those animals vocalizing within the atopical space of the *neutre.*

19. For a development of the distinction between the writer's social self and his *moi profond,* see Marcel Proust, "La méthode de Sainte-Beuve," in *Contre Sainte-Beuve, suivi de Nouveaux melanges,* pref. Bernard de Fallois (Paris: Gallimard, 1954), 132–36.

20. Franz Kafka, *Tagebücher 1910–1923,* volume 7 of *Gesammelte Werke,* ed. Max Brod (Frankfurt am Main: Fischer Taschenbuch Verlag, 1976), 414.

III. COMMUNITY AND DEATH IN KAFKA AND BLANCHOT

At the end of "Josefine" the protagonist disappears; her song is lost for the mouse-people, who, in their practical slyness, will continue along their habitual path. The final four short paragraphs of the story are replete with the logical hesitations and paradoxical formulations that had characterized the tale throughout, but in this case the narrator's language focuses almost exclusively on the problem of history ("Geschichte") as memory *and* forgetfulness. We are told, in the final sentence of the story, that since the mouse folk has no interest in history, Josefine, like the previous heroes of her race, is bound to be forgotten. Since we are in the realm of the *neutre,* however, since we are beyond the horizon of balanced polar opposites, this forgetfulness of Josefine should not be equated with her "tragic destiny." That is: forgetfulness is not the negative opposite of memory (memory understood positively as the capacity of a people to sustain through the interiorization of consciousness the essential life of its heroes). This is why the final paragraph of the narrative exhibits a Blanchot-like tranquillity:

> Vielleicht werden wir also gar nicht sehr viel entbehren, Josefine aber, erlöst von der irdischen Plage, die aber ihrer Meinung nach Auserwählten bereitet ist, wird fröhlich sich verlieren in der zahllosen Menge der Helden unseres Volkes, und bald, da wir keine Geschichte trieben, in gesteigerter Erlösung vergessen sein wie alle ihre Brüder. [216]

> So perhaps we shall not miss so very much after all, while Josephine, redeemed from the earthly sorrows which to her thinking lay in wait for all chosen spirits, will happily lose herself in the numberless throng of the heroes of our people, and soon, since we are no historians, will rise to the heights of redemption and be forgotten like all her brothers. [376]

The notion of "redemption" ("Erlösung"), which in a Judeo-Christian context would be linked to the preserving power of memory (when a people is redeemed, that is, "bought back," "ransomed" by a Savior, it is exonerated of its sin and allowed to continue, to further its existence and even, in certain scenarios, to obtain everlasting life), is here linked to the notion of forgetfulness. Josefine will be redeemed insofar as she is forgotten, insofar as her appeal-for-difference, her naïve belief in her identity as a "chosen spirit," are subsumed within the in-differentiating force of the masses. A detailed stylistic analysis of the verb tenses in the final section of the story would show that there is no precise moment, no dramatic point at which Josefine does, in fact, disappear. Rather, she slips between the interstices of the narrative texture: she has, so to speak, always been lost for the mouse folk.

In turning what the *voix narratrice* would have represented as the tragic end-point of death into an unlocalizable "disappearance," the *voix narrative* may have recovered the spectral and uncanny truth of death, its essential neutrality, its luminescent exteriority beyond the oppositions of light and dark, inside and outside. Although, as Heidegger would have it, I die my own death, which is mine and mine alone, there is an important dialogic relation between the one who dies or disappears and the one(s) who remain(s) behind: and it is in this relation and only in this relation that what we call "community" can arise. The relation that binds together Josefine and the mouse folk—an indifferent forgetfulness—may seem strange to the reader whose universe is that of the *roman;* but in the *récit,* this relation (*rapport*) has, in Blanchot's words, all the power and meaning of the secret, of mystery. Let me conclude with a fragment from Blanchot's *L'attente l'oubli*[21] that rewrites, in concentrated abstraction, the enigmatic ending of Josefine, the mouse singer, whose fate will have always been to disappear within her people, to lose what has always been lost—her precious identity:

> We do not go toward forgetfulness, no more than forgetfulness comes to us, but suddenly forgetfulness has always already been there, and when we forget, we have always already forgotten everything: we are, in the movement toward forgetfulness, linked to the presence of the immobility of forgetfulness.
>
> Forgetfulness relates to that which forgets itself. And this relation, which renders secret that to which it relates, holds the power and the meaning of the secret. [87]

21. Maurice Blanchot, *L'attente l'oubli* (Paris: Gallimard, 1962); my translation

IV. Attentions

THOMAS SCHESTAG

Mantis, Relics[1]

> Il lisait. Il lisait avec une minutie et une attention insurpassables. Il était par rapport à chaque mot, chaque signe du texte dans la situation où se trouve le mâle par rapport à la mante religieuse au moment d'être dévoré.
>
> He was reading. He was reading with unsurpassable meticulousness and attention. He was, in relation to each word, each sign in the text, in the situation in which the male praying mantis finds himself in relation to the female at the moment he is being devoured.
>
> —Maurice Blanchot, *Thomas l'obscur*

The sentence in which the praying mantis appears identifies an unmistakable symmetry—emphasized by the repetition: "par rapport à . . . par rapport à [in relation to . . . in relation to]"—to clarify the facts of reading, at this moment, by way of the parallel with the insect. The sentence, it appears, elucidates how Thomas reads. His relation to every word, to every sign in the text is as is the relation between the male mantis and the female when the male is about to be devoured. Is as is. But *how,* as? What, at first glance, through the offered comparison with insects, leads to an insight into Thomas's reading, remains veiled when one looks at it again. The analogy relates the parallels in a crosswise fashion around a *situation* in the middle. Thomas was, before every word and sign of the text, *in the situation* in which the male praying mantis [*Mantis religiosa*] finds himself when he is about to be devoured by the female. However, the situation on which the clarification of reading depends in this passage remains in darkness. Nothing

1. This essay is translated from a longer essay bearing this same title and that appears in "fila sonantia," *Der Prokurist* 18 (1996), ed. Thomas Schestag. In the longer essay, the section on Blanchot is followed by one on Paul Celan and immediately preceded by a reading of Jean-Henri Fabre's *Souvenirs entomologiques* (1879), ed. Yves Delange (Paris: Robert Laffont, 1989), traces of which are found throughout these pages. The epigraph is from Maurice Blanchot, *Thomas l'obscur* (Paris: 1941). The passages discussed here and in the following pages are found in the fourth chapter of this *roman,* 21–26. All translations from the German and the French in this essay, unless specified otherwise, are mine. Trans.

YFS 93, *The Place of Maurice Blanchot,* ed. Thomas Pepper, © 1998 by Yale University.

is said about it. The sentence that appears to clarify how Thomas reads remains dark. Obscure. Precisely for this reason, however, it seems to coincide with the title of the novel, *Thomas l'obscur.* For the situation of the title—the relation of *Thomas* and *l'obscur* to each other, just as the relation to *Thomas* here, to *l'obscur* there, taken in isolation—is no less opaque. It brings into view different possible readings, without, however, replacing or supplementing one reading with another. *Thomas l'obscur* may mean that the title designates Thomas as the obscure, the opaque one: *obscuritas* uncovers Thomas in his essence, uncovers his essential characteristic. Thomas—l'obscur: this title says in all clarity and precision—that is, it reveals—who and what Thomas secretly, essentially is. Thomas—the Dark: this is the truth about him, the epiphany of his essence (his reading included), and the book fans out, page by page, word by word, and sign by sign, the spectrum of this appearance. The title, however, can also mean the reverse: not that Thomas's essence is found in his opacity, but that his essence remains opaque, dark. Obscure. What appears in the one interpretation to be the uncovering of Thomas's essence becomes, in the other interpretation, the documentation of the opposite: not only does Thomas's essence remain dark, but Thomas himself remains hard to see, darkened, obscure. And, in a more irritating repetition, with darkness and light crossed over: Thomas appears in darkness. Where *Thomas l'obscur* appears—as a reminder, the book *appears* in 1941, bearing the title *Thomas l'obscur*—two opacities, so it appears, divide the glance; the glance divides two opacities. Not only does the title turn appearance and darkening inside one another, but, moreover, the appearance of opacity, even more opaquely, turns two opacities inside each other: the darkness, declared to be essential, in the fullness of its negative light, lightless clarity, namely pure darkness, which not only is in contrast with light, but also allows the day, woven into the night, originally to dawn out of the night, and makes appearance appear (close to that night, the essence of the sublime, out of which the command *fiat lux* is issued); and a peculiar darkening of darkness, which does not resemble the resolution of darkness in light, but rather, clouds light and darkness, day and night, both taken in isolation and in their relation to each other. Repeated differently, the title relates, closer to the crossed-over interpenetration of the opacities: the appearance of opacity, and the opaque appearance: the appearance (of opacity), and the (opaque) appearance (of opacity); (the appearance of) opacity, and (the opaque appearance of) opacity: *l'obscur.*

The interpenetration of the two opacities into each *other* does not produce a synthesis out of two given opposites, no original third or preprimary *state* from which the oppositions would result; rather, this interpenetration clouds, in both states, light as well as darkness, the *signified* oppositions, and even signification itself, since it is signification that dawns [*anbricht*] yet breaks off [*abbricht*], breaks off yet dawns, neither (both) dawns nor (and) breaks off in this crossing over, in this *situation.* This moment, which ruins the contour of a rhetorical figure, the sharpness of the oxymora, that clear obscurity of the first interpretation, the silhouettes, and which fans out: scatters hesitation—*mora*—in the outline of two elements that are, from extremely close up, related to each other—aspectrally—this moment is neither *aurora* nor *crepusculum,* neither dawn nor dusk, but simply twilight: twilight, twi-night [*zwienächtig*], twi-day [*Zwietag*], hybrid [*zwittrig*], twin [*Zwilling*]: *Thomas.* The twilight alludes not to the dawning of a night that would correspond to the imperative *fiat nox,* but to the space of an echo, a space that undoes the relation [*Verhältnis*] of *nox* and *lux,* of nothing (or night) and light, to each other, making it the dying away of a sound [*Verhälltnis*], which undoes the *-halt,* hold, into a *-hallt,* an echo. In this passage, which sketches the disaster of the *perhaps* starless heaven, the constellation of the title, which interprets *Thomas* as the star, *l'obscur* as the satellite, disperses; Thomas—Didymos—becomes a twin [*Zwilling*], the proper or other name of *obscuritas,* the *obscuritas* becomes the twin of the proper or other name Thomas. *Thomas: l'obscur.* The inversions move into each *other.* The slingshot [*Zwille*] of the title does not simply split up its own initial, the cross of Thomas—T—, but every letter, not just those of the title, making each letter into a breaking seal, into an Ynitial. In the passage just quoted, which describes Thomas reading, and which compares reading to the moment in which mantis and mantis swallow one another, what actually happens is that the title of the book—*Thomas l'obscur*—reads the book by this title; here the reading of books, reading in general perhaps, is signed *Thomas l'obscur:* what is seen and what is seeing in the glance are defined more precisely as double-edged opacities. Seen in this way, it seems that the reason for the quoted *situation* is found in *Thomas l'obscur,* which cannot simply be understood as either the title of a book, or the book by this title, either the reader or what is read, either beginning to read [*Anlesen*] or reading out [*Ablesen*], or reading to the end [*Auslesen*].

Only recalling the pages on the mantis, in Fabre's *Souvenirs ento-*

mologiques among others, only looking in another book, dissolves the opacity of the situation and deciphers the *obscure* situation as an *obscene* one: the moment of the mixing of sexes, which seems to unveil the obscure moment of reading to be copulation; to unveil, in the relation between the reader and the page he looks at, between Thomas l'obscur and the open book, the *generative* act of meaning, to bring into view the *begetting* of signification. But first it introduces, in the word *obscene,* another mantis relic. For *obscenus,* an adjective that seems to correspond in this passage to the word *situation* in the same way as *Thomas* to *l'obscur,* before meaning the ostentatious and shameless showing of the genitals [*Scham*], names in the language of Roman augurs—the mantes—the catastrophic, inauspicious sign or omen. Inlaid in the situation that introduces mantis and mantis, of both sexes, into each other, the word *obscenus* interprets the praying mantis as the catastrophic omen to which the male mantis remains blind. It shows the seer not in the moment of interpreting a fact as an *obscene* sign, and not as blind seer: rather, the sign remains obscure to the seer—even to the blind seer. In the sign of the obscene sign even the blind seer goes blind, the one who does not see the genitals [*Scham*], but rather—as though the shame [*Scham*] were going to survive him, pulsates into them at the moment of decapitation. The moment of reading. The clarification of the situation, which compares the moment of reading the open book to the moment of the mixing of the male and female genitals [*Scham*] of the mantis in copulation, interprets the reading glance to be the male genitals, the open book the female, but it also unveils the two sexes in each *other:* it obscures the situation and gives more precisely the adjective *obscene* as the synonym of the adjective *obscure.* Not least, the syntactical and semantic porosity of the end of the sentence, beyond the end of the sentence—*au moment d'être dévoré*—disrupts what seemed to be the mixing of two sexes, turning it into the impossibility of breaking up the moment into these or those genitals. *Au moment d'être dévoré:* at the moment of being devoured. The turn of phrase carries a hiatus that delays with respect to the moment the impossibility of delaying the devouring that will happen momentarily, the devouring in this moment; it makes the moment late with respect to the moment, but most of all—if one looks at the moment of reading—divides the reference that points back to devouring and devoured entities, making it unable to reach its goal. It is the verb *dévorer*—to devour—that confuses the situation. For, on the one hand, on the basis of its lack of syntactical ambiguity, it means—and it has, through the memory of Fabre's entomological memories, the appearance of evidence—the literal devouring of the male mantis inside and by the female, which—similar not only to the open book, but to every word, every sign in it—dismembers and consumes the reader, lover, in the moment of the *act,* in order to decompose, to discard that which it has incorporated, and to remain behind. On the other hand, however, and too equal [*zu gleich*], the verb *dévorer* entwines a semantic nuance that affects or attacks the eyes, that makes the eyes into things that grab or attack. Emile Littré records, close to the evangelist in the moment of revelation, in the eyes' consumption of the book—"Dévorer un livre" [to devour a book]—a synonym of reading—"le lire avec avidité" [to read it avidly]—, and quotes, further down, in order to give evidence for the devouring with the eyes—"Dévorer des yeux, jeter des regards pleins d'ardeur et de convoitise [to devour with one's eyes, to cast glances full of ardor and desire]"—one of Montesquieu's *Lettres persanes,* not far from the loving, syncopated mantis—*la mante* [the mantis]/*l'amante* [the female lover]: "Ici une amante . . . une autre dévore des yeux son amant [Here a female lover . . . an other devours her lover with her eyes]."[2] The situation of the sentence quoted from *Thomas l'obscur* blends the literal and the metaphorical nuance. In this sentence the female mantis devours, no, it is about [*auf dem Sprung*] to devour the seer, but at the same time, again based on our memory of Fabre's entomological memories, the seer is about to devour the mantis with his eyes: "Il lance des oeillades vers sa puissante compagne. . . . En cette posture, immobile, longtemps il contemple la désirée [He casts glances towards his powerful companion. . . . For a long time, in this posture, immobile, he contemplates the object of his desire]." In this sentence every word and sign devours, no, every word, every sign is about to devour the reading Thomas, but at the same time, too, the reader is about to devour: every word and sign. The situation sketches sexes and eyes—open, directed (toward)—about to devour each *other:* it ruins the contour of the generative, cannibalistic and *act*-character—of reading as of loving—in one (compound, divisible) word of *philology,* the philology that it sketches by suspending the decision about location and relation to each other of male and female, active and passive, reading and read entities: *au moment d'.* The moment of this situation does not describe the *completion* of the decapi-

2. Emile Littré, *Dictionnaire de la langue française* (1876), vol. 2 (Paris: Gallimard, 1961), 1846–47.

tation of the seer by the mantis, nor the devouring of the mantis by the seer's glance, nor the reading Thomas's being absorbed—into the devouring, eye-directing, eye-opening word and sign, nor the devouring of sign and word by the eyes of the reading Thomas: this is underscored by the sentence immediately following, which puts the stress on the eyes [*Augen*] at the moment [*Augenblick*], *about* at the moment of their mutual devouring: "dévoré. L'un et l'autre se regardaient [devoured. They looked at each other]." Both looked at each other. The opaque situation of this moment, of the thomised moment, signed *Thomas,* of the moment of the encounter, no, of the devouring of one *another* of eyes and moments, is what the lines started by the succinct sentence "L'un et l'autre se regardaient" attempt to develop by crossed-over enlargement and microscopy of the moment, of the divided moment, not *a-* but *tom*ized:

> Les mots, issus d'un livre qui prenait soudain une puissance mortelle, exerçaient sur le regard qui les touchait un attrait doux et paisible. Chacun était comme un oeil, à demi fermé, qui laissait entrer le regard trop vif qu'en autres circonstances il n'eût pas souffert. Thomas se glissa donc dans les couloirs obscurs et tranquilles. Puis il alla plus avant. Il s'enfonça, sans défense, jusqu'à cet instant singulier où il se sentit regardé à son tour par l'intime du mot. Ce n'était pas encore effrayant, c'était au contraire un moment presque agréable qu'il aurait voulu prolonger. Le lecteur considérait joyeusement cette petite étincelle de vie qu'il ne doutait pas d'avoir éveillée. Il se voyait avec plaisir dans cet oeil qui le voyait. Son plaisir même devint très grand. Il devint si grand et si impitoyable qu'il ne put que le subir avec une sorte d'effroi parce qu'il ne réussissait pas à la faire partager à son interlocuteur. Le moment où il fit à celui-ci un signe de complicité sans recevoir de réponse fut un moment insupportable. Il s'aperçut alors de toute l'étrangeté qu'il y avait à être observé par un mot comme par un vivant, et non seulement par un mot, mais par tous les mots qui se trouvaient dans ce mot, par tous ceux qui l'accompagnaient et qui à leur tour contenaient en eux-mêmes d'autres mots, comme une suite d'anges s'ouvrant à l'infini jusqu'à l'oeil de l'absolu. Pourtant il ne cessa pas de vouloir s'emparer du texte. Avec une terrible obstination il refusa de retirer son regard, croyant encore être le lecteur profond des mots inépuisables, alors que les mots s'emparaient déjà de lui et commençaient de lire. A cet instant il se sentit pris dans un corps à corps absurde, mordu par une dent pleine de sève, pétri par des mains intelligibles. Il entra avec son corps vivant dans les formes anonymes des mots, leur donnant sa substance, formant leurs rapports, offrant au mot être son

être, possédé après chaque mot par le serpent de la phrase. Pendant des heures il se tint, comme un mort, avec à la place des yeux de temps en temps des mots yeux; il était immobile, fasciné et dévoilé. Pourtant, même lorsqu'il se fut abandonné et que, regardant son livre, il se vit avec dégoût sous la forme du texte qu'il lisait, il garda la pensée qu'en lui, privé de sens, et presque de vie, demeuraient des mots obscurs qui veillaient profondément. Ces mots poursuivaient une vie sourde qu'il nourissait tout en restant étranger. Dans l'état incompréhensible où il se trouvait, alors que le mot *Il* et le mot *Je* montaient sur lui comme de gigantesques cafards, et, juchés sur ses épaules, commençaient un interminable carnage, il reconnaissait le travail de puissances indéfinissables qui, âmes désincarnées et anges des mots, l'exploraient.

The words, coming forth from the book which all of a sudden was taking on deadly powers, exercised on the glance that touched them a gentle and peaceful attraction. Each of them was like a half-closed eye, which let in a too intense glance which it would not have tolerated in different circumstances. So Thomas slipped into the obscure and tranquil hallways. Then he went further. He sank into them, defenseless, until that peculiar moment when he felt that he was being looked at in his turn by the innermost part of the word. It was not yet frightening; on the contrary, it was an almost pleasant moment that he would have liked to prolong. The reader joyfully contemplated this little spark of life, not doubting that he had awakened it. He saw himself with pleasure in this eye that saw him. His pleasure became even very great. It became so great and so pitiless that he could bear it only with a sort of terror because he was not able to make his interlocutor share it. The moment when he made toward his interlocutor a sign of complicity without receiving a response was unbearable. He perceived then all the strangeness that there was in being observed by a word as by a living being, and not only by one word, but by all the words that were in that word, by all those that accompanied it and that in turn contained in themselves other words, like a procession of angels that opened out ad infinitum to the eye of the absolute. Nonetheless he did not cease wishing to seize hold of the text. With terrible obstinacy he refused to withdraw his glance, still believing himself to be the deep reader of inexhaustible words, while instead the words were already seizing hold of him and beginning to read him. At this moment he felt himself taken into an absurd wrestling match, bitten by a vigorous tooth, kneaded by intelligible hands. He entered with his living body into the anonymous shapes of the words, giving them his substance, forming their relationships, offering the word being his being, possessed after each word by the snake of the sentence. For hours he stayed there like a dead man,

> with, from time to time, in place of his eyes the words eyes; he was immobile, fascinated, and unveiled. Nonetheless, even when he had abandoned himself and when, looking at his book, he saw himself with disgust in the form of the text he was reading, he retained the thought that in him, who was senseless and almost lifeless, obscure words dwelled and were on deep watch. These words pursued a deaf life that he nourished while remaining a stranger to it. In the incomprehensible state in which he was, while the word *he* and the word *I* climbed on him like gigantic cockroaches and, perched on his shoulders, began an interminable carnage, he recognized the work of indefinable powers, which, disembodied souls of angels of words, explored him.

These lines describe the moment of reading, the slipping and sinking into the moment of reading. They break apart the fissure [*Sprung*] in the expression of *auf dem Sprung* [about], to read, and in this way produce the appearance not only of enlargement but of lengthening. They write the dispersion of magnifying glasses for space and time, of *tempus* and *templa,* of props of the mantis, beyond the seer and back before the seer. The path into the moment of reading irritatingly dissolves its frame. It isolates and frees, in the open book, the words from the page, and enlarges each of them almost into a physiognomy, into a face, and further into an eye. It's not a question of not losing sight of the word [*das Wort nicht aus den Augen zu verlieren*] but of seeking the eye in the word. The moment [*Augenblick*] of reading seeks the moment of the word. This moment leads, by an inversion, from the comparison of words with eyes—"Chacun était comme un oeil [each was like an eye]" to the disruption of the eyes, to their replacement, from time to time, with words, with the words *eyes:* "avec à la place des yeux de temps en temps les mots yeux [with, in place of the eyes, from time to time the words eyes]." Each word *like an* eye—in place of the eyes *the words* eyes. No word is a face, and there is no pair of eyes in it, but it does come out of the face, strewn with eyes, of the open page, mantis- and Midas-text at once, pulled out of it by enlargement, *like* an eye, and like *one* eye. Thus the beginning of the sinking into the moment. In place of the eyes, however, one finds, from time to time, *the words* eyes. *Eyes* is word, but not *a* word: rather, more than one, less than one. Multiplicity of eyes, eyebreak. Thus the end of the sinking into the moment. The ends, however, hold each other up, interrupt each other's words, leap to each other's eye. Neither eye nor eyes, neither words nor word. Each word is like an eye—*eyes,* however, is, at times, a word. Each word, eye—each eye, word. The addition, however: not *one,* distorts the inversion: no word is *one,* at the limit no *word,* not even *eyes.* Wordbreak. The ends of the act of sinking into each *other* hollow out, disrupt the schema of the substitution of word and eye for one another, crosswise, from the end: in place of eyes, from time to time, the words eyes. In place of the eyes: eyes. It is Thomas's—the twin's, Didymos's—reading, the sinking into Thomas's reading that seems to lead to this peculiar, uncanny doubling: untenability of the eyes; untenability of the word. The ends of the moment: *divid.*

Thomas's reading, it appears, seeks from the beginning not to read meaning out of words, not to grasp the word's meaning in and through the word, not to leave the word behind, to drop it, as soon as the meaning is reached and to close the book, read to the end; but rather, it seeks, in the word, the eye, the word *as* eye, seeks the moment [*Augenblick*] or split in the eye [*Augenspalt*] in order to penetrate the word. The divided, half-closed, half-open eye guardedly attracts the glance that tries to see it; it mixes invitation and reservation, hesitation and compliance, holds up the penetrating and pervading glance by attracting it, draws and entangles it in the depth of a surface, and takes away initiative and direction from the intention of the glance. The inconspicuous pull into the opacity of the eye-word (which in place of the colors—*couleurs*—in the eye opens the eye up to hallways—*couloirs,*—obscure rows) pauses in a passage that names the beginning of the *mantic* layer in the moment. It is the beginning of the *consideratio* in the reader: "Le lecteur *considérait* [The reader *considered*]." A moment [*Augenblick*] in which the reader does not contemplate [*ins Auge faßt*] a star, but rather, it is the glance that awakens a flash, interprets it as a spark of life, which the glance believes to have fathered in the cell of shame [*Scham*]. Thus the mantic layer slides, without transition, into the generative and specular layer, into the mirror stage of the moment. In the awakened glance the reader sees himself seeing. A moment of speculative self-generation: *as* birth of a star in the glance [*Blick*], the reader comes out of the eye [*Auge*] in which it penetrates, and approaches himself. He saw himself with pleasure in this eye that looked at him. He saw himself grow, and his desire grew in this seeing. The approach, however, becomes threatening. The approach deprives the reader of the initiative of the glance over something that comes and that he believes to have awakened—and in it himself. The reader does not succeed in focusing his growing desire on what is approaching, in enveloping it, in communicating the focused desire of what is approaching for him. The sign of complicity that he makes to what is replying remains without reply [*Entgegnung*], gets lost in what is approaching, comes away without an answer. It unsettles, without consolidation, the assumption that, in what approaches him, the reader encounters *himself.* It is the—unbearable—moment of the reply [*Entgegnung:* literally, taking away of the opposite] that breaks the appearance of *making, giving, trans*mission of signs, of *com*munication and *con*sideration, of originally synthetic apperception and of the wished-for synthesis of those who encounter one another into *co*-members of a common situation, possible to overlook, *in* the eye. It is the moment in which the appearance, on the grounds of the eye into which the reader slides in order to become aware of his own glance collected into a star, is extinguished. In it the description of the mantic moment, between mantis and mantis, about to complete their copulation, in Fabre's words, is discussed. "Le lecteur *considérait* [the reader *considered*]," one reads in *Thomas l'obscur;* "longtemps il *contemple* la désirée [for a long time he *contemplates* the desired female]" in the *Souvenirs entomologiques.* However, the sign that divides and transforms the mantic profile of both situations is given, in the *Souvenirs,* by the female mantis (which corresponds to the word in *Thomas l'obscur*) in order to be reciprocated—"l'amoureux cependant a saisi un signe d'acquiescement, signe dont je n'ai pas le secret [The loving male, however, has noticed a sign of acquiescence, a sign whose secret I don't possess]"—while in *Thomas,* on the contrary, it is given by the reader and remains without reciprocation—"Le moment où il fit à celui-ci un signe de complicité sans recevoir de réponse fut un moment insupportable [the moment when he made toward his interlocutor a sign of complicity without receiving a response was unbearable]." In the *Souvenirs entomologiques,* the sign leads to the copulation of the sexes, to the disastrous fulfillment of the (implied) specular moment, of successful communication. In *Thomas l'obscur* the sign gets lost: what seemed to be a mirror and, in the mirror, a mirror image, opens its eyes, the mirror layer in the moment is defined more precisely as original ecstasis, eye and eyed as ecstases which do not refer back to given existing entities, but rather ex-pose [*aussetzen*]. Sliding forward into the moment enlarges this ecstasy into the metamorphosis of the word, which does not remain word but opens up into words inside the word, to a pocket-word that contains not contents but other words containing other words. What seemed to be word, to keep its word, opens up into words that accompany one another, that slide into one another, that scatter the appearance of a given contour of the one or the other word, the one or the other content. The goal that this flight from words made of words, from words in words, seems to have, and that provokes the comparison of words with angels, is the eye of the absolute. But this detached, unsettled eye does not keep its promises. The eye of the absolute, relic of the speculative layer in the moment, interrupts [*bricht ins Wort*] the reader from the beginning of his absorption, opens up into the word *as* eye, in order to penetrate it, which aspectralizes the appearance of givenness of the *one* word—*eye,* for instance—into words made of words.

In this moment—of the untenability even of the absolute (a word *as* eye), of the alignment of the rows of words into mediators, but without communication, into messengers, but of no message, and while Thomas, blind to the counter-glance from the word, insists on exploring the essence of the word—the words begin to read the reader who opens up into a word—*as* eye. . . . The reader mutates into a word, the word into a reader. The scheme of inversion, however, fails here as well. In the moment of the inversion not only reading and read entities are lost, but also the original ecstases, defined more precisely as divisible ecstases. The word *obscur* clarifies this. At the beginning, Thomas slides into the eyed words as though into opaque hallways—*couloirs obscurs*—, and the glance remains unscathed, intact. Later, however, the word opens into words made of words, and the opaque words—*mots obscurs*—start to move into Thomas, the reader, whom they start to read. Thomas attains the opacity that attains him: *Thomas l'obscur.* The opacity does not lead two given magnitudes, Thomas and words, into each other, in order to divide and reunite them, but rather it splits the outline of both. It is, to be precise, interrupting translation and communication with the word, not words that remain in Thomas, that find residence, settle there, but: *mots.* It is not the one or the other reader who penetrates the word, who opens up in the word that opens up into words made of words, but *Thomas.* Thomas penetrates the word—*mot,*—words—*mots*—in Thomas. Thomas—*mot. Mots*—Thomas. At this moment *mots* and *Thomas* slide, not taken at their word [*wörtlich*] and not figuratively, but literally [*buchstäblich*], into each other. In the *word,* the meaning word and that which the word means—*word*—suspend each other. In *Thomas,* the decision about whether a word takes the place of a bearer of the word, signified by the word, or whether *Thomas,* impossible to interpret unambiguously as word and bearer (of a meaning) divides the glance, is lost. In both—*mots, Thomas,*—the ecstasis, nothing other than: *mots,* nothing other than: *Thomas,* yet at the same time the *divisibility* of the ecstasies, from their closeness to one *another,* the ecstasis splits the glance [*Blick*]. It is the moment [*Augenblick*] of the asymmetrical doubling of the word—*mot*—, a doubling signified in Thomas *as* word—twin, Didymos—; this word breaks doubly: it does not get resolved either in its interpretation as word (to be semiotic bearer of semantic content) or in its interpretation as word (to be what is meant by the word), but remains other. This other; more irritating, remaining, an imperceptible drawing-closer that falls apart in coming closer, attacks in the seam of the quoted sinking into the moment, most overtly, first of all *being* and the *eyes.* Thomas, at the moment when the word opens up into words made of words, when *mots* penetrate *Thomas* and begin to scatter the appearance of a given shape, replaced by a word, even by a proper name—Thomas offers to the word, which at the moment of the opening, of the impossibility of its unambiguous interpretation as a word, takes on peculiar corporeality and liveliness, while Thomas's corporeality and liveliness threaten to die out: "Pendant des heures il se tint, comme un mort [for hours he didn't move, like a dead man],"—Thomas offers his being to the word being, in order to fill the empty word that is coming closer with that whose loss appears to him to be near, the substance that is his own, a content grasped in *Thomas* in whatever way or fleetingly: "offrant au mot être son être [offering his being to the word being]." And the next sentences repeat the doubling, in reference to the *eyes:* "avec à la place des yeux de temps en temps les mots yeux [with, in place of the eyes, from time to time the words eyes]." In place of the eyes, from time to time, the words *eyes.* In place of the eyes: eyes. The sinking into the moment of the word, and the enlargement of the word, defines more precisely and opens up in the reader, *Thomas,* the word to words that open up into words. No word is resolved by being explained as word; it is neither resolved by being explained as a signifying word nor by being explained as the thing meant (by the word). In reference to the eyes, this means: the words *eyes,* precisely in place of the eyes, undo the understanding of the eyes, both as signifying word (for each word opens up to words made of words), and as the thing signified, the eyes. What remains, however, where *eyes* remains or remain (in this moment the possibility of counting, counting out, and recounting is also lost), freed from the frame of the interpretation, remains unforeseeable, opaque, open. Precisely *because* the text speaks of *eyes* as words or as word—the difference loses its meaning—, *eyes* is not, eyes are not resolved in their explanation as word. For each word—and, *a fortiori, word*—shares the eyes' impossibility of being interpreted unambiguously as eyes. Thomas attempts—thereby freeing *mot(s)* that move into Thomas from the frame of their explanation as word, and freeing *Thomas* from the frame of its explanation as a proper name or as a signified body and word-body—to save *himself* at this moment by offering to the word *being* what he—who begins to shatter in his becoming aware of the *mots* that are opening up and introducing themselves into *Thomas*—believes not to be able to keep a moment longer, to contain a moment longer: his being [*sein Sein*]. He attempts, through a transfusion, to have brought to safety in the other word substance, weight and meaning, the ideal, the ideal content [*Gehalt*] of his own splintering form, *contents* [*Inhalt*]. However, Thomas's offer to entrust his being to the word being, to have rescued (in the other word) the content (of the one word) through the shattering of its form, involuntarily traces tears in the ontological joint of the language of words. The offer comes too late. For *being*, too—content or form, either way—does not get resolved by being explained as a word. The irritation about this beginning—yet breaking off being makes the sentences adjacent to the quoted sinking in, lengthening and magnifying of the moment in which the word (no less than the reader called *Thomas*)—breaks open, starts strangely to stammer. That which does not stop coming closer to Thomas, even at the moment of the loss of the contour of the word, of any word, of the signifying and signified sphere, even there where the glance avoids the open book, is called at first "quelque chose . . . d'absolument étranger à tout être [something . . . absolutely foreign to any being]": something foreign to all being (*être*, however, oscillates between a being and Being), foreign to all beings, that neither *is* nor *is not*. Although Thomas in the same sentence denies existence to this presence—"cette présence," as it is called a little earlier—"il pouvait dire qu'il n'existait pas [he could say that he didn't exist],"—the next sentence grants to this presence precisely that which the previous one had denied it: "cet être [this being]." This close thing, this thing coming closer is understood as a being, as Being, and speech [*Sprechen*] stops between denying and granting [*Ab- und Zusprache*]. This *être*, however, appears to Thomas to have been replaced by another—"un autre être [another being]," of which it is said that it is *obscure* like the replaced being, yet different. Another nuance in that which, it is said, does not exist, a divergent way to be absent—"d'être absent." The near, nearing thing is exposed between presence and absence. The entity of the anonymous narrator or reporter oscillates in the estimation of that which comes closer, between "incommensurable being, incommensurable Being" and "this *être,*" between defense against deixis and deixis. Thomas, in the report of the narrator, oscillates between the asserted nonexistence of this presence, its substitution through another, no less obscure *être,* between its closer definition as a modification of absent being—"*être absent*"—, and again as this being, this Being—"*cet être*",—that, according to the report, does not stop coming closer to Thomas—"invisible and certain." The evident uncertainty of these lines, the stammering breaking open of the lines around *être,* and the breaking open of the word *être* in these lines, impossible to interpret unambiguously as a word, in the very enlargement of the lines, deprives the layers, which acquire contour, standing out against each other, in the glance directed toward the page of the open book *Thomas l'obscur,* as narrator, protagonist and plot line; it deprives the layers of the appearance of their composure into entities. The enlargement of the lines, close to the enlargement, described in the text, of the word in the reading moment signed *Thomas,* defines more precisely the supposed instances [*Instanzen*]—narrator, story, protagonist, and author,—too close to each other, as *divisible* ecstases, defines every stamp [*Stanze*] as a word that is *opening up:* it introduces the describing and the described sphere into one another. What is described here is a signed reading, a reading of names, Thomas's reading, which enlarges, into a divisible ecstasis, the moment that compares each word to the mantis, the mantis however to an eye, and which penetrates this eye: the ecstasis of penetrating the awareness of the experience that each word opens up into divisible words made of words that begin to read the reading *Thomas,* of penetrating Thomas, a word that is like an eye; of breaking the seal, the sealed moment of reading, the signature of the moment: *Thomas.* At this moment, which bends into each other *mots* and *Thomas,* the described reader of described letters, which opens a caesura in the comprehension of *mots* as words, of *Thomas* as protagonist, reader and letters, the *described* microscopy moves into each word of the *description.* And it moves in the question of how to read the *novel* with the title *Thomas l'obscur* by *Maurice Blanchot* from the point of view of the description of the reading Thomas in it, a description in which the *agonal* understanding of the relation between reader [*Leser*] and letter [*Letter*], the *ergonal* understanding of the writing as work, and moreover the understanding of the *Par*erga—of the name in the title and the name of the author—as *-erga,* namely as words, is lost. For the described enlargement of the word opening up in the moment opening up pushes off balance the intermittent relation, the rhythm between the sinking into the word (which stops unforeseeably and unaccountably, in a way impossible to locate, impossible to give a word to, and irresponsible) and the (foreseeable, ac- and recountable, possible to locate, give a word to, and take responsibility for) going and going over into the next word. The more incalculably the described microscopy penetrates each word of the description, the more immeasurable and unplaceable it becomes, not only the closeness of word and word, in the sentence, to each other, but also the tear [*Riß*] in the outline [*Aufriß*] of intimacy, in the outline of each and every word about to unite itself to itself and become the word itself. And the less possible to interpret unambiguously the text as text, the novel as novel, the title as title, and the author as author: the word—*mot*—does not break in only in *Thomas*, and does not open up only the comprehension of Thomas as word, but rather, the divided, divisible going into each other and separating of the word—*mot*—in Maurice Blanchot disrupts the intention to grasp before and after, beginning and end of the proper name, to grasp in the proper name the contour of the word—*mot,*—to fit inside the word that is opening up—*mot*—the proper name: *Mau . . . ot.*

The irritating doubling, the oscillation between doubling and splitting, in the place where the absorption into the moment becomes aware of the *divisible* ecstasis, where the word is not resolved by being explained, either as signifying or as signified—this doubling seizes, in the quoted passage that describes the moment, not only the *eyes* and *being,* but also *time.* Time *and* being. Being and time. And eyes. The enlargement affects the outline of time as ecstasis; it affects the appearance of distinct times: of the time of narration, narrated time, and the time of reading *in* the described enlargement. The sentence that writes the eyes apart, not by turning them into a differential definition of eyes—here word, there thing—, but by writing them as nonunifiable indifferentiability, as *eyes* that open up in the glance, as *breaking* eyes, the sentence that disrupts the appearance of a distinction between word and thing, implants between eyes and eyes the phrase "from time to time." Quaking discussion of time, of the word time, that makes doubling and division oscillate: "avec à la place des yeux de temps en temps les mots yeux [with, in place of his eyes, from time to time the words eyes]": *de temps en temps.* The phrase emphasizes, at first glance, the discontinuity between eyes and eyes: however, the fact that the (words) eyes take on the place of the eyes only temporarily traces at the same time the discontinuity in the outline of time, of the word time. *Tempus.* The discourse from time to time defines time more precisely as meantime [*Zwischenzeit*—literally, time in between]. Between time and time [*Zwischen Zeit und Zeit*] time stops, a gap or pause remains, a caesura, which opens, yet also cuts off the appearance of temporalization [*Zeitigung*], the interpretation of the pause as a *tendency.* The pause temporalizes [*zeitigt*] just as much as it detemporalizes [*entzeitigt*]. Repeated otherwise: it remains open whether the pause can be brought into a relation of condition with time—possibility or impossibility, no matter. The caesura disrupts time. It does not mark the contours of the time out, but rather marks time, as the pause of pause, as porous time. As a sieve. The question of the outline of time, of the word *time, tempus*—a word whose origin is found from time to time in the root of the word *templum,* that relic of ancient mantic art—recurs in the only description that tries to comprehend Thomas's reading—the moment of sinking [*Vertiefung*] into the word, the moment of the enlargement of the word—more precisely. There one finds: "Il lisait. Il lisait avec une minutie et une attention insurpassables [He was reading. He was reading with unsurpassable meticulousness and attention]." Both words that accompany and describe reading, *minutie* and *attention,* aim at the heart of the discussion of time. Of the word. *Tempus.* For its origin oscillates between *spanning* and *splitting.* Between the interpretation as a time *span,* which pulls through the word *attention,* whose closeness to the Latin verb *tendere*—to pull, extend, tend, long, span—shines through (an origin that is preserved by other Indo-European words in the root **temp-*), and the interruption of this interpretation as span and tendency, evident in the word *minutie*—which deciphers the *minute,*—whose derivation from the Latin verb *minuere*—to split—remembers the root **tem-*—to cut, to divide, to split, to slaughter, from which at the time both *tempus*—understood as cut and segment, but also as tailor, as reaper—and *templum,* derive. In Thomas's reading, which deepens [*vertieft*] the moment that enlarges every word, not last *mot* and *Thomas,* into divisible ecstasies, the two mutually exclusive semantic tendencies summoned up to grasp time, the word time, cross each other. More exactly: tending (toward semantics: the framing of the span of a word, of the word time and any other, into its ends), and the interruption of tending. At this moment time starts, yet stops. For in the crossing over of spanning and splitting the insight dawns that they do not stand in an exclusive relation to one another, but cut through one another. No span without starting or breaking off. No cut that does not spread the appearance of a beginning or an end—of a span, of a word. Yet the declaration of these two words as synonyms, span of cut, cut of span, does not come off: in the cut, another, third dimension divides the outline of the span. The irritation between spanning and splitting in the outline of time—in the eye of the reading Thomas—pushes into view a phrase of Rousseau's, which Wartburg's *Französisches Etymologisches Wörterbuch* quotes in order to illustrate the slurred meaning of the word *minutie,* common in French starting in 1768: "application attentive aux menus détails [attentive concentration on small details]."[3] In this definition, the word *attentive* leaps to the eye. But even the word that is to be defined—*minutie*—shows up, furtively, in the definition: in the adjective *menu,* which enters the French language from the past participle *minutes* (cut up into pieces, detailed, small, tiny, insignificant) of the verb *minuere* (to split). The definition attempts to understand *minutie* as a synonym of *attention.* Its attempt at understanding, however, oscillates between in- and exclusion: it attempts to exclude from *minutie* the moment of cutting into pieces, the detailing *in sight* [*im Blick*], to the advantage of the directed, intensive [*angespannt*] glance at the *menus détails* (almost a tautology), at cut-up processes of cutting up, detailed details, details of details—or whatever other splits this composition provokes. Too equal [*zu gleich*], however, it includes *menu* in the definition and in the intent glance at the detail, and defines the detail more precisely, underhandedly, as a splittable part, the glance as a cutting one. The *minutie* wanders, it records the border of the tranformation even of the smallest *significant* details into the *insignificant* and trivial, yet interpretable [*deutbare*] detail: it stops between mantic and semantics. And is about to split even the smallest iota [*Deut*] (*Deut* is the piece that has been knocked off, cut off, split off), even a hair, an H. It is even about to disrupt the iota [*Deut*] and the interpreter [*Deuter*]. Referring explicitly to literary writings and their meaning [*Bedeutung*], Wartburg records for the adjective *minutieux:* "without importance or signification (said of a story)." In the parade of the attempts at defining the word, *minutie* oscillates between deep respect and dismissal, until the latter takes the upper hand, as though in the divisible detail the glance and the sense of measure for the size [*Taille*] of any details threatened to get

3. Walther von Wartburg, *Französisches Etymologisches Wörterbuch,* Volume 6/2 (Basel: Zbinden, 1957), 131.

lost, as though the glance that measures, practices moderation and is authoritative [*der messende und maßhaltende, -gebende Blick*] were to shatter or crumble. As though measurement [*das Vermessen*] were to shatter into presumption [*zum vermessenen*]. The sinking into small, smaller, and most small dimensions—and into the detailability of the smallest things—disfigures what appeared to be a sign into a monstrosity. In another, similar passage of the same chapter that inscribes in the reading glance, crossed over, *minutie* and *attention,* a sentence—as though it attempted to follow through with the Rousseau quotation in Wartburg's *Französisches Etymologisches Wörterbuch*—cuts off, a little further down, the interpenetration of spanning [*Spannen*] and splitting, and exiles *minutie* from the reading glance, which it isolates as an intent [*gespannt*] glance, as the glance in the sign of the *attente* [wait]: "Mais ni les minutes ni les heures n'épuisèrent son attente": Neither minutes nor hours exhausted his wait (for) [*warten (auf)*]. The sentence tends forward from minutes to hours, toward the growing time *span,* which is outgrowing, outlasting division. It identifies the *minutes,* but in them *minutie,* as the counterpart of the *attention* to which it remains external. Thomas's wait, however, tends toward an *être* of which it is said that as it approaches its *monstrosity* grows: "de plus en plus monstrueux [more and more monstrous]." It is the isolated, obscure prosopopoeia of the *minutie,* a prosopopoeia exiled from the glance, that Thomas's waiting aims for: the spanning of the eyes is directed toward the splitting, nothing other than that, of the span. The longer Thomas waits [*attente*]—this wait is a *seeing* into the night—the closer monstrosity comes: the *minutie* in the sinking into the moment, in the moment of the ecstasis of the eyes. It is said that the encounter of the *attente* with *minutie* requires "l'infini du temps [the infinity of time]," and that *minutie* exists "hors du temps [outside time]": outside the span and the wait (for), which however tends toward nothing except *minutie.* Speaking of the *infinity* of time infinitesimalizes, in this passage, the relation of spanning to splitting. This discourse attempts to stall monstrosity, having *demonized* it. For fear accompanies the *attente* [wait] of the eyes for the monstrous approach of the *minutie.* A detachment provokes both a repulsion and an attraction; both a repulsion and an attraction, having become intolerable, provoke a detachment and remove Thomas from Thomas: "Attente et angoisse si insupportables qu'elles le détachèrent du lui-même. Une sorte de Thomas sortit de son corps [Wait and anguish so intolerable that they detached him from himself. A sort of Thomas came out of his body]." This opening of the body and eclipsing, at the moment of the most extreme *attente,* which comes close to a doubling in Thomas and to Thomas, is alluded to by the entry of *minutie* into the semantics of proper names—Thomas, Didymos: it renews the memory of the Greek word *temnein*—to cut, to slaughter, to split—synonym of the Latin verb *minuere,* in the background of the exiled *minutie,* in *Thomas.* The removal of *minutie* from Thomas's eyes arrives too late. From *Thomas,* from the word that opens up—to'am, ta'om, temnein, tomós, tomé, tomás, tà éntoma, tmesis . . . —, the word that causes part (or span: *attente*) and divisibility of the part (or splitting: *minutie*) to oscillate, splitting moves into the span of the moment. Against this *too late,* against the ruin of time in the origin of time, the lines adjacent to the removal of *minutie* from Thomas's attempt to postpone eyes intent [*gespannt*] on the *attente* (nothing except it), on the wait (for nothing except *minutie*), to postpone the moment of the encounter of *attention* and *minutie,* to put down between *attente* and *minutie* the continuum of the span of the delay—*mora.* Thus it is said of Thomas's eyes: "Ses yeux essayèrent de regarder non pas dans l'étendue, mais dans la durée et dans un point du temps qui n'existait pas encore [His eyes attempted to look not into the expanse but into the duration and toward a point in time that did not yet exist]." Against the *too late* the sentence puts up a *not yet.* The point, however, at which the uninterrupted drawing of a line—in space (*étendue*) or in time (*durée*), no matter (since the sentence puts both under the sign of the span)—aims, is not (in the sentence: *not yet*) the point that, as a point in time, one day will pass into the continuum of the line that, so to speak, waits in the future for the time-train [*Zeitzug*]; almost in reverse, it is the incision of the acute, of acupuncture into the appearance of given spans composed of points: the break-in of *minutie* into the tending moment, into the time-train [*Zeitzug*] and moreover into the delay [*Verzug*] (of time)—understood as a span. The sentence that describes the moment of the encounter of the intent eyes with the opaque visage of *minutie* defines the point at which the waiting seeing aims—more precisely, as eyes, eyes from which the description exiles *attention,* into which it enters *minutie.* It calls the eyes tiny: yeux *minuscules:* "C'est dans cet état qu'il se sentit mordu ou frappé, il ne pouvait savoir, par ce qui lui sembla être un mot mais qui ressemblait plutôt à un rat gigantesque, aux yeux minuscules et perçants [It was while he was in this state that he felt himself bitten or hit, he couldn't be sure, by what seemed to him to be a word but which was rather like a gigantic rat with tiny, piercing eyes]." The adjective *perçants*—piercing, drilling—grants to the eyes precisely what causes tininess, the incisive, detailing *minimizing* in the glance, which divides down to the smallest detail. Not a mimetic, but a minimizing, faculty of *diminution* [*Minution*]. An opaque faculty, and precisely for that reason a faculty on the verge of leaving the faculty behind. In the encounter with that which appears to Thomas to be a word—*mot*—but which the anonymous narrator or patronymous author, Maurice Blanchot, finds similar to a gigantic rat—*rat*—, the will to distinguish between large and small, the will to measure and stipulation [*zum Maß und zur Maßgabe*], to the span and to the measurement of that which divides the intent [*gespannt*] glance, collapses. What oscillates between *mot* and *rat* is: *gigantesque* aux yeux *minuscules:* it mixes indistinguishably the huge and the tiny. In the hesitation between *mot* and *rat,* in the incipient conflict of the interpretations between *Thomas* and *literature* (a *roman* [novel] which *Maurice Blanchot* signs and publishes), the sentence describes and writes precisely the moment that it tries to exile from Thomas's eyes, starting out from the entry of the mantis, in order to attribute *attente*—tension, strain—toward the word to Thomas, and in order to attribute *minutie*—fragmentation—to the eye of the mantis, which oscillates between word—*mot*—and rat—*rat.* The sentence—detailed detail of a *novel,* part of the literature of the *novel,* divides, by writing, the ecstasis of the word—mante, mot, rat . . . —the ecstasis of the reading eyes into splintering ecstases divides, by writing, the asymmetry, open toward spanning, in the crossing over of *attention* and *minutie* in Thomas's eyes. It writes, in the mutual interruption of *mot* and *rat,* the splintering delay: **mo**(t)-**ra**(t). The cutting closeness to one another of **Th**o**m**as and **mot,** the cutting closeness to one another of **rat** and litté**rat**ure, undoes the appearance of givenness of both, of a protagonist in his proper name, of a novel, belonging to literature, signed and published in the proper name of its author, Maurice Blanchot. The attempt to divide the crossing of *attention* and *minutie* by dissociation—that is, splitting—of the reading moment into two spans or two entities, into mantis and mantis, to attribute *attente* to the mantis-Thomas (title and proper name of a book, protagonist and reader of the book, described in the book) and *minutie* to the mantis-literature (which contains Thomas, which shares [*teilt*] each word—*mot*—that moves into Thomas and divides [*teilt*] the outline of the word *Thomas*), this attempt fails: it fails because of the opening-up first name, in the pressing forward and penetrating of the opening-up *mots* into *Thomas,* a pressing forward and penetrating out of which the exiled minutie returns and disrupts the association of mantis and mantis into a symmetrical, tense dissociation of the moment into reader and word; it fails because of every word defined more precisely as an opening-up one, words out of words, words that disrupt the appearance of givenness even of the *novel,* composed of countable words, self-same and the same as the meaning that they contain; they disrupt the understanding of the whole novel as a part and detail of the whole *literature;* it fails because of the opening-up *-rat-* in literature, the fraying emblem of rotting, gnawable letters in the glance. What is lost because of the closeness to the *mante*—impossible to interpret unambiguously in the feminine or masculine span of the word—is, not least, the understanding of the *Roman* [novel] as a (male, female) *Romantis,* as a member or noun [*Hauptwort*] of a literary *genre.*[4]

4. To register in the pause or gap between enlargement and reduction, between the one and the other, old and new version of *Thomas l'obscur:* The crossing between *attention* and *minutie* in the glance (through the microscope)—about to be understood as *feminine,*—a crossing that interrupts time and the time *span* traverses, between *obscuritas* and *claritas,* on the threshold of blinding, discreetly, Jules Michelet's book *L'insecte* (Paris: Hachette, 1858): "Les yeux et les mains des femmes, fines et faites aux petits objets, au travail à petits points, sont éminemment propres à ces choses [dealing with insects, T.S.]. Elles ont plus de respect aussi, d'attention, de condescendance, pour les minimes existences. Les études microscopiques spécialemet veulent des qualités féminines. Il faut se faire un peu femme pour y réussir. Le microscope, amusant au premier coup d'oeil, demande, si on veut en faire un usage sérieux . . . surtout du temps, beaucoup de temps, une complète liberté d'heure, pouvoir répéter indéfiniment les mêmes observations, voir le même objet à différents jours, dans la pure lumière du matin, au chaud rayon du midi, et parfois même plus tard . . . ces études demandent . . . qu'on soit . . . hors du temps. . . . Le détail minutieux de l'infiniment petit . . . le grand Swammerdam . . . d'un oeil perçant . . . sur ce fond douteux, obscur, il saisit les premiers linéaments de la vie, et en eux les caractères décisifs et profonds qui sont le mystère de l'insecte . . . *l'insecte et le fils de la nuit* . . . à peine de douteux linéaments qu'on voit ou que l'on croit voir. Dans quelques temps, vous pourrez, avec une fine aiguille, isoler ces je ne sais quoi, et vous figurer que ce sont les membres du futur papillon. Lacune effrayante. Il y a (pour beaucoup d'espèces) un moment où rien de l'ancien ne paraît plus, où rien du nouveau ne paraît encore. . . . Swammerdam, devant l'infini du monde microscopique, paraît saisi de terreur . . . insatiable observateur du plus minutieux détail . . . percer d'un fin regard le menu détail, Swammerdam créa la méthode du grossissement successif . . . il fixa ces choses éphémères, obligea le temps de faire halte et força la mort de durer . . . je ne sais quelle tendresse, une sensibilité féminine (dans un mâle génie scientifique). . . . Il lui semblait que la science, lancée par lui, . . . le menait à quelque chose de grand et de terrible, qu'il n'aurait pas voulu voir: . . . le microscope . . . On comprend parfaitement l'absorbant attrait qu'il exerce . . . [Gallery of blinded seers, or going blind—T.S.] Le premier, Huber, de bonne heure a été aveugle. L'illustre auteur du grand ouvrage sur le hanneton, M. Strauss, l'est devenu à peu près. Notre pâle et ardent Robin est déjà sur cette pente, et poursuit sans s'arrêter. . . . J'allais dire: L'insecte est

The deep irritation produced by the *minutie* crypted in the intent glance for the appearance of given entities, of the protagonist and title—*Thomas l'obscur,*—of the protagony of the novel, for the novel, for anonymous narrating entities of either gender, for the patronymous entity of the author Maurice Blanchot, is pushed into view by a book by Maurice Blanchot published in 1950 with the same title, *Thomas l'obscur,* which is called again and still a *roman* [novel], and so adds to literature, but which bears, on the cover page, between title and genre, the additional note *nouvelle version.*[5] This new version originates, at first comparative glance, by way of cuts in the first or other, published in 1941, which it reduces in length to about a third. A tighter, tense [*gespannt*] version, resulting from cuts. Span resulting from cuts: *at-*

femme. . . . Pour les instruments qui percent, taillent, scient, etc., malgré tous nos progrès, l'insecte a peut-être encore aujourd'hui un peu d'avance sur l'homme. . . . [. . . Women's eyes and hands, fine and used to small objects, to stitching, are eminently apt for these things [dealing with insects—T.S.]. They have also more respect, more attention, more condescension for the smallest beings. . . . Microscopic research especially needs feminine qualities. One must become woman a little if one wants to succeed in them. The microscope, amusing at first glance, requires, if one wants to make serious use of it . . . above all time, much time, a complete freedom with one's hours, the ability to repeat indefinitely the same observations, to see the same object on different days, in the pure light of the morning, in the warm rays of noon, and sometimes even later . . . these studies require . . . that one be . . . outside time. . . . The minute detail of the infinitely small . . . the great Swammerdam . . . with a piercing eye . . . on this unclear, obscure background, he seizes the first traits of life, and in them the decisive and profound characteristics that are the mystery of the insect . . . *the insect is the offspring of night* . . . barely unclear traits that one sees or thinks one sees. In a while, you will be able to isolate this je ne se quoi with a fine needle, and you can imagine that it is the limbs of the future butterfly. Terrifying gap. There is (for many species) a moment when nothing of the old appears anymore, when nothing of the new appears yet. . . . Swammerdam, in front of the infinity of the microscopic world, appears seized by terror . . . insatiable observer of the most minute detail . . . to pierce with a fine eye the minute detail, Swammerdam created the method of progressive enlargement . . . he stopped these ephemeral things, forced time to halt and death to last. . . . I don't know what tenderness, a feminine sensitivity (inside a male scientific genius) . . . It seemed to him that the science he had launched . . . was leading him to something great and terrible that he would have preferred not to see: . . . the microscope . . . One understands perfectly well the absorbing attraction it exercises . . . one cannot come away from it. . . . How many workers it has deprived, if not of life, at least of their eyes! [Gallery of blinded seers, or going blind—T.S.:] The first Huber, soon became blind. The illustrious author of the great work on the maybug, Mr. Strauss, almost did. Our pale and ardent Robin is already headed in this direction, and continues on without stopping. . . . I was going to say: The insect is woman. . . . For the instruments that pierce, cut, saw, etc., despite our progress, the insect still today perhaps has some advance on man. . . .]" (x-xi, 53–54, 56, 73, 97–98, 106, 112–13, 180)

5. Maurice Blanchot, *Thomas l'obscur* (new version) (Paris: Gallimard, 1950), 27–33.

tente from *minutie.* In reference to the reading scene of the fourth chapter of both versions: the new version originates by way of cuts, of splits in the intent [*gespannt*] glance at the open book, *Thomas l'obscur,* by way of diminutions that dissect, in the glance, the tension as well as the composition—each word, each letter—of the old version. It disfigures the first or other version by that *minutie* in the intent glance that both versions attempt to fade out of Thomas's eyes. While the first version inscribes the *minutie* that is in the word *minuscules* in the eye, cut up or doubled into eyes, in the mantis (in the eye of the reading Thomas), namely further down, in place of the mantis in that which seems to Thomas to be *mot,* but seems to the anonymous or patronymous literary figure [*Literat*] to be *rat,* to be at least close to *rat,* the new version is traversed by one more cut: this version cuts the adjective *minuscules* from the eyes of the *rat* and calls, evidently in order to avoid the conflict with *minutie* in Thomas's eyes, only the left-over *perçants:* "un rat gigantesque, aux yeux perçants [a gigantic rat with piercing eyes]." The exclusion of the word *minuscules* here, from the eyes of *rat, mot,* and *mantis,* the eclipsing of that word in which *minute* and *minutie* dawn, that names cutting and splitting, documents the attempt to deny *minutie* to the open book that Thomas reads, as well as to the novel with the title *Thomas l'obscur.* The denied *minutie* affects, in the reprint of the new version, also *literature:* on the title page of the reprint the genre designation *roman* [novel] has been cut out and is missing. This moment cuts the book with the title *Thomas l'obscur* out of its binding, out of a literary genre and literature in general. More precisely: it cuts literature apart. In the glance that divides *minutie, dis*poses the frame of literature, of each and every letter. The tendency of the cuts to ban *minutie* not only from Thomas's eyes but also, in the new version, from the eyes of the mantis, of the rat, of literature, to deny the cutting glance both to the reader and to the text, pushes, obliquely, opaquely, eyes into view that can be looked for in the signature *Maurice Blanchot.* The new version, much thinner, almost a miniature of the first, is in precisely the same relation to the first as the female praying mantis is to the reading Thomas in the description of the scene of reading in both versions. The new, thinner version, *Thomas l'obscur,* cuts up *Thomas l'obscur,* the old and longer one. Thus the new version puts the first published one, from the viewpoint of the *Souvenirs entomologiques,* not so much in the position of the female mantis but of the ash-colored migratory locust, that so much more voluminous prey of the mantis, and inscribes in

Fabre's formulation that in the mantis the axiom of semantics is reversed—"du contenu moindre que le contenant [content smaller than container]"—a paradoxical echo: the smaller the container, the larger the content. The second, or new, version, produced from the first by way of cuts, contains, holds the first as much as it withholds it: it has devoured it. At first glance, anyway. What, however, is (with)holding, what (with)held in it? Do the parts of the second version compose the body of the triumphing mantis as an exhibit of the pieces of its prey, incorporated and exposed in its body, and does the blank between the letters and words trace the seam toward the untouched remainder of the consumed book *Thomas l'obscur*? Or does the second version, in reverse, show the untouched remainders of the dismembered prey, what is left over—*tà éntoma,*—sacrificial pieces, insections, of the consumed book *Thomas l'obscur,* and does the blank between letters and words sew the seam in the direction of the consumed part of the prey, no longer available to the glance, the seam toward the invisible, transfigured body of the praying mantis? The new version oscillates between mantis and mantis: between a triumphant female reader, who beheads, takes apart, and consumes all coming male readers—or will the new version, sooner or later, become the prey of a later, thinner version?—and the dismembered remainders of the infatuated reader, laid out for consumption, for reading. The new version, however, in spite of all the difficulty in interpretation and the opacity of what it offers to the eye, proceeds from that which both versions, in a passage of the fourth chapter, call a *carnage* between the word *he* and the word *I,* a massacre (the first version defines it more precisely as *interminable,* and as the massacre between two *cockroaches,* two words that the second version cuts off): another, blunt word for *minutie.* What the *minutie* that the second version results from tends toward, the *minutie* that is exiled from the eyes of the mantis (Thomas), as well as from the eyes of the mantis (mot : rat : literature), and that holds open the interpretation of the second version to both, to the remainders of the consumed male mantis as well as to the body of the consuming female, is what the tense, concise new version of the sentence introducing the mantis alludes to. The first version spoke of word and sign—"chaque mot, chaque signe [each word, each sign]" in the eye of the reading Thomas; the second version cuts or splits off the word—*mot*—, and keeps only the sign—*signe:* "Il était, auprès de chaque signe, dans la situation où se trouve le mâle quand la mante va le dévorer [He was, in relation to each sign, in the situation of the male mantis when the female is going to devour him]." The second version cuts *mot* from the figure of the praying female mantis and carves it into the figure of the captured male. It identifies *mot* (in *mot,* however, every word) as a prey, as prey of lite*rat*ure (this assumption is held by the new version until the moment that splits off the word *roman* [novel] from the title page). By being the only one that identifies the sign—*signe*—as a signifying one, with the mantis, it turns its attention [*Augenmerk*] from the moment [*Augenblick*] signed *Thomas* (l'obscur) to the signature of the book, *Maurice* (Blanchot). The mantis of both versions moves into the signature of the book. However, it hurts or consumes neither the moment signed *Thomas* nor the title of both versions: *Thomas l'obscur.* As though the signature, fortified, as though it were a faculty, with *minutie*—Maurice Blanchot—was hindered by a timidity in detailing, cutting out, or splitting up the title. As though the title, *Thomas . . .*, made it necessary to leave on even the genre designation *novel,* even the belief in *literature* in order to rescue at least the signature—Maurice Blanchot: the second version, too, does not touch, in the sentence that precedes the introduction of the mantis, the crossing over of *attention* and *minutie* in the reading moment signed *Thomas.* Thus both title and signature trace the outline of an apotropaic situation: *minutie* against *minutie,* mantis against mantis, *Thomas . . .* against *Maurice. . . .* As though in *Thomas* the *opening-up* word, forestalling the intended, meticulous [*minutiös*] splitting *in the name* of the author, were attempting, from the page under consideration [*im Blick*], to understand the—opening up—word as a proper name.

The only—at first glance, the only—addition in the new version, which appears to have been produced by way of cuts and abridgments from the previous version, is an endpaper that acts as a theoretical hinge between the two versions, in the position of the rapidly extending forelimbs, so to speak, if the second version takes, with respect to the first, the position of the praying mantis, *about* to cut the first version. A miniature theory of the version, of the relation between the two versions, *Thomas l'obscur* and *Thomas l'obscur,* to each other. More precisely and more opaquely: miniature theory of diminution—of that which the version into version, into more or less tense *attente,* cuts out. "Il y a," thus begins the subsequent endpaper exposed between all the versions, "pour tout ouvrage, une infinité de variantes possibles [for each work an infinite number of possible variants]." The sentence introduces a distinction between *ouvrage* and *variante,* text and variant; it calls the text one, the variants infinite, without mentioning a criterion that would prevent each variant, *as* text in its turn—intersecting with the infinity of the variants of that text—from triggering infinite variants: the introduced distinction *splinters.* The following sentence, however, by way of dates, appears to recall the contours of the original variant, the beginning and end of the first published text: "Aux pages intitulées *Thomas l'obscur,* écrites à partir de 1932, remises à l'éditeur en mai 1940, publiées en 1941, la présente version n'ajoute rien [To the pages written starting in 1932, turned into the editor in May 1940, published in 1941, the present version adds nothing]." The present version adds nothing. It adds nothing, except—among other things—the sentence that says that it adds nothing. If the new version adds nothing, however, what does it subtract or cut off? Which sentence does it undo, which word does it cut out, cut apart, which does it replace, and for what reason? The sentence goes on: "mais comme elle leur ôte beaucoup, on peut la dire autre et même toute nouvelle, mais aussi toute pareille [but since this version takes much away from them, one can say that it is different and even all new, but also just the same]." The present version, because it is much indebted to the one that precedes it, that underlies it, can be said to be different, in fact completely new, but also the same. The adjectives *different, new,* and *same* are not synonyms of a pretended [*vorgegebenen*] or a pregiven [*zuvorgegebenen*], nor of an open, renounced [*aufgegebenen*], single, or diverse signification; rather, they are *in-different.* They mean nothing. The version published in 1950 is essentially no different from the one published in 1941; thus it is also not the same, but the relation of the two versions to each other is *in-different.* All the same. The sentence grounds this peculiar indifference of the two versions to each other by the following addition, which concludes the sentence and the endpaper: "si, entre la figure et ce qui est ou s'en croit le centre, l'on a raison de ne pas distinguer, chaque fois que la figure complète n'exprime elle-même que la recherche d'un centre imaginaire [if one has good reason not to distinguish between the figure and that which is or believes itself to be the center, each time that the complete figure itself expresses nothing but the search for an imaginary center]." The version may be said to be the same, all the versions may be said to be indifferent to each other, when one has good reason not to distinguish between the figure (or version) and that which is, or appears to be, its middle; all the more so when the complete figure (or version) expresses nothing other than the search for an imaginary middle. The versions circumscribe a middle from which they (seem to) originate, and toward which—and it is indifferent whether they are called old or new, other or same—they move. The versions mean nothing, except that middle that they seek, out of which they seek to originate, to which they seek to belong. However, the dating of the versions drives a wedge into this indifference, and poses the question of the origination of the versions out of each other. Out of the scene of reading, around mantis and mantis, in the fourth chapter of both versions, the one that is always dated earlier assumes the position of the prey (one more voluminous in relation to the preying glance and body, *a limine* similar to the ash-colored migratory locust) of a future, thinner, diminished [*diminuiert*] version—and it is indifferent, whether it offers to sight the unused or related pieces of the one that already exists and underlies it, oscillating between in- and exclusion. The tendency—*attente*—of the dated series of the versions aims, infinitesimally, toward a most thin word-piece, fragment, detail, which, impossible as it is to interpret unambiguously with the version, contains not only all the published and underlying versions, but also all the possible versions; versions, or spans, that originate from the division of the middle, from the di-minution of the tiniest thing. This tiniest thing would be, in accordance with the formulation of the endpaper, original and internal image [*Ur- und Inbild*], imago of all versions understood as visions in the endpaper, which equalizes—defines more precisely as *obscure*—the difference between vision and hallucination, between phenomenal and phantomatic appearance. The *visio,* or span—*attente*—each version (infinite variants, according to the formulation of the endpaper), originates from the *divisio,* or splitting—*minutie*—of a most tiny, most divisible detail, not from a version. And if from an image [*Bild*], then from a splintering one, from the ability of all images to splinter. No matter whether ad-image, internal image, to-image, copy [Am-, In-, Ad-, Ab-, *-bild*—a reference to *Aminadab,* Blanchot's second novel—Trans.]. This detail, coming out of the moment of the scene of reading in all versions—around mantis and mantis—fades out in *Thomas.* It comes out of the opening-up moment, signed *Thomas,* that scatters every word—*mot*—that penetrates it, and that divides the outline of the signature, writing it apart into words out of words; yet it also scatters in these words the opaque origin—*minutie*—of all versions. Toward this detail—*Thomas*—, however, the tendency of the scene of reading to subtract *minutie* from *Thomas,* and to inscribe the *mot* that mutates into a *rat,* repeated in an opening-up word, spans, or waits. And finally, in the moment that loses even the belief in the possible givenness of literature, which cuts out the word *roman* from the title page of the new version, the tendency to seal *minutie* in the book's signature, *Maurice Blanchot.* As though the signature, the *splintering* seal, mustered in *Maurice* the description of a more unregulated, more opaque divisibility of each word—*mot*—against *Thomas,* namely against the *tmesis* decipherable in the *opening-up* signature. Exposing *Maurice* in, and between, two—among other, all other—languages: *Mot-Riß* [word-tear] (too close to the tearing apart of the word—*mot*—in *Thomas*—T.om).

A track in this agonal silhouette, the outline of a shadow, a rip in a pocket [*Schatten-, Taschenriß*] which disrupts, between the signature and the title of the book, in all versions, even the appearance of the structuring into *agon,* just before the *moment* [*des Augenblickes* auf dem Sprung], is left by a passage toward the end of both versions, which *Thomas* explains as a word—*mot*—in the version published in 1941, but complements with the word *vide* in the version published in 1950. A passage that—in the opening-up word and moment, between mantis and mantis, between *Thomas* and *Maurice*—opens the question of the end of literature, of the beginning of literature, the *beginning/ending* [*anfangende*] question: that of the *name.* After the end: the 1941 version closes, after and under the end of the last sentence, with the word FIN [end], which is missing in the 1950 version, as though it had lost, with its composure, the belief in the end, in dated and datable ends, beginning and end—of the novel, of literature. (The endpaper functions, precisely for this reason, like a fascinating ocellus. The new version, in the eclipsed end—FIN—of literature, touches on the *affinity* in the outline of each word, each letter; the *affinity* of beginning and end of literature. The affirmation, defined more precisely as *affinition,* of each word as opening-up words out of words, in the moment. What is affined is what crosses the intent glance, what breaks apart, breaks out of the span of the explanation of it as word. It affines—or sifts—the expectant, intent glance into a detailing one; it divides the binding separation in the inside and outside of the glance, the inside and outside of the word, it minutiates [*minutiiert*] the ends of language.[6]

In the seam of both versions there is talk of people breaking out, of a city, emigrants, those who were already called *nomads* when they lived

6. The lines on *Affinition,* here, trace—among other things—*affinity* to what Werner Hamacher develops elsewhere with the word *Afformativ* (Werner Hamacher, "Afformativ, Streik," in Christian L. Hart Nibbrig, ed., *Was heißt "Darstellen"?* (Frankfurt a.M: Suhrkamp, 1994) 340–71.

there, nomads "in their own houses," who shatter the word Oiko-*nomie,* who break forth from the word, who scatter the explanation of word and language as house, scatter the economy of the language of word; these "nomads" rise up, "comme des astres"—like stars or like disasters—oscillating between star and unlucky star, *astres* and *dé-sastres,* they rise up into constellations setting off [*aufbrechenden*] into Thomas's eyes, Thomas, of whom it is said in the next sentence—in a manner true to the novel's tendency to register *attente* in Thomas's eyes, to fade *minutie* out of them—that he, as a shepherd, leads and accompanies the constellations, and attempts to steer the stream of man-stars into the first night (the night of the description of the moment of reading, between mantis and mantis). And both versions pause, as they speak of what breaks out toward this night, over the difference between *word* and *name.* They pause in a sentence that *Thomas* concludes: affines both times. In the first version: "d'autres qui répétaient avec acharnement leur nom pour le retenir, perdirent cependant le souvenir de la parole, des sons, de la bouche, alors qu'ils continuaient à faire retentir *le mot de Thomas* [my emphasis] [others, although they relentlessly repeated their name to retain it, nonetheless lost the memory of the spoken word, of sounds, of the mouth, while they continued to intone *le mot de Thomas*]." Besides rearranging, leaving out, and substituting a few words in the sentence, the new version complements the phrase *le mot de Thomas* with the word *vide* [empty]: "d'autres qui gardaient avec acharnement leur nom, perdirent la mémoire de la parole, tandis qu'ils répétaient *le mot vide de Thomas* [others, who relentlessly held on to their names, lost the memory of the spoken word, while they repeated *le mot vide de Thomas*]." A German translation of the new version attempts to render the phrase thus: "während sie Thomas' leeres Wort wiederholten [while they repeated Thomas's empty word]." But the phrase is not resolved in this span. The first phrase already oscillates between "Thomas's word" and "the word *Thomas.*" Between Thomas, the word, and Thomas, the name. Between Thomas and Thomas: Thomas interpreted as *word* and Thomas as *setting off.* The second version however interrupts the oscillation between two spans, or interpretations. In the addition, which at first glance hollows the word—no matter whether it is Thomas's (unnamed) word or the word *Thomas*—into an *empty* one, and posits as absolute the *attente* in Thomas, the ruin of *attention* appears: the beginning of a third interpretation in the intent glance deciphers in *vide* precisely the word that the formulation of the first version, from the angle of its explanation as Thomas's word, withholds: *vide* is Thomas's word, which those who are setting off repeat. The repetitions, however, direct the glance toward the deviations in the return. The word *vide* opens up. The word, which is meaningful in the context of the other interpretations of the semantic status of the word, the word that calls the questionable ones—the word *Thomas,* Thomas's word—*empty,* devoid of content, defines more precisely every word as one that *opens up:* if the questionable words are *empty,* yet *empty* remains a word, the questionable words burst out [*brechen . . . auf*] into words out of words; the expectant tension is directed at the emptiness itself, at the word *empty* itself, and the halves of semantics, the signifying and signified spheres, are out of joint. Repeated otherwise, the *word* bursts out [*bricht . . . auf*] into *name* (in accordance with an opaque closeness that suggests a similarity between the *name* and the *nomads* setting off, but a similarity, in them, to the *Nehmen* [taking]: *nemein*[7]—meaning to divide, to slaughter, to split, but also, next to *legein,* the more cutting-off reading[8]—, in *nemein* however less to the *semantics* of the break than to the dawning, but also breaking off, of semantics and mantic): *vide* opens up. In the context of the French language, *vide* means *empty,* yet it traces, splintering the frame of the one language, too close to the word of another, close language, the Latin *vide*: *see!* In the moment of departure [*Aufbrechen*], between two languages and versions, in the seam of the shattering imperative—see!—which is issued out of the deciphered text toward the moment signed *Thomas,* the *visio* of the one or other interpretation breaks up [*bricht . . . auf*] into *divisio,* and every span—whether a word, a letter, a point—breaks up into a more detailable one. In the *attente,* in the intent glance seeking to see, the unpreventable *minutie* breaks up. The word breaks up into an opening-up one; in the word, the name. Thomas breaks up into the divisible *tmesis*—of literature. In Thomas, the *di-vide*-seeing breaks up.

7. On the discussion of the correspondence to one another of *nemein* and *Nehmen,* starting from their closeness to the *name,* see my *Parerga:* Friedrich Hölderlin; Carl Schmitt, Franz Kafka; Platon, Friedrich Schleiermacher, Walter Benjamin; Jacques Derrida. Zur literarischen Hermeneutik (Munich: K. Boer, 1991).

8. On the discussion of the correspondence to one another of *némein* and *légein,* see Jesper Svenbro, *phrasikleia* (Paris: La Découverte, 1988), esp. Chapter 6: "Nómos, exégèse, lecture," 123–36: "Now, from the moment that one examines, in its entirety, the list of Greek verbs meaning 'to read,' one realizes that *nómos* could very well be the noun of action of one of them and consequently present a situation analogous to that of *lex.* For one of these verbs—though not very frequent in this sense—is precisely *némein*" (124).

Out of the *opening-up* word in the moment signed *Thomas,* which provokes the taking back of the word FIN from the first version, the taking back of the word *roman* from the title page of the new version, which *affines* the will to language and literature, *Thomas l'obscur,* which, in the diminishing sequence of all the versions, with the mantis in mind, sketches the silhouette of a notice, narrowed to the duel between two first names, an agonal, apotropaic notice, *Maurice* (Blanchot) against *Thomas* (l'obscur), author's name against title, in order to preserve *minutie* as the faculty of a named entity expressed in words, in order, on the contrary, to ban the *opening-up* word in the glance—*Thomas*—to the empty span—*attente*—, to the opening credits [*Vorspann*], between mantis and mantis, *Thomas l'obscur,* not finally, but after the end, not at the beginning, but before the beginning, touches, in *Thomas,* on the beginning/ending [*anfangende*] question of the name.

—Translated from the German by Georgia Albert

HANS-JOST FREY

The Last Man and the Reader[1]

Thinking the last man means thinking any man as the last one. The only thing that distinguishes the last man from others is the fact that he is the last. The peculiarity of being the last consists precisely in the loss of meaning of the peculiarity of this man with respect to man as such. The death of the last man is not only, like the death of any other man, his own: it is the death of man in general. The end of the last man is the end of humanity. This end is in no way accessible to man, since it is his own. This is true, of course, for every death, but the

1. All references to Maurice Blanchot, *Le dernier homme,* are given here with the page number for the first edition (Paris: Gallimard, 1951), followed by the page number for the new version (Paris: Gallimard, 1957), followed by the page number for the English translation by Lydia Davis, *The Last Man* (New York: Columbia University Press, 1987). References to Blanchot, *L'espace littéraire* are abbreviated *EL,* followed by page numbers from the first edition (Paris: Gallimard, 1955), from the collection idées edition (Paris: Gallimard, 1968), and from the English translation by Ann Smock, *The Space of Literature* (Lincoln: University of Nebraska, 1982). Translations of both works have been slightly modified. [Editor]

YFS 93, *The Place of Maurice Blanchot,* ed. Thomas Pepper, © 1998 by Yale University.

death of any one man is survived by the humanity of other men, in whose memory death lives. In the case of the last man there is no such backward glance toward the end. Humanity, of which he is a part, cannot continue and preserve itself in other men: it ends in him. Beyond the last man there is nothing human anymore—only what is beyond man. In the last man, death as the limit of humanity appears. Mortality—the mental anticipation of one's own death made possible by the backward glance at the death of others—is human. Death, however, is not: to the extent that it is possible to think the last man, death is the end of humanity.

But what was often strongest was the thought that in him we had been dead for a long time: not in that exact form, which would have been almost easy to accept, but in the reflection I read with uncertainty, with resentment, on our faces, that at that point we too had allowed something to die in us that should have found support in us, something that was not only ourselves, but our future and the future of all men and also of the last man. A thought that did not yet allow itself to be thought. (59/56/32)

The last man, the man at the limit of humanity, who is open to the no longer human, lacks self-reflection. But it is not reflection understood as that which is human that ends with the last man. The issue is not to say what humanity is, it is that it ends. However, it does not end so long as reflection takes place. The lastness of the last man is neutralized as long as he is accompanied by an entity, even himself, which perceives him as the last man. Reflection belongs to mortality, not to death. It hinders the opening toward the no

He wasn't to split in two. This is the great temptation of those who are approaching their end: they look at themselves and talk to themselves; they turn themselves into a solitude peopled by themselves—the emptiest, the most false. (24/24/11)

longer human, which the last man, as a dying one, and the dying man, as the last one, already nearly attains. In reflection, humanity endlessly obstructs the end of humanity. Someone is always still there who obliterates the end by limiting it.

The question about the witness is the question about the narrator. The last man does not see himself. Thus, only someone else can tell his story [*Erzählung*]. But this only reproduces the doubling that is already present in self-reflection. Now it can be said that the last man does not see himself, but the accompanying narrator must survive the last man in order to be able to tell about him, thus obliterating him as the last. Thanks to the transfer of the reflective capacity onto the narrator, the last man's breaking glance is preserved unbroken, but only for a glance that, simply by existing, shows everything that it sees as the last thing to be an anticipating fiction. The narrator, whose ability to tell of the last man consists only in his imaging him in anticipation or in his looking back to him, must annihilate himself, in order not to contradict the truth of his story simply by telling it. One could also say: the last

"I can't think about myself. . . . " (8/8/2)

I was there, not in order to see him, but so that he wouldn't see himself. . . . (24/23/11)

. . . so that his face would remain bare and his gaze undivided. (24/22-3/11)

. . . I was there—the "I" was already no more than a Who?, a whole crowd of Who?s—so that there would be no one between him and his destiny. . . . I was there . . . so that it would be me he saw in the mirror, someone other than him—another, a stranger, nearby, gone, the shadow of the other shore, no one—and that in this way he would remain a man until the very end. (24/22-3/11)

man has no history [*Geschichte*], since, as the last man, he leaves behind no narrator who can remind himself and others about him. The "story" ["*Geschichte*"] of the last man is without witnesses, cannot be told, is without a narrator.

But slowly—abruptly—the thought occurred to me that this story had no witness. . . . (23/22/10-11)

The elimination of the witnessing narrator opens up the question of where the narrative about the last man comes from. It is a first-person narrative—though with occasional switches to the third person,—yet the told story cannot be traced back to a stable entity. It is a feature of the figure of the last man that he is no longer accessible to any human glance, not even his own. The dimension beyond man that is involved in the idea of the last man pulls all that is human to the border of its end, where its special quality pales and it begins to become simple presence. In the wake of this idea, the characters in Blanchot's narrative, since all they are is dying, have become impersonal. Who they are no longer has any importance: it is just that they still are. The narrator, too. The word "I" is no longer a pronoun, but has become hardly more than the sound *je* that is produced by the breath as it passes through

I owed him a limitless distraction, and even less, the opposite of expectation, the reverse of faith, which wasn't doubt: ignorance and neglect. But still this wasn't enough: this ignorance had to ignore even me and leave me to one side, gently, uncertainly, without any sense of exclusion or aversion. (23/21-2/10)

And who is talking? Is it you? Is it me in you? Is it the murmur that keeps passing between us and whose different echoes reach us from shore to shore? (148/138-39/83)

But how the word I vibrated between her teeth, passing like a breath. . . . (30/28/14)

the teeth. I no longer stands for a name—at most, it stands for its absence. It designates the smallest possible difference from the anonymity beyond humanity. In and out of this beyond is where one should tell of the last man, except that thinking and speaking beyond humanity is also a mental anticipation, just like the thought of the last man. Thinking the last man means thinking the end of man. The end of man renders necessary the question of the dimension beyond the border of man. But the latter is defined as what is beyond man and therefore inaccessible to him. It is available to the anticipating thought only as that which is essentially out of reach, never available to him.

This unreachable element can be experienced through the last man, not because it becomes accessible, but because it remains withheld as that toward which the text is unwaveringly underway. The problem for Blanchot's text is to say what cannot be said without losing it as unsayable by saying it. Blanchot's text is not so much about saying what the unsayable is, but rather how it is able to appear. That is, the question is about the particular form of cata-

That I—this is what I can't say—was terrible: terribly gentle and weak, terribly naked and without decency, a tremor alien to all pretense, altogether pure of me, but of a purity that went to the far end of everything, that revealed and delivered over what was altogether dark, maybe the last I, the one that will astonish death, the one that death draws to itself like the secret that is forbidden it, a piece of flotsam, a still-living footprint, a mouth open in the sand. (31/29/15)

chresis as which this text constitutes itself.

* * * * *

I: no personal pronoun, but a sign for the dissolution of what it should stand for: the personal. The last man no longer says I: he is without standpoint and without world. Almost. So much so that he needs the other, who still has a remainder of world, in order not to go under in the lack of differentiation. I is the sign not only for the dissolution of the person, but also for the remainder of the one who dissolves. Not only does the person disappear in "I": that which is still left of the person also turns into a personification of disappearance, a becoming-worldly of the one who is without world, the visage of the invisible, the humanization of the non-human.

We: not a plurality of people, but an impersonal generality in which people get lost. Not I and you and you . . ., but neither I nor you. No longer I and no longer you in the drunkenness of we. We, however, also as the appearance of the I and you that have disappeared in it. We: no longer the community of people that will be named and not yet the anonymous gener-

He was there, entirely there, and yet someone who was less himself, who gave less certainty of being himself, someone absolutely insufficient, without reliance on himself or on anything else, without even that fullness of suffering visible on certain faces when for one instant, through some unknown grace of being, the greatest suffering is contained and endured. Then why did he impose himself to such an extent? How was he present, with that simple, evident presence, near us, but in some sense without us, without our world, maybe without any world? (56/53-4/30)

But he really didn't have any world, that was why she tried to give him hers. . . . (32/31/16)

It was as though some instinct had told her that in his presence she should say I, only I, that he was fascinated by this light word over which she herself had so few rights and which she pronounced in such a way that it designated almost someone else. (30/28-9/14)

This "we" that holds us together and in which we are neither one nor the other? (49/46/26)

. . . this drunkenness that always says We. (131/122/73)

. . . as though, confronting him, what had been I had strangely awakened into "we," the presence and united force of the common spirit. (9/9/2)

ality of the impersonal. Its appearance as pronominal remainder.

The depersonalization of the personal pronoun is, in the opposite perspective, the personalization of the impersonal. Just as the loss of name leaves behind the pronoun as the remainder out of which it can be read, this personification in Blanchot's text is not only the substitution of the invisible with a visage, but just as much the figure of its failure to materialize. The second part of the narrative is principally an apostrophe to the immobile thought and hence its personification. But the you inserted as an interlocutor by the address does not succeed in acquiring a visage. The prosopopoeia remains a wish that is never quite fulfilled. The visage remains invisible. But precisely this preserves the possibility that the appearance does not obliterate the invisible that is supposed to appear in it. For the invisible, appearing is doom. The visage of the invisible as such can only bear the traits of its refusal to appear. It is not so much the invisible that appears in it, but its inability to appear. The *you* in Blanchot's text is not only the personification of thought, but also, and more so, the per-

Motionless thought. . . . I want to talk with you, you who do not answer. (127/119/71-2)

It is true that I, too, still have the desire to talk to you as to a face confronting me over there on the horizon. Invisible face. (150/140-41/85)

Maybe there are many faces, but only one face, neither beautiful, nor friendly, nor hostile, simply visible: this face I imagine you are, even the face that you certainly are, because of this refusal to appear that is in you . . . (153/144/87)

sonification of the impossibility of the personification of thought, the visage of the absent visage of the invisible. It is not what cannot appear that appears, but its inability to appear. But the inability to appear does not appear only by being an object of communication, but in the failure of the figure that makes the invisible appear to materialize completely—for example, in the fact that the *you* does not acquire any contours. The figure of the invisible is figure not because it makes the invisible visible, but because the invisible remains withheld in it. The completed figure presents the danger of deception. It is taken for that for which it stands, as though it were the overcoming of the inability to appear. Blanchot's text, which constitutes itself as the continual nonreaching of the complete figure of the invisible, unwaveringly undermines the fiction it builds, and thereby remains open to that which it allows to appear precisely by not saying it. This opening toward what remains unsaid is the impossibility of closing off a text that can only say the unsayable by not saying it and therefore is incomplete. The incessant non-arriving is a basic characteristic of Blanchot's narrative.

* * * * *

What is experienced as the difficulty of Blanchot's text is based on the expectation that there is a hidden meaning that should be brought to light. Understanding would, then, require the removal of an obstacle that blocks access to the meaning of the text. The beginning of *Le dernier homme* speaks of this obstacle when the last man talks of the fact that he cannot think about himself. Thus the idea that there is still an obstacle that blocks access to myself remains very much presupposed, but the obstacle here consists precisely in the fact that there is none. If something is in the way, one can fight it and perhaps overcome it in order to go further. What hinders now, however, is precisely the lack of a resistance that helps to go on: the absence of an obstacle that one does not encounter, through which one cannot locate oneself, and past which one falls into emptiness. This means, to turn it differently, that it is precisely the obstacle that allows access to that for which it is an obstacle. What is beyond the obstacle is only accessible

And if he hadn't said to me one day: "I can't think about myself: there is something terrible there, a difficulty that slips away, an obstacle that can't be met"? (8/8/2)

as that to which one's progress is hindered. If the obstacle is absent, there is nothing. For this reason precisely the absence of obstacles is what withholds, but in such a way that there is no hope to advance, by overcoming a resistance, toward something that has been withheld, because there is no resistance and nothing is withheld.

Blanchot's text functions like the obstacle one does not encounter. It is difficult not because there is a hidden meaning one needs to discover, but because one cannot arrive at what matters by clearing obstacles out of the way. The text makes available what matters to it precisely through the fact that it does not make it available: not because it withholds it, but because it does not have it. It remains unsaid, not because it is kept quiet, but because it cannot be said. The accomplishment of the text does not consist in attempting to say what cannot be said, but in leaving it unsaid and in keeping present that which is out of reach for it by never allowing it to crystallize into an unambiguous statement.

Such a text is figurative in the sense that what it says is not what it means. It would be misleading, however, to inter-

And only what is disturbed can appear. (154/144/87)

. . . and what held me back was—I don't know what—something too easy, in that approach, which left it without defense and me without decision. It was too simple. (116/108-9/65)

pret what the text says as a figure for what cannot be said. Although what is said sets one in motion toward what cannot be said, it does not mean it. Because the point is not to say the unsayable, the access to it is not opened even by an interpretation of what is said. There is no access to it at all, but only the possibility of experiencing it as inaccessible. This experience cannot consist in saying, and thus denying, the unsayable, whether as such or through figures that take its place; rather, the experience perceives the unsaid that is absent in what is said. What is there is open toward something that is present in it as lack, but which cannot be ascertained by any interpretation. The text is, then, also *not* figurative, since what it says precisely does not mean the other thing that appears in it. It is not possible to interpret what is said in the direction of the unsayable. It is rather the case that one experiences the unspeakable through the impossibility of interpreting what is said. The text does not mean something other than what it says. But it happens by saying something, as the constant not-saying of the unsayable, which is inherent in what is said as the impossibility of interpreting it.

The text is not interpretable. Not because the difficulties it poses for interpretative skill are too great, but because it is too simple. Not because it is incomprehensible, but because it offers nothing to understand. Here reading can no longer be conceived as understanding. What is there cannot be penetrated, evaluated, categorized. It must be accepted as what is written and does not lead beyond itself. Yet it is not sufficient. The lack of what is not said, which is at work in it, keeps it open toward that which it cannot convey in any way. When the text cannot make available what is most important (to it), perhaps one comes closest to it by always looking slightly past what is there. The glance that goes by what is said is not a searching, possessive one, but a distracted one that slides off into uncontrollable dimensions. The will to understand peters out when one is distracted. The distracted person does not assert himself. He does not create a circle for himself in which he is master. Everywhere a little out of it, he is where the statement that is a product of concentration cannot arrive:

I couldn't interpret that scene, or understand it, only remember it . . . and seeing that I kept coming back to it, she added: "It's nothing. What do you want to understand? There's nothing to understand." (85/80-1/47)

Maybe he always chose someone else in you. Maybe, by this choice, he made you into someone else. It was the look by which one would most have wanted to be observed, but which perhaps never observed you, still gazed only at a little emptiness near you. (26/24-5/12)

I owed him a limitless distraction, and even less, the opposite of an expectation, the reverse of a faith, which wasn't doubt: ignorance and neglect. But this still wasn't enough: this ignorance still had to ignore even me and leave me to one side, gently, without exclusion and without diversion, by an uncertain movement. Then who was encountering him? Who was talking to him? Who wasn't thinking of him? I didn't know. I only felt that it was never I. (23/21-2/10)

outside that which can be and is said. The distracted reader does not relate to the text in a questioning or dismissive manner, which would require concentration. He accepts what is there without dealing with it in an interpretive or critical effort. Only such an acceptance of what is said makes it possible to look past it.

* * * * *

Blanchot describes reading in *L'espace littéraire* in a way that suggests connections to *Le dernier homme.* A reading is not an interpretation. Reading is not a phase of a conversation in which those who participate strive toward an understanding. A reading does not open up what the author has intended. On the contrary, it frees the work from its author: this is its achievement. Reading frees the work from all intention and allows it for the first time to be what it is. This liberation of the work from its dependence on a personal act, be it that of the author or that of the interpreter, moves reading to the end of the world, in the worldlessness of the last man. The space for work and reading is anonymity. The attitude of the reader who leaves open this space for himself by not intervening in

Reading is situated beyond or before comprehension. (EL 205/261/196)

It would seem, then, that to read is not to write the book again, but to allow the book to *be:* written—this time all by itself, without the intermediary of the writer, without anyone's writing it. (EL 201/256/193)

The singular property of reading demonstrates the singular sense of the verb "to make" in the expression "it makes the

the work with his grasp of it, is the simple assent to what is there. The reader makes it possible for the work to be by leaving it in peace: by letting it be. The simple "yes" to the work is not the business of the specialists, whose understanding and concentration on the meaning are always a gesture of power—or a submission. The one who comes closer to the work is perhaps the distracted reader, who is never quite with it but always also elsewhere and a little out of it. In the wish of authors for attentive readers it is always the author who would like to be taken seriously, although reading needs precisely to leave him out, and this might be easier to manage for the inattentive reader, who gets distracted.

work become a work." The word *make* here does not designate a productive activity. Reading does not produce anything, does not add anything; it lets be what is; it is freedom, not the freedom that produces being or grasps it, but freedom that welcomes, consents, says yes, can only say yes and, in the space opened by this yes, lets the work's overwhelming decisiveness affirm itself, lets be its affirmation that it is—and nothing more. (EL 202/257-8/194)

What appears in reading is that the work is—before all statement, meaning, and personal coloration. In the "yes" of the reader the mere presence of the work, the work as mere presence, takes place. This presence is calm, calming, not subject to the wake of negativity that pulls everything made of language into its own failing, the quiet middle of the storm. Reading is staying safely in the presence of

. . . the calm centre of measureless excess, the silent Yes at the center of every storm. (EL 205/261/196)

language without precipitating into the absence of meaning.

* * * * *

The distracted reader does not understand. What he reads is not communication for him but simply language taking place. Because language takes place as communication, one can only read its taking place out of communication, but this is not possible if one concentrates on that which is communicated and which, through the weight of its content, precisely covers up the fact that it is being communicated; it is only possible by ignoring, by looking past that which is communicated, of which there remains only the fact that it is communicated. Perhaps it is possible to put off the temptation to understand this process as reflection. It is not a question of turning one's glance from what is said back toward the act of saying. What is in question is not an act at all—neither the act of perception nor the act as what is perceived—but simply what is there. The reflexive endeavor remains a gesture of power. It strives for the mastery of understanding. Reading is simple assent to what is there, and not an effort to grasp it. This is why the reader does not reflect, but rather is distracted, absent-minded. This distinguishes him from the author, who, as creator and active entity, is attentive to his activity, and to whom the simple "yes" to his work is barred precisely for this reason. The author as author cannot read himself. The reader—even if he happens to be the author—is always someone else.

The distracted person is out of it [*daneben*]. Distraction has in common with reflection that attention is not directed at an object. But while the one who reflects shifts his attention to his relationship to the object, the distracted person loses it completely. The fact that the latter looks past the object does not mean that he is attentive to what is beside it [*daneben*]. The consequence of this would be merely that the state of being confused [*Danebensein*] would become an object, and he would become attentive to it. But the distracted person does not have a center anywhere. He is always somewhere other than where he is. Only the one who is not concentrating is out of it. Only the one who is distracted can have access to the state of being beside [*das Daneben*], since it is not possible to concentrate on it. The

. . . the writer never reads his work. It is, to him, illegible, a secret, before which he does not stay. (EL 14/13/23)

The writer can never read his work for the very same reason which gives him the illusion that he does. "He is," says René Char, "the genesis of a being who projects and of a being who contains." But in order for the "being who contains," the being who gives form and measure, the form-giver, the "Beginner," to attain the ultimate metamorphosis which would turn him into "the reader," the finished work has to escape from him, to escape from the one who makes it, complete itself by putting him at a distance, culminate in this "distancing" which disposes him conclusively, this distancing which then, precisely, takes the form of reading (and in which the reading takes form). (EL 209/268/200)

beside [*Daneben*] is never there. The one who is distracted is never with that which is there, but also not with that which is beside it. He is never with anything, and always beside everything. What is beside everything is the fact that everything is. Distraction is perhaps the experience of presence without something—an experience that the distracted person can make only because it is not what matters to him. The presence of the work as what matters opens up to the distracted reader precisely because it is not important to him, in the distracted unconcernedness of the assent to that which is there. On the side.

* * * * *

What Blanchot describes as the reader is the experience of Blanchot's reader. His narrative texts are of such a nature that it is possible to have access to them only when they are read in Blanchot's sense. It is not that reading is a method, described in *L'espace littéraire,* that one could use as a set of instructions for reading his stories. Reading cannot be learned and, as a process, cannot be captured in rules. It cannot be mastered, and the only way to let it happen as that nonunderstanding straying into which it slips away is to renounce the attempt to learn it. The essay "Lire" only presents what has always already taken place when a literary text is accepted without being pinned to a meaning and thus missed.

What is peculiar in Blanchot's texts is perhaps that they continuously suspend, more than others, the possibility of understanding. At no point does the text make available what would be necessary for the understanding. One reads on without ever having understood, but looking forward to a future understanding, which however never presents itself. The movement of reading is here not a process from what one has understood to what one must still understand, and even the retrospective position of what one reads later does not make what one read earlier more understandable. Understanding is always later; it is endlessly ahead. Reading happens through the suspension of understanding; it goes on in spite of this cessation, or because of it, outside the understanding. It may be the hope of a later understanding that drives it on; but in the not yet of the understanding each next step of the reader can be nothing other than

Later, he asked himself how he had entered the calm. He couldn't talk about it with himself. Only strange joy at feeling he was in harmony with the words: "Later, he. . . . " (157/147/89)

the unconditional acceptance of what is there. Postponing understanding makes room for the simple "yes" of the reader to the presence of words that do not yet mean, but which in the postponement of understanding have no other meaning than "later." Later makes the present free for what is present. The happiness of saying "yes" is the pleasure one takes in the calm of presence before the understanding takes it apart.

The happiness of saying yes, of endlessly affirming. (12/11/4)

Happiness of always saying Yes, of endlessly affirming. (125/117/70)

. . . oh, the happiness of always saying Yes . . . (131/123/74)

The "yes" of the reader is the "yes" of the last man. Assent to mere presence without anything that could appear, on the margin of the world constituted by man, as the ocean [*Meer*] and more [*Mehr*] into which the world passes. Like the last man, the reader arrives to the end of the world, which is the border of what is human, a border on which he is already almost nobody, or more than somebody.

As though his presence was all there was of him and did not allow him to be present: immense presence, even he did not seem able to fill it, as though he had disappeared into it and been absorbed by it slowly, endlessly,—a presence without anyone, perhaps? (53/50-1/28)

How was he present, with that simple, evident presence, near us, but as though without us, without our world, maybe without any world? (57/53-4/30)

But the reader's task, reading, is the work, which is a human construct and belongs to the world. By letting the work be—by leaving it in peace he allows it to be—he appears to be at home in the human sphere. And when the work does not show itself as this or that to the assent of the reader, but asserts itself in its mere presence, this appears to be an experience that could also be made with any other object. But what is peculiar to the work is perhaps that it does not simply make possible the step from "what" [it means] to "that" [it is], but makes it inevitable, since it is what it is only when reading allows it to assert itself in its mere existence. The work is that human thing that leads to the limit of the human. Hence the reader is the last man: on the boundary of the possible, where understanding stops without everything having come to an end, and where the presence that is still there cannot be contained in a human order.

* * * * *

The "yes" of the reader is light. It is light because it does not have the weight of the assent to something said, to these or those judgments or opinions; beyond the contents, which evaporate, it is a consent purely to the linguistic event. Where not only what is said begins to blur in the leveling murmuring of being said, but where forms, peculiarity, and characteristics acquire the undecided uniformity of mere presence, everything loses its weight. Lightness is a preliminary phase of disappearance.

What becomes lighter is less there. When it gets lighter, the Something, which is still that, begins to become more rarefied and to dissolve in undifferentiated presence. The last man lives, dies in this transition. Everything becomes light for him, because he does not hold any views and has no responsibilities. Everything that can be held and for which one needs to take responsibility becomes endlessly light in the face of its ending peculiarity, too light to be still measured by the seriousness of a moral. Of course in the lightness of what is almost at its twilight the thoughts retain something human and, in their lightness, something bitter, a regret about their lack of weight; but this bitterness is also a light one, like everything else.

If I ask myself: did he think more than you think?, I see only his spirit of lightness, which made him innocent of the worst. A being so irresponsible, so terribly not guilty . . . (13/12-13/5)

He would express some thoughts: how light they are, how they immediately rise, nothing disturbs them, nothing imposes them. "But isn't that what makes them bitter?"—"Bitter?" "Slightly bitter." (13/13/5)

The spirit of lightness can concentrate on something only in distraction. Distraction makes light what it concentrates on. People too become light to each other when they encounter each other. It is their characteristic that they are at their own limit and already imbued with their imminent disappearance. When they look at each other, they simultaneously look past each other; precisely because they

Perhaps it is this lightness that isolated them from us, a lightness that she did not take directly from herself, but received from him, as I observed without bitterness but with the impression that this was how he bound himself to her, by a bond so light that she saw only the absence of a bond, not noticing that now he spoke only to her and looked only at her. She said, on the contrary, that he did not look at her often, and never directly, but a little bit sideways, "toward you, I feel it,"—and perhaps, in fact, once or twice, I thought I had caught a tired gaze seeking me out, but this was a gaze which, once it had found you, did not let you go, perhaps

do not see each other, they see what connects them as people on the verge of disappearance and meet each other as people who have a missed encounter, without making each other happy but also without feeling neglected by the other.

because of its fatigue or simply because it was not looking at you. (75/70-1/40/1)

The happiness of the last man is always only the happiness of saying "yes." But this "yes" is a yes at the limit. It affirms everything, but everything has become light, transparent unto its absence which its differentiation pales into, and in which it agrees with everything else in contentless presence. If the "yes" affirms banal things, this is less because of a preference than because lightness makes everything indifferent and banal. To the extent that this "yes" is directed to things, there is in it a worldly remainder, just large enough that someone can still say "yes" to something, since what is approved with this "yes" is not things as what they are, but their being at hand [*Vorhandensein*], the presence that can manifest itself only in this being at hand, and in which things in their peculiarity are destined to come to an end. If the "yes" were only the assent to what each thing is, it would have to take lightness hard and

I believe there were days when the simplest person would have found him too simple and when chatting about the most unimportant things occupied him completely, gave him a pleasure people don't understand: though not with everyone, or only with everyone? The happiness of saying yes, of endlessly affirming. (11/11/41)

But the calm must pour into the heart, therefore the mysterious gift, the free judgment must be accomplished: oh, the happiness of always saying Yes, the surprise of these new bonds and the certainty of what is older; the appeal for a new lightness that comes to me from the first lightness, the thought that is not thought by me, that is already returning to the upper reaches, leading me up with a mad promptness, not altogether leading me up. (131/123/74)

be burdened with the regret that form is undone. A consent to pure presence, free from regret, is on the contrary the carefree movement toward this presence, a kind of drunkenness of the going up in it; for the "yes" also renders the one who consents lighter and lighter, draws him to his own limit and would already have made him disappear if he were not still able to say "yes."

The transitional zone in which everything is light opens on two sides: toward the solid reality of things, which begins to blur in it and which can leave behind a painful memory as it is exposed to corrosion; but also toward the empty, undifferentiated presence, into which everything that crumbles sinks back, and whose closeness, which announces itself in its lightness, initiates an ecstatic becoming one with it. The simultaneity of these two opposite orientations is the light hesitation of the person who is no longer alive and not yet dead.

When in such a hesitation the memory of what has been left behind and the intuition of what is ahead come together, that is only another, last and light attempt to put into words a state of mind in which even time has lost its dimensions,

She seemed to me then to be of an essence I couldn't call childish, but so unbound by thoughts of the future, so present and yet so scarcely burdened by the present, so gravely, so unknowingly insouciant, that I could only look at her with a certain drunkenness, and without a doubt this is what gave her this feeling of lightness that made her almost drunk, too, yes, in the long run, as though she were abandoned to a spirit of lightness she wasn't always sure she could control. (107/101/59-60)

He walked with a light hesitation; his very strange step gave the impression that only for moments at a time did he stop at our level, but that he came from very far down and that it was always by virtue of a very strong stubbornness that he came. And yet this wasn't the motion of a man about to fall: it was another uncertainty, because of which one became uncertain of oneself, an uncertainty sometimes painful, sometimes light and a little drunk. (28/26-7/13)

in which one cannot remember; but the lack of memory does not mean that one has forgotten, for one neither remembers nor forgets. The opposition between remembering and forgetting is invalidated just like that between attention and distraction, concentration and negligence, care and lack of cares. Here is just as much beside the point [*daneben*] as, yesterday and tomorrow, is today. There is no situation because there are no reference points. This is the condition of eternity, which is no longer a condition since everything has stopped without anything having begun, and everything would be without end or beginning if a lament were not still putting into words the loss of time.

One can't remember someone who is only present. But, contrary to what it sometimes had seemed to me, I didn't forget him either: forgetting has no hold on presence. (62/58/33)

. . .the calm that was confided to my negligence. (114/107/64)

And the calm, too, is uncertain, in the midst of which we are reborn ceaselessly into the lightness of ourselves: the large question, steady and indestructible, perhaps entrusted to our negligence. (143/134/81)

But the lament I suddenly hear: in me? in you: *"eternal, eternal, if we are eternal, how could we have been? how can we be tomorrow?"* (151/141/85)

* * * * *

Frivolity almost leads to the point where self-forgetfulness turns into that whose disturbance I was. The self-obliteration in forgetfulness, which frees the memory of what is pre- and posthuman, is death: convergence of forgetting and remembering, entrance into the unreachability of what is always beyond, of the impossible, which takes up all possibility and which can only, in the realm of the possible, be

Frivolity is what is best about us. (122/114/68)

First to forget. To remember only there where one remembers nothing. To forget: to remember everything as though by way of forgetting. There is a profoundly forgotten point from which every memory radiates. Everything is exalted in memory starting from something forgotten, an infinitesimal detail, a miniscule fissure into which it passes in its entirety.

If I must eventually forget, if I must remember you only in forgetting you, if it is said that he who will remember will be accepted with a "yes" over and over again. It is the monotony and the suspense of Blanchot's narrative that it constantly remains in the greatest closeness to a point that is never reached, a point that brings together what can only be thought and said separately, since thinking and saying must be the separation of that which they could not make appear if they were the same as it.

profoundly forgotten by himself and by that memory which he will not distinguish from his forgetting, if . . . (151/142/85-6)

The approach to the limit of what is humanly possible and the assent to pure presence without something, whose impossible experience becomes, in *Le dernier homme,* the experience of writing, is related for Blanchot to what happens when one reads. The lightness of the unconditional "yes" connects the man at the furthest limit to the reader of the literary work. That the work emerges in this vicinity is not surprising. It originates and has a deep relation to the *désoeuvrement,* an in- and preoperative state where no activity yet produces the shape in which the work comes to itself by leaving behind, in its beginning, its own possibility, which it has lost, and constitutes itself into what has always already begun. The perspective of beginning,

. . . eternity is achieved, but grows on ceaselessly. Such a discovery is accepted

emerging, and appearing is not completely absent in *Le dernier homme.* Although the thought of undifferentiated presence consolidates itself more and more rigidly and does not admit of anything still beginning, the possibility of departure is still contained in it, and even in the consenting movement toward the end of forms, the temptation to, at least, make disappearance appear, does not disappear completely. But in general the last man tends toward the end, and ending is closer to him than beginning.

Precisely in this, however, he is close to the reader. For the writer the work is originating. He exposes himself to the unreachable anonymity of the origin out of which the work begins. To the extent that it gains shape and enters the world of appearances, the work moves away from its initial closeness to that which enters into it as what came before and is withheld; but Blanchot has always identified the particularity of the poetic work in the fact that it remains a beginning one, and that what is visible, graspable, understandable in it does not cover up closeness to what is unavailable in its origin. The reconstitution of the work in this

right away. No beginning and yet the soar of a perpetual awakening. No end, but an always satisfied and always desiring aspiration. (122/114/68)

I think this is what tempts us both: I, that you be a face, what is visible in a face, and you, to be a face for me once more, to be a thought and yet a face. The desire to be visible in the night, so that it will invisibly fade away. (150/141/85)

closeness is the reader's business. His "yes" to the work is not an assent to what is said, signified, and intended, and does not at all concern the fact that the work is a construct and the product of an ability, however much this deserves respect and consideration—it only says "yes" to the fact that the work is, to the fact that it was able to begin. In order to have this attitude to the work, the reader must disregard everything, or see through everything, that establishes the work in the world of the visible, and listen to what, in the work, can only be perceived as an echo of the unmasterable preworldly. Thus the reader of the work, like the last man, must dismantle a constituted world in order to come close to the neutral presence out of which the work—no longer as that of an author—breaks forth, inexplicably and overpoweringly initial.

Such a correspondence between, on the one hand, that which is told by and as the last man and, on the other, the reader, as Blanchot understands him, seems to suggest that it is possible to read *Le dernier homme* as an allegory of reading. However this conclusion, which is difficult to avoid, introduces the difficulty that in this case the text has precisely not been read but interpreted. But it is not sufficient to establish this without reflecting on the peculiar character of the meaning that is attributed to the text with this interpretation. If the text signifies reading, it signifies a relation to the text that is not of an interpreting nature. The result of the interpretation ends up in opposition to the act thanks to which it has come about, because the text now signifies the impossibility of its own interpretation. But by signifying that it precisely cannot be reduced to its own signification, it leads back, past what it signifies, to the reader, that is, to that element in the text that is not its signification and that does not communicate itself to the interpreter, but only to the reader. The literary text can and should in no way, since it is made of language, cease to signify; but it finds here in Blanchot a chance to signify in such a way that it is able to free up what is not significant in it and offer it to the reader's "yes."

—Translated from the German by Georgia Albert.

Contributors

GEORGIA ALBERT is a graduate student in comparative literature at the University of California, Irvine, and is the translator of Hans-Jost Frey's *Interruptions* (SUNY Press).

ANN BANFIELD teaches literature and linguistics at the University of California, Berkeley. Author of *Unspeakable Sentences* and translator of Jean-Claude Milner's *For the Love of Language,* she has recently completed a book on Virginia Woolf, Post-Impressionism, and Cambridge theory of knowledge.

SIMON CRITCHLEY is Reader in Philosophy at the University of Essex. He is author of *The Ethics of Deconstruction* (Blackwell, 1992), and *Very Little . . . Almost Nothing* (Routledge, 1997). A volume of his essays is forthcoming from Verso. He is coeditor of *Re-Reading Levinas* (Indiana, 1991), *Deconstructive Subjectivities* (SUNY Press, 1996), *Emmanuel Levinas: Basic Philosophical Writings* (Indiana, 1996), and *A Companion to Continental Philosophy* (Blackwell, 1997).

DAVID ELLISON received his Ph.D. in French literature from Yale University and taught at Mount Holyoke College before moving to the University of Miami, where he is Professor of French and Comparative Literature and Chairman of the Department of Foreign Language and Literatures. He is the author of *The Reading of Proust* (Johns Hopkins, 1984), *Understanding Albert Camus* (University of South Carolina Press, 1990), and *Of Words and the World: Referential Anxiety in Contemporary French Fiction* (Princeton, 1993). Currently he is working on a book project tentatively entitled *Ethics and Aesthetics of European Modernism.*

YFS 93, *The Place of Maurice Blanchot,* ed. Thomas Pepper, © 1998 by Yale University.

HANS-JOST FREY teaches comparative literature at the University of Zurich. Two of his books have been translated into English: *Studies in Poetic Discourse* (Stanford University Press, 1992), and *Interruptions* (SUNY Press, 1996). His most recent book, *Der unendliche Text* (Suhrkamp, 1990) will be followed in 1998 by *Die Autorität der Sprache.*

DENIS HOLLIER teaches in the French Department at New York University. His latest book, *Absent Without Leave (French Literature Under the Threat of War)*, an expanded version of *Les déposédes* (Editions de Minuit, 1993), has recently been published by Harvard University Press.

LYNNE HUFFER is Associate Professor of French at Yale University. She is the author of *Another Colette: The Question of Gendered Writing* (University of Michigan Press, 1992) and *Maternal Pasts, Feminist Futures: Nostalgia, Ethics, and the Question of Difference* (Stanford University Press, 1998). She is the editor of an issue of *Yale French Studies* entitled *Another Look, Another Woman: Retranslations of French Feminism* (1995).

JEAN-POL MADOU is Professor of French at the University of Miami, Coral Gables, and has taught at the University of Nijmegen. He is the author of *Démons et simulacres dans l'œuvre de Pierre Klossowski* (Paris: Meridien-Klincksieck, 1987) and *Edouard Glissant* (Atlanta: Rodopi, 1996), and is currently working on a study of the double modernity of French poetry in Mallarmé and Rimbaud.

THOMAS PEPPER teaches in the Departments of Comparative Literature and Nordic Philology at the University of Aarhus. He is the author of *Singularities* (Cambridge University Press, 1997), as well as of essays on Althusser and Levinas and Merleau-Ponty and Lacan. He is currently at work on a study of Kierkegaard, as well as on a study of the relation between paranoia and repressed homosexuality in modern philosophy.

DOMINIQUE RABATÉ teaches at the Université Michel-de-Montaigne, Bordeaux III. He has published *Louis-René des Forêts. La voix et la volume* and *Vers une littérature de l'épuisement* (Corti, 1991), and has edited three books, including *Figures du sujet lyrique* (Presses Universitaires de France, 1996). He is currently at work on a new book on the modern and the contemporary novel as specific modes of literary enunciation.

THOMAS SCHESTAG is visiting professor of German at New York University, and has taught at the Lajos-Kossuth University, Debrecen

(Hungary), and at the University of Michigan, and the University of Virginia. He is the author of *para- Titus Lucretius Carus, Johann Peter Hebel, Francis Ponge- zur literarischen Hermeneutik* (1991), *Parerga:* Friedrich Hölderlin; Carl Schmitt, Franz Kafka; Platon, Friedrich Schleiermacher, Walter Benjamin; Jacques Derrida. Zur literarischen Hermeneutik (1992), *Asphalt* (on Walter Benjamin, 1992), and *buk* (on Paul Celan, 1994).

JAMES SWENSON teaches French at Rutgers University. He is in the process of finishing a book manuscript on contradictory readings of Rousseau during the French Revolution.

MICHAEL SYROTINSKI teaches French and Francophone literature at the University of Aberdeen, Scotland. He has published on Blanchot, Paulhan, Caillois, Derrida, and V. Y. Mudimbe. His critical study of Jean Paulhan, *Defying Gravity,* is published by SUNY Press (1988).

DEBORAH TREISMAN is the Managing Editor of Grand Street. She is also the translator of Vincent Kauffmann, *Post Scripts: The Writer's Workshop* (Harvard University Press, 1994).

HENT DE VRIES is Professor of Philosophy at the University of Amsterdam and Chair of the Board of the Amsterdam School for Cultural Analysis (ASCA). He is the author of *Theologie im pianissimo: Die Aktualität der Denkfiguren Adornos und Levinas's* (an English translation is forthcoming from the Johns Hopkins University Press). He is coeditor, together with Harry Kunneman, of two volumes with essays on the concept of Enlightenment and the debates between Frankfurt School Critical Theory and recent French thought. He is also the coeditor, with Samuel Weber, of a volume entitled *Violence, Identity, and Self-Determination* (Stanford University Press) as well as the coeditor, with Mieke Bal, of a new book series, *Cultural Memory and the Present,* to be published by Stanford University Press. He has just completed a book entitled *Philosophy and the Turn to Religion* (forthcoming from the Johns Hopkins University Press).

The following issues are still available through the **Yale French Studies Office,** P.O. Box 208251, New Haven, CT 06520-8251.

19/20 Contemporary Art $3.50
33 Shakespeare $3.50
35 Sade $3.50
38 The Classical Line $3.50
39 Literature and Revolution $3.50
41 Game, Play, Literature $5.00
42 Zola $5.00
43 The Child's Part $5.00
44 Paul Valéry $5.00
45 Language as Action $5.00
46 From Stage to Street $3.50
47 Image & Symbol in the Renaissance $3.50
52 Graphesis $5.00
53 African Literature $3.50
54 Mallarmé $5.00
57 Locus in Modern French Fiction: Space, Landscape, Decor $6.00
58 In Memory of Jacques Ehrmann $6.00
59 Rethinking History $6.00
61 Toward a Theory of Description $6.00
62 Feminist Readings: French Texts/American Contexts $6.00

Add for postage & handling

Single issue, United States $3.00 (Priority Mail) Each additional issue $1.25
Single issue, United States $1.80 (Third Class) Each additional issue $ .50
Single issue, foreign countries $2.50 (Book Rate) Each additional issue $1.50

YALE FRENCH STUDIES, P.O. Box 208251, New Haven, Connecticut 06520-8251
A check made payable to YFS is enclosed. Please send me the following issue(s):

Issue no. Title Price

____

____

Postage & handling ____________

Total ____________

Name ____

Number/Street ____

City ______________________ State __________ Zip ______________

- -

The following issues are now available through Periodicals Service Company, 11 Main Street, Germantown,N.Y. 12526, Phone: (518) 537-4700. Fax: (518) 537-5899.

1 Critical Bibliography of Existentialism
2 Modern Poets
3 Criticism & Creation
4 Literature & Ideas
5 The Modern Theatre
6 France and World Literature
7 André Gide
8 What's Novel in the Novel
9 Symbolism
10 French-American Literature Relationships
11 Eros, Variations...
12 God & the Writer
13 Romanticism Revisited
14 Motley: Today's French Theater
15 Social & Political France
16 Foray through Existentialism
17 The Art of the Cinema
18 Passion & the Intellect, or Malraux
19/20 Contemporary Art
21 Poetry Since the Liberation
22 French Education
23 Humor
24 Midnight Novelists
25 Albert Camus
26 The Myth of Napoleon
27 Women Writers
28 Rousseau
29 The New Dramatists
30 Sartre
31 Surrealism
32 Paris in Literature
33 Shakespeare in France
34 Proust
48 French Freud
51 Approaches to Medieval Romance

36/37 Structuralism has been reprinted by Doubleday as an Anchor Book.
55/56 Literature and Psychoanalysis has been reprinted by Johns Hopkins University Press, and can be ordered through Customer Service, Johns Hopkins University Press, Baltimore, MD 21218.